VINTAGE
CLOTHING

1880-1980
Identification & Value Guide

by Maryanne Dolan

3rd Edition

ISBN 0-89689-109-7

BOOKS AMERICANA
INC

DEDICATION

for my mother,
'A FASHION PLATE'

ACKNOWLEDGEMENTS
WITH VERY SPECIAL THANKS TO:

BUTTERICK FASHION MARKETING CO., NEW YORK.

BUTTERFIELD & BUTTERFIELD, SAN FRANCISCO, CA., particularly Douglas Sandberg and Patrick Sumner for their photographs of the Harrah Museum auction and Patsy Irvine, curator of Vintage Clothing, for the fashion photographs

CHRISTIE'S EAST - Elise Luray of CHRISTIE'S EAST and Nancy Sullivan, now with CHRISTIE'S WEST (Beverly Hills) for the photographs of the Joan Crawford auction.

M.H. DeYOUNG MUSEUM, GOLDEN GATE PARK, SAN FRANCISCO, CA - Melissa Leventon for the photographs of the wonderful gowns donated to the Museum by Mrs. Nion R. Tucker and Mrs. James Caldwell in memory of Sara Bard Field Wood, I Magnin and Co., S.F. and Mrs. Eloise Heidland.

WILLIAM DOYLE GALLERIES, NY, whose M.J. Flanagan supplied the photographs of the Ruth Gordon auction.

FOLKWEAR PATTERNS formerly of San Rafael, California.

RICHARD KNAPP who owns and wore the Vargas shirts

LEVI STRAUSS CO., of San Francisco, California whose Dori Wofford provided the contemporary fashion photos as well as the historic photographs from the Levis Strauss Museum in San Francisco.

PETRA MARTIN for the photographs of her own splendid garments pictured in this book, and also for the use of the photos of the garments consigned to Butterfield's.

MARYMOOR MUSEUM of REDMOND, WASHINGTON - MARJORIE COLL AND PEGGY HANSEN who supplied the photos from the Museum's impressive collection.

MONTGOMERY WARD of Chicago - SARINA BUTLER of MONTGOMERY WARD for her generous cooperation which enabled use of the company photographs.

THE MUSEUM OF THE CITY OF NEW YORK for the photographs of the magnificent WORTH gowns

THE SIMPLICITY PATTERN CO. ARCHIVES, NILES, MI, and Anna Morris whose cooperation permitted the use of the SIMPLICITY fashions SOUTHERN OREGON HISTORICAL SOCIETY, Jackson, Oregon.

SPIEGEL, JOHN Shea, President and Cris Crockett for permission to use the Spiegel Co. photographs

DONNA VERNER of DRESSING UP, formerly of Oakland, CA

VINTAGE FASHIONWORKS, Vallejo, CA, Shelley Antilla whose fashions and models enliven this book.

BETTY WILLIAMSON of Grass Valley, CA, who caters to the special needs of the Vintage car collector.

TO MY FRIENDS WITH GRATITUDE FOR THE LOAN OF THEIR TREASURES:

Marlys Aboudara

Nan Almeida

Susan Bachelor

Linda Baker

Sally Baker

Virginia Cox

Beatrice Deasy

Pat and Henry Ewald

Clarice Hart

Richard Knapp

Betty Krueger

Pat LePage

Dorothy Malott

Thomas A. McGovern

Fred McLorn

Pearline Munson

And to all of those who modeled, you make it all beautiful

PREFACE

'Fashion is as Fashion Does' goes the adage and indeed in 1995 Fashion is doing all sorts of unexpected things.

But in 1880 fashion was an established mode, deviation from the fashion rules was not encouraged and fashion at all levels was so well delineated one's social standing could be assessed immediately by the clothing a person wore.

It was not really until the 1920s that independence in dressing became a standard and as time moved forward, the clothes we wore became less a badge of our station in life than a statement of what we believed in and who we felt we were.

By the 1950s non-traditional clothing was making an impact and during the late 1960s wearing anything one pleased in any condition became the norm among certain segments of society. Not all, there have always been those who clung to traditional values and the fashions which reflect them, but unfortunately it was the media with its constant coverage of the 60's unrest which has left us with the most lasting images of the clothing (if not fashion) of that era. No one who saw it will ever forget the costumes of the Woodstock generation. A composite of those fashions could certainly be put together to make a cohesive exhibit, but many of those garments are available by virtue of their condition even then and the mis-matched ensembles can only be duplicated by acquiring pieces here and there.

By the 1970s fashion had resumed its normal niche but that period was neither particularly innovative nor impressive. It had reverted to traditions, more or less. Overlaid by the new feeling that we could wear whatever we liked, whenever we liked to whatever place we wanted to go. That feeling still persists and gives all new fashion an energy which drives the fashion industry to show clothing which ordinary humans could not possibly wear but which is amusing and often very expensive. The philosophy of the bizarre does lead to sensible adaptations which can be very pleasing, so the famous designer fashion shows which may leave us gasping do have a practical purpose. But as one pundit has it "the masses yawn at the mandates of fashion designers".

One overriding reason Vintage Fashion has become so desirable is because the glorious influential days of the really great designers seem to have passsed, so the things they made and the times that clothing represents is like all else that is gone forever, highly attractive to us. We ever cherish the mysterious past and that is what vintage high fashion represents. These vintage garments continue to go way over estimate at auctions, and auctions overall tell us the truth, vintage fashion has arrived as a prime collectible and as my mail continues to tell me it has a fascination and beauty and something else, a mystique which thrills us and stirs our sense of history and challenges our imagination. Ah, the good old days. And oh, the charm and glamour of the garments of those times.

As we move well into the 1990s, who knows where fashion will wander - the acceptance of travel in space will ultimately have some impact, the rise of technology which will lead to more and more people working at home will certainly influence fashion, especially clothing of the work place; the clothing children wear has already been strongly influenced by an asexual approach, the rise of sports such as soccer now sees strong sales of the typical uniform shirts worn by the well known teams - just visit London and check out the big stores - tennis wear has changed not only in color but style, surfing wear, largely unknown a few years ago is now a big seller, so the popularity of heretofore little known sports will have an effect.

So will travel wear reflect the new emphasis on comfort - Europeans say they never have any doubts about who is American, they know them by their Nikes, or Reeboks. Many new developments will change our clothing ways, but even when we think we are breaking from tradition and being totally independent we are really becoming more uniform. Jeans still persist, the jogging suit seems entrenched even if the wearer never jogs, the baseball cap is now a passion (even worn backwards does not a fashion radical make, it is still a baseball cap). High heels except for very special occasions seem to be disappearing, hats make a feeble comeback here and there but seem genuinely to be cast aside forever as a major fashion accent - what we probably will never see again in any numbers are the fans, the tiaras, the bustles, the truly wonderful hats, the high button shoes, the paisley shawls with their long fringe, the corsets (was that a collective sigh of relief?)

Fashion has shown us many faces, demure, provocative, elegant, saucy, opulent, simple - even now, you make your own image and when we move into the arena of Vintage your image of yourself can match your fantasies. That is the ultimate plateau, transform yourself, (if even for one night at an Art Deco ball) into the creature you keep buried deep inside your prim daytime suit, metamorphose into that sleek coquette or into some other being who exudes power along with charm.

The magnificent possibilities of collecting vintage clothing not only for wearing but for beauty and investment are not endless, while new pieces keep coming into the market place, the really stupendous garments are disappearing into collections and museums. But if you want to enrich your life, educate yourself about times past and their history, if you want to learn about fabric and the art of dressmaking (good tailoring is truly an underrated craft), the incredibly creative art of design, and take yourself out of the everyday mundane world, Vintage Clothing is for you.

This, the third edition of this book, is intended as a guide to ease your way into this engrossing, historic, beautiful world of Vintage Clothing. It is a never ending world, it is constantly surprising, it is all things to all collectors and with you, I feel it is a passion and a delight. Let us all enjoy this particular cosmos.

AUTHOR'S NOTE: Vintage Clothing collectors and museum curators and those of you who are simply interested in this subject in an abstract or historic way, thank you for your letters and phone calls, for your gifts and good wishes, thank you for being such an appreciative, intelligent audience. No book has validity until someone reads it and reacts. My very deepest gratitude to you for reading and reacting in such a positive way. My greatest wish is to meet you so we can share our thoughts on this, our very special world of Vintage Clothing.

138 Belle Avenue
Pleasant Hill, California 94523

INTRODUCTION

Collecting vintage fashion becomes the art of the possible. The very material of which most clothing was made lends itself to destruction and the need to be in fashion which caused so many beautiful gowns to be discarded and neglected has left us with many gaps in our collection wardrobes.

Even the Smithsonian Institution has not been able to fully round out the Inaugural Gown collection of the First Ladies. Some of the gowns currently on exhibit were never worn to that First Ball, but are simply dresses of the period. So it is with the collector; if a primary sample of a period piece is not available, we must make do with a secondary example, or a dress or suit of the same period.

Indeed, so much High Fashion has been chronicled that a whole new wave of collectors dealing only with every day garments has surfaced, but most collectors today are seeking good samples of the great design periods, and this is a challenging, but rewarding task.

It can take you from specialized shops, to flea markets, to thrift shops, to second hand clothing stores and to friends and relatives with bulging closets or attics.

Competition in this field is becoming much keener and it behooves you to be pleasant to Aunt Minnie who may be harboring a Balenciaga somewhere.

Fortunately for us, many people refuse to discard anything and it is to them that we owe a large debt of gratitude for much of our older clothing. In most cases, since these people bothered to save it, they also took care of it.

Unless you are blessed with great skill at needlework, older clothing is often difficult to repair and restore with authenticity. The old taffeta, for example, had metallic thread to give it that rustle, but it also caused it to rot away, so you seldom see an old taffeta dress in mint condition and it is almost impossible to repair. The best advice is to take your restorable, valuable clothing to an expert. In many cases museums dealing with vintage clothing offer such services, and if they do not, can probably recommend a specialist in this narrow field.

If the price is right, and the damage slight or not too obvious, buy the piece and then think about restoration. "If the Price is Right" should be emblazoned above every clothing collector's closet these days when the large auction houses are organizing special auctions of high fashion vintage clothing and selling it for high sums.

The average collector today should keep in mind the fragility of his or her collectible, the competition for this clothing, the escalating prices and need for less procrastination. Someone, if it's a fair price, will buy that gorgeous gown before you can say Schiaparelli.

Collectors should look for rare pieces in good condition, the choice Victorian pieces or the 20's dresses that are beaded and in excellent condition. Remember that all of the 1920's dresses were not hand beaded but that does not seem to be of tremendous import to collectors; what should rank very high on your list of requirements for any garment is the basic design, the material, and the way the garment was made.

The vintage clothing collector has chosen a field which excels in great beauty and interest; it deals with design, with fabrics of types sometimes rare and expensive, with braids and lace, and feathers and beads; it makes a definitive comment on history and what people did and what they wore for their work and leisure. It is often a collectible of remarkable elegance and above all it is a reflection on the collector, for anyone who chooses this field must be a person of awareness and taste.

The collection should speak for itself, through you, and the statement it makes says as much about you, the collector, as it does about the person who originally wore it.

CHAPTER ONE
1880-1900

The primary collecting area in the field of Vintage Fashion occurs after 1880, beyond that we are dealing with the very rare and expensive garment which has now become the province of the museums and affluent collector. True, the occasional 1860's or 1870's dress or hat or bonnet will turn up to lend excitement to the chase, but the practical collector will choose a later period which lends itself to easier acquisitions.

By the 1880's the bustle using a wire support was back in style and the feet were visible below a slightly shortened skirt. That seemed to be as far as women were allowed to display any part of the anatomy, and unfortunately for females of the 1880's and 1890's, fashion dictated such a plethora of clothing for ordinary wear that one wag was inspired to say that planning the Parthenon probably took less time than his wife's daily toilette.

Too true, imagine yourself day after dreary day preparing to go outdoors; the corset, the drawers, the bodice, petticoats and more petticoats, and often so many buttons down the back help was needed to dress.

The Victorians loved clutter in all things, their houses were shrines to that particular god, knick-knacks everywhere, not an inch of shelf or table space left unoccupied. It seems fitting then that the women who dictated these arrangements also cluttered their persons. Not only was the clothing complicated and overdone, but the coiffure was also a tribute to the complex, calling for front curls and whatever one favored in back. False hairpieces were popular, some made from the combings of the Victorian woman herself; braids, or plaits as they were referred to, chignons, loops; the more elaborate the better.

Ribbons and feathers and flowers were much in evidence on the bonnets which were so varied and eyecatching they are greatly prized today by collectors.

The 1880's bustle differed from that of the 1870's, but the whole effect in the first years of the 1880's was one of rigidity and stiffness, which ironically or not, complemented the Victorian attitudes.

Dresses were heavier, and skirts began to increase in size.

Men's clothing was somber and conformed to the new image of the successful industrialist. Single-breasted jackets and straightline, longish, frock coats, worn with straight trousers without a crease, prevailed. The clothing atmosphere was one of inflexibility and propriety, and in female fashion, not always particularly pretty.

From her well-shod feet to her beribboned bonnet, the lady of the 1880's was as encased by her clothing as she was by the conventions of the day. For the collector of the fashions of those years, the clothes are highly desirable, but not readily available. It is wise to comb attics and old trunks, especially if your family has been an acquisitive one, for it is usually in this way that the collector has the best chance of coming upon these treasures.

To us, in 1995, they seem as other-worldly as the 17th century laces and satins must have seemed to the Victorian, they were uncomfortable, restrictive and not overly flattering, but they appeal to our fantasy lives, says one dealer, and the best of the clothing represents good workmanship and often good design in what was an era of peace and plenty and sturdy family life. The garments are part of that nostalgia, they have an aura of stability.

One of the loveliest of all collectibles springs from the 1880's – the shawl. Shawls are still worn today, they are useful and graceful, but the biggest thing in shawls for the Victorian lady was Paisley. The colorful, swirled patterns of abstract, curved shapes are felt to have derived from the patterns of Persian rugs and the name itself from Paisley, Scotland. It was far and away the most popular type, although these shoulder coverings came in a great variety of sizes and materials. If the budget does not lend itself to the dresses and suits of the Victorian age, try shawls, with their heavy fringes and bright colors they can be used in a variety of ways, even as wall hangings. They are still fairly easy to find although serious collectors have long been seeking them and there are now many museum displays which feature them. They are without doubt one of the genuine markers of the age and some collectors use them as a backdrop to a clothing collection.

As the 1880's gave way to the 1890's the silhouette began to show signs of adapting to the emerging woman. Paris still had a firm hold on the fashion world, although women were showing signs of making their own decisions about what they wanted to wear and how they wanted to look. Men, too, began to feel stifled, but in spite of the tendencies of a group called the 'Aesthes' with their fancy vests and velvet jackets and their preference for color, the basic shape did not change much. The accessories were engaging though, and lent an air of the rakish to the men of fashion – the cane, the elegant watches, the fobs, the hats – all of which are diligently hunted today.

By the 1890's the shape of the female gown had become softer and looser. The sleeve, always a good indicator of the period of early clothing, now showed some fullness at the top and by the late 1890's had expanded considerably.

But the biggest revolution in clothing was caused by the wheel. Or two wheels – the bicycle. It became an absolute passion and while we may find it hard to conceive of cycling with large, veiled hats and full length skirts and often rather formal looking blouses, think of the men doomed to hats and coats and ties while they pedaled. Still, after being repressed for so long the bicycle must have seemed like the ultimate in freedom. Where the wealthy had their horses and carriages, now everyone could indulge the craving for mobility at little expense. Naturally, not everybody was content to ride as if dressed for a party, so it was only natural that clothing modification would follow.

The bustle disappeared. Knickerbockers became the number one item on the fashion agenda. Both men and women wore them and the difference was the women's were much fuller. Hats were still worn, and jackets but men adopted the cap too, and younger boys really admired this casual style. The whole 1890's world was cycling, everybody was on the move. Skirts eventually replaced the knickers for women and they were full and easy to manage. Women's Lib wasn't even a gleam in the female eye, but the clothes were telling us something.

The 1890's female preferred such materials as gauze, and the old time silk warp challies, black taffeta was still popular and cashmeres and organdies and a new canvas cloth in fancy weave called 'Mouline natte' flourished. Transparent fabrics such as grenadine, mousseline de soie, chiffon and the small standing collar became part of the fashion scene, especially for Spring. Flowers, vines, scrolls, trimmings of blossoms and leaves covering these light fabrics lent a feminine look.

"Eighteen ninety eight," boasted a woman's magazine, "was a time to buy stripes, and all cord effects are safe for the coming season. Tucks will run crosswise on waist and sleeves and around the skirt, while braids, insertions, ruffles and all decoration will follow in the same path." Ruffles did indeed flourish in every possible width on that year's Summer fashions to such an extent that they often overshadowed the gown itself. Collectors today who find a gown of that era in less than repairable condition, tend to strip it of its laces and ruffles for possible use elsewhere. Do not overlook the possibilities of a gown in very poor condition which may cost too much to have refurbished. If the price is right, its trimmings, even to the buttons, can be useful as a collectible.

The seven gore skirt was in vogue and if you have the good fortune to own or to be able to examine a skirt made in this way, it is clearly a clever way of fitting the garment smoothly across the front and hips and giving it a graceful fullness at the back. For those interested, not only in the clothing of the day, but the way it was made, this type skirt has a dip in the back which is given more by the bias back seam than by the added length at the bottom. In certain materials, such as wool, this was a rather flowing cut and flattering. Wool was a favorite for clothing of this period and much of it is still in surprisingly good condition.

The late 1800's allowed for almost any color, any material or shape in women's dresses, although black dominated colorwise and the foulard again was gaining favor. Although the name 'foulard' is used again and again in fashion writings of the day and we can assume that it communicated itself immediately to the women who read the writings, it is not something most of us hear much about today. It encompasses several fabrics, it is a lightweight twill or plain woven silk, or silk and cotton, and it usually has a small printed design. The fabrics used in the more expensive gowns of the late 1800's were made over using the original material. Sometimes this was done more than once so if the needlewoman was skilled, we often cannot date a dress accurately.

White crepe de chine sounds seductive now, and indeed it was meant to be then. Dresses made of this often have fascinating trim, narrow lace ruffles, or deep ruffles edged with lace. This silk crepe makes any garment we find today expensive, but it is usually quite beautiful.

Sleeves of that day were distinctive and more than anything else give the garments the look we most associate with the period. They were generally long and trimmed at the top, cuffs or edgings were usually seen at the wrist. By the turn of the century, the ideal, unrealistic goal in waistlines was 19 inches. There were cases of ruined health by women seeking the impossible.

The designers were handling fashion as if it were great art. The upper sleeves were very large and full and balanced horizontally with the hem of the skirt, but the eye was drawn inevitably to the tiny waist. It is an exercise in proportion and these designers did their work so well that it is the silhouette which comes to mind, rather than individual garments when we think of the late 1890's.

It would probably send the Victorian lady in a state of shock if she realized that collectors of 1995 are madly seeking her underwear. Back to Basics might well designate collections of undergarments of the 1880-1890 period. There is more underclothing available to the collector than would seem possible, probably because women wore so much of it, a goodly quantity of it has survived. The underthings were cleverly engineered to nip in or add on, tighten or disguise. Nobody's perfect, so there was plenty of it made, and plenty of it now to choose from.

The corset is legendary and one wonders today how women were ever coerced into wearing them. They were linen covered, shaped with whalebone or steel. The whalebone lent flexibility to the corset and was not so heavy as the steel, but in either case the corset could be considered a dangerous garment. Smelling salts were big sellers and it probably had to do with the tight corset.

Today we look on these as high collectibles, particularly from a museum standpoint. Several major museums have mounted showings of the corset, and in this kind of viewing they do have a certain fascination, and in the abstract, were often beautifully made; from a practical standpoint women of the 1990's should give daily thanks for their liberation from this undergarment.

It's questionable who suffered more from this fashion – the Right Whale which almost became extinct or the woman who wore the corset. It is not rare to find these, especially those with the steel ribs. Some have been found in the original boxes in pristine condition. Even then there were women who refused to conform or was it just faint heart?

Drawers, which are simply a takeoff of longish underpants are a wonderful addition to a collection. They are charming in an innocent, long-ago sense. They were meant to cover the 'limbs' and were popular for a very long time. Most of the surviving drawers, and indeed a surprising number have survived, are elegantly ribboned and trimmed with lace, but even the simpler ones are real conversation pieces. These undergarments, unless unusually elaborate, are more easily cared for than the dresses or suits since their basic material was cotton or muslin. It is a fast growing segment of the vintage clothing field.

Another interesting and overlooked collectible is the apron.

For everyday household chores, the apron was in full swing in the 1880-1890 period. The lifestyle of women still dictated their almost total commitment to the home and although women were beginning to emerge into the workforce, house and hearth was still the lodestar of their existence. So aprons were not only necessary, but fashion magazines of the day spent much space discussing this covering. Nowadays the apron is an anachorism except the frothy little concoctions we tend to don during the holiday season, or the barbecue aprons sported by men who feel more in the cordon bleu spirit when the voluminous garment is covering them.

The 1890's lifestyle dictated the use of the apron.

Afternoon tea was an ordinary aspect of life and demanded a covering for the dress of the young lady who did the pouring. These were fancy, net or lace, made in any way the owner chose, but reaching to the knee and made rather narrow. Some exist of Valenciennes or Brussels lace with very elaborate trimmings. There were fancywork aprons for needlework – embroidery was popular because even at leisure hands should not be idle – and, of course, the ordinary work-a-day aprons. These were generally about two-thirds length and were made of lawn, nainsook or dimity, but were also trimmed to relieve the plainness. These materials could be laundered fairly easily, a necessity for the working apron.

The apron wardrobe was large and diverse. There were sewing aprons, servants aprons, nurses aprons, the aprons artists wore, kitchen aprons, children's aprons and most interesting of all as a social commentary, the aprons worn by the new young women who were beginning to take jobs. They worked behind the counters or were moving into offices as 'typewriters'. To cover their clothing they wore simple aprons of black cambric or sateen which was made of 2 lengths of material hemmed together to a belt and either buttoned in back or tied with long, black strings. These reached the bottom of the skirt and had at least one pocket. These intrepid women also wore cuffs which often matched the apron.

Very few vintage clothing collectors have, as yet, focused on this area, but it is interesting and often delightful. It is challenging too, but a good, representative collection of aprons could be made from the 1880's to the 1980's, and it is yet an inexpensive way to collect.

Aprons are beginning to appear in the shops, many reminiscent of a very different lifestyle. Not so glamorous as the designer clothing, or even the less costly pretty day dresses, aprons are a relatively untapped field, different, and because they are available and reasonably priced, rewarding.

These lesser collectibles within the large category of Vintage Fashion can be formed into deep and valuable categories of objects, certain to appreciate in value as well as interest, so always keep the accessories in mind when you buy older clothing.

Accessories were abundant in pre-1900 America. There was such a myriad of things with which to complement an ensemble that the mind boggles. Fashion maintained that these little trifles could be added to suit one's individual taste, and so the belts were often jeweled with precious gems or imitation stones, but silver and turquoise were favorites for the shirtwaist costume, emeralds and gold for blouses of velvet. Gold filigree belts were in vogue and the waist fell to the hemline and all manner of clever sash arrangements, as well as chiffon or lace or silk neck arrangements which tied under the chin were worn. Such short tie arrangements are still seen.

Veils were considered in fashion although ladies were warned that if the veils were dotted and "if the dots are too close, they will throw shadows on the face, but if scattered widely will have a flattering effect." Another typical fashion which seems forever etched in our consciousness is the empire scarf which was over 2 yards long and was meant to be fastened about the brim of the hat, crossed at the back and brought around and knotted on the left shoulder. A very romantic picture this, but not many seem to have survived. A favorite for this kind of scarf was Palin Brussels net so we are sometimes deceived into looking for chiffon and gauze and bypass the net.

Somewhat larger fans, feather ones or net or silk or gauze; suede gloves and suede dancing slippers were all the crack, and are all to be ardently embraced when discovered. Fan collectors have long been active, but gloves are still, for the most part, lying in piles in out of the way boxes in shops, and they are still in the bargain category.

The freedoms which were coming were certainly manifesting themselves in fashion. Whereas black stockings had been de rigueur, now plaids or stripes, even embroidered effects replaced the rather elegant black, and polka dot hosiery was said to be a big seller. For the collector, finding a pair of hose of this era is a tremendous find. Usually when they are available, it is hosiery which had never been worn and simply laid away. Just as today the stockings were not much considered, and having served their purpose were discarded. Probably it is best to consider the hosiery a bonus to your clothing collection, never stop looking for it, but don't expect to find it too often. Recently I saw a pair of Victorian spats for $30. Condition was excellent and before I could say, "I'll take them," they were bought by someone more decisive than I. Anything to do with the years 1880-1890 will sell because it can no longer be treated lightly, it is definitely museum bait.

Combs, too, have always had their devotees. The comb suited the pompadour hair style very well and were ornate and bejeweled and bedazzled the onlooker with multi-colored stones. There are many quite large and lovely comb collections already in existence, and not every clothing collector includes examples, although a comb lends authenticity to the dress. In collecting garments it is well to remember their context and if possible, to add a few of the accessories typical of their period. Even the august Smithsonian Institution has begun to equate the First Ladies gown collection with the rooms and artifacts of their times. If a collector strives to add some good quality items which tend to be silent pointers to the era it can only add interest and piquancy.

Children's fashions have always had appeal. Probably during the 1880-1890 period it was Kate Greenaway who most influenced their design. The popular artist of the 1890's depicted children dressed much as they would have been a century earlier, in the 1880's the Little Lord Fauntleroy look was introduced by the illustrations in the novel, the black velvet suit with a lace collar and plumed hat. A television rerun of the old film recently held a group of young people in thrall, so who knows what the future holds for little boys clothes.

Children seem always to have had more freedom in their clothing than the adults of the same time, and of course the infants were dressed in long dresses regardless of their sex. One of the great guides in this field are the old catalogues if precise dating is desired, but in the case of children, clothes were often handed down and may have been worn years after their purchase. From about the end of World War I, the whole world wanted to look young, and both children and adults wore much the same styles. Children's clothing is rather specialized, it tends to be expensive when the garment is old and attractive, and not all dealers handle it. It certainly lends authenticity to a collection and should be actively sought out if your aim is for all clothing of a certain period. People who love this type of apparel could not choose a more endearing type, if you do buy the dresses and suits worn by youngsters, search assiduously for the shoes, they are very special.

As in any collecting field, the fashion collector should be aware of developing trends. Today the Victorian wedding gown is one of the most desired of all garments. Young women are buying them to use just as they were originally intended and this fits into the general passion we all have for nostalgia.

Actually, the white gown and veil with orange blossoms was a Victorian invention. The gown was not meant to be put away after the wedding. It was to be used as a formal dress, or evening dress. My great grandmother's wedding dress of the 1880's shows much wear indicating it did double duty long after the wedding itself, it was not put away after the ceremony in tissue and into the cedar chest. It had never been intended for that fate.

The Victorian wedding dress can be magnificent, the best of them are overwhelming. The long train, the sleeves, full at the top, the luxurious fabric and the veil, often of precious lace crowned with either artificial or real orange blossoms. Not all of them had the large sleeves or the train and some are very simple, which proves once again that accurate dating in clothing is sometimes difficult.

While details have significance for the collector, it is more important to try to date by period divisions as suggested in this guide, otherwise, overlapping motifs which appeared and reappeared, and the fact that not everyone was prosperous enough to keep up with minor stylistic influences makes the average collector's task a considerable one. Even museums, unless given exact dates by the donor, generally use at least a decade time span.

Underwear is a good example of difficulty in precise dating.

Much of it was handmade following broad fashion dictates and while seeming to conform to a specific time, can often stem from an entirely different time, so it is best to use the famous 'circa' instead of dealing in specific years.

As 1900 dawned the most memorable thing about the late 1800's left its imprint. It was the shape of the female form. As sleeves continued to grow larger at the top and the skirt narrowed over the hips, the emphasis shifted to the tiny waist. Mention the gay nineties to anyone, the vision it conjures up is invariably that flamboyant, wasp waisted charmer.

1879-1880. Left to right, Cashmere dress with crepe; cashmere imported from India. The girl's dress is a copy of adult style, also made of cashmere with grosgrain and lace trim. Note oriental doll and clocks in hose. This dress is of satin with chiffon and velvet; the little girl's coat is velvet with fur trim, bonnet has large, curling feather; the woman's cloak is of heavy silk. This type of dress in excellent condition is almost unattainable, should such costumes become available value can vary considerably dependent upon geographical location and condition. Minimal prices should be $2000-3000.

These, and the gowns on page 7, are magnificent and feature satin, satin and silk, tulle, grosgrain, fine gauze and faille. Fine examples of the styles of 1880.

Children of 1879-1880. Boy's suit sports large brass buttons both on jacket and pants, the dresses and coats the girls wear are all high priced, very high fashion clothing of the period. Prices vary on any garments of this type but the dresses should begin at $850. $750 for the boy's suit of this era.

PARISIAN FASHIONS OF 1885. Left, walking dress of silk with tiny flower print. Bow trim in back, cut velvet accents. Paris label. Value $2,000 minimum. A very elegant 'dressy' costume of fine wool with lace ruffles on the skirt. Large bustle. Blouse has pleats down front. This was the very latest style in 'fancy' dress in 1885. Paris label. Fan has oriental motif. Value $3,000 minimum. Right, cut velvet trimmed with jet and made to fit over the bustle. Long front panel heavily decorated with jet beads. Lined with silk. The skirt is silk with gold threads and lace insets. Paris label. Should a garment such as this become available with the genuine jet trim it should have a starting price of $4,500. Museums are fast becoming the primary purchasers of this type period clothing.

8

C. 1885. These ladies wear two piece dresses with pleated skirts, a fairly common fashion at that time. Button trim as well as trimmings of beads and braids were also popular. These dresses are wool, floor length for the older woman, shorter for the younger. Boning in the waists helped minimize the waistline. Value of each $1,200-2,000. To contemporary eyes these dresses look quite fussy but often were considered 'house wear'.

Little Lord Fauntleroy had nothing on this young boy who wears a heavily starched white linen and eyelet trimmed collar and cuff set over his suit. Replete with large bow his costume overshadows that of the little girl. Her dress is linen with ruffled yoke and high neckline. The boy's high shoes lace, the girl's button. Collar and cuffs $350-450, girl's dress $200-250.

The flounces, the ribbon and lace inserts, the button trim, the shorter length considered appropriate for the younger woman all point to the style and quality of this dress. Silk and taffeta c.1884-1885. $1,500-2,500.

Although this figured satin dress probably dates from 1894 to 1896, tradition has it that this picture was taken in 1898. This illustrates the continuing fact of life that fashion may dictate a certain style but women wear what they must, or what they love, regardless of 'official judgment.'
Notice lace handkerchief pinned at neckline.   Value $1,800-3,000.

Purple was an 'in' color at the turn of the century. Taffeta, well-made, unusual buttons of abalone, bows, heavy silk fringe, on the bottom, velvet accents and of course the bustle. This piece of dress-making is a tribute to the skill of the modistes of the time. Every Vintage Clothing collector is looking for at least one of these. So is every museum curator, movie producers, clothing rental shops, historical societies, and apparently just plain folks. Value $3,000-3,500.

Supposedly a photograph of Grand Duchess Louise. Certainly the dress is worthy of a duchess. It is an extravagant creation of striped silk taffeta, heavily beaded with lace insertions, tassels and lace at sleeve ends and with a flounced train. Magnificent. $3,500-5,000.

Most collectors can only fantasize about owning garments of such beauty from the 1895-1896 period. Lavish does not begin to describe the best of them and they are scarce and almost unobtainable. Most which are found require restoration and that is a project for the skilled professional.

An early Autumn toilette from Paris, 1895. This gown is from Maison Worth of Paris and is a golden brown faille. It was recommended for use on cool days. It has embroidery of silk and of spangles done on the faille in straight bands of galloon on the sleeves, the corsage front is a pointed bolero which turns back in narrow revers and a square collar from a full chemisette front of Pompadour taffeta. The front is here obscured by a large Louis XVI cravat which was then all the rage. The craval is lace and ruffles. The skirt is cut in one of the new techniques Worth was then using, with a seam down the middle of the front and pocket-like pieces trimming the hips. A large round leghorn hat in a natural grayish shade. Altogether magnificent. Value $6,000-10,000.

In the 1890s even the youngest children were sometimes put into mourning clothes. This girl wears a frock of black Henrietta cloth with a short circular skirt and a waist with a blouse front. The round yokes of French crepe are surrounded with crepe pleating. The hat is similarly overdone but from a collecting standpoint would be worth going the proverbial mile to acquire. Dress $1,000-2,000.

The woman wears a mourning gown of crepon with a crepe collar. Wide circular skirt, square lace over collar. Value $3,000-4,000. There are now collectors specializing only in these mourning costumes.

Ladies' Polonaise with adjustable pannier - front and back view. A complicated dress to make - it required almost 10 yards of lightweight goods and was considered a summer garment. Beautifully tailored with heavy fringe and print trim. 1880. $2,000-2,500.

11

A bit overdressed for croquet? Oh yes, but such a picture of elegance and grace. And such vintage clothing treasures. This summer toilette is white mohair made with a plain full godet skirt and a belted waist which has a full vest, gathered at the neck, shoulders and belt. The fronts roll from the vest in revers, which are faced with embroidered white silk and which expand into epaulettes over the full sleeves. Three straps of white ribbon caught with rosettes cross the vest and a narrow belt of ribbon goes around the waist 1895. Value $3,500-4,500.

The tan colored serge gown on the right made in simple tailor style has a round waist with three box pleats at the front and one at the middle of the back. The middle pleat of the front is caught down with clustered rows of small pearl buttons. Between the pleats are bretelles of tan moire ribbon with double loops drooping at the top. Collar and belt are of the same material stitched to fasten in a point. Perhaps simple by 1895 standards but a magnificent gown. Value $2,000-2,500.

Front and back view of a Princess style dress of the 1880-1881 period. The Princess style is very flattering to the woman with an excellent figure and it has always been popular. This one was considered useful for at home wear although by our standards it is quite elaborate with its many bows and train. This is black twill. 1880. Value $1,500-2,000.

This costume was considered 'simple' in 1880, but at the same time stylish and attractive. It illustrates the prevailing style of materials, the mixture of solid color and busy Oriental fabrics. It was an outdoor outfit so was made of suiting material. Value $1,500-2,000.

12

The cape was a 'fashionable wrap' in the early 1880s. The satin bow finishes off the layers of ruffling which make this cape so appealing. Shown front and back. Value $350-550.

Another morning costume of the 1880 period. This is cambric and considered 'pretty' with its long row of self covered buttons, pockets with bows, large bottom flounce, and sprightly trim. A pleasing costume. Shown here both back and front. Value $1,200-1,800.

A SPENCER waist. The spencer is a term frequently misunderstood. It is a short tight jacket which could also be used as a waist. This one is cambric trimmed with piping of a contrasting color and very popular item in the early 1880s. Value $200-250.

Right:

The opulence and exquisite tailoring of these complicated gowns of 1895-1896 has to be seen to believed. The nipped waist emphasized the wide skirts, the scallops at that waistline were considered a slenderizing touch, the sleeves, the high collar, the hat and parasol all combine to make these custom made garments national treasures. This is black taffeta. Value $3,500-5,000.

Top Right:

This 1895 Fall fashion is electric blue cloth trimmed with black fox fur. The flared skirt is banded with the fur, the waist is pleated at the front and plain in back, and is fastened at the side. The yoke has a high collar of blue velvet, the draped collarette is of broche shot silk in green, blue and black and is edged with fur. Value $3,500-5,000.

Dresses of the 1884-1885 period all reflect excellent workmanship and meticulous detail. Left is rep wool with lace at neck and cuffs. Bottom flounce has small tassels for trim. The secret of this clothing lay in the fit. Standing for fittings was a tedious process. Waist is boned. Value $1,000-2,000.
Right has the recurring button trim on a cut velvet over silk bodice. Bottom flounce and of course the front drape gathering to a bustle in back. Value $1,500-2,000.

If daisies could tell, this young lady of the 1880's could describe her feelings about the tight corseting of the day which gave gowns such as she wears their unique look. The dress is two shades of satin with a fairly flat bustle. This dress does not sweep the floor. Button trim, lace at high neckline. Value $1,500-2,000.

14

1883 dress, taffeta, ruffled at neck and sleeve edges, fullness at top of sleeve, tight at wrist, self rosettes on circular skirt. Value $1,000-1,200.
Man's suit, wool, double breasted, long jacket, high buttoned. Value $400-600.
Child's cotton dress, simple but with ruffled neckline, worn over embroidered-edged petticoat. Value $145-195.

Brown and beige striped taffeta robe, c. 1850-1860, the boned bodice and bell-shaped loose sleeves trimmed with navy and white ruching, the hand stitched skirt lined with brown glazed chintz. Bodice relined at a later date. This robe sold at auction for $400 and is valued at $1,000-1,800.

A turkey red calico with a small white print makes up this house dress or wrapper of 1885-1905. The yoke is white with ¼" red embroidered flowers. The gathered yoke of the red material has a 1" wide ruffle of red embroidered and scalloped edging. The dress is semi-fitted princess style in front and flares to a full skirt. The back has a 5" wide inverted pleat from the shoulders. It is tucked at the waistline. Full leg-o-mutton sleeves taper to a white cuff of the same embroidered ruffle. An amazing amount of work was expended on the tailoring of these 'at home' garments. Value $400-650.

15

Visiting costume c. 1880. Satin striped brown and lavender satin trimmed with silk patterned in pastel colors and silk fringe. Label: Worth, Worth being the great Parisian couturier. $7,500-10,000.

Evening dress by Worth, c. 1885. Crimson figured silk with skirt panel of 18th century point d'Angleterre lace, trimmed with red ostrich plumes. Label. $8,500-12,000. Courtesy of Museum of the City of New York.

C. 1900. Silk Chiffon "one of the fancy new materials" at the turn of the century. Dress, $2,000-2,500

C.1897-98 straw hat with plumes, $250-400. Wool poplin suit, $950-1,500. Notice jeweled belt, often these were genuine stones. Kid gloves, French, $45-55.

1894 advertisement. Coats and cloaks of this type are now in the $800-1,000 range without fur, with fur trim depending on the kind, the price rises at least to the $1,000-1,500.

1883 Black Mourning dress, gathers in front, ornamented back, trimmed with black jet beads. Value $1,800-3,000.

An autumn fete costume, 1894. Cocoa brown with very large leg-o-mutton sleeves. Velvet, striped ribbon trim. Value $2,500-3,800.

Latest fashions of 1891. The garment on the left features the very popular ¾ length jacket and the tailored look. The center dress is of silk and the colorful costume reflects the bright and often unusual color combinations worn during this era. The walking dress on the right is of faille and shows the hip detail emphasized during the 1890's. The hats are worn perched squarely on top of the head which was the millinery mode. The shoes were either laced or buttoned and all the ladies wore gloves. Any garment bearing a Paris label of this vintage and obvious quality ranges in price from a minimal $3,500-6,500.

Figured silk apricot colored gown, 1890. Value $850-1,000. Photo by Kenn Knackstedt. Courtesy Southern Oregon Historical Society.

1884 Wedding dress. Satin and lace, fichu at neck. Value $2,000-3,000. Parasol $200-250.
Photo courtesy of Southern Oregon Museum, Kenn Knackstedt, photographer.

21

c.1918-1921 wedding party. Each dress is different, each pair of shoes differs from the others. The bride is quite nicely dressed but the individual costume touches on the attendants (the cameo e.g.) are rather distracting from the main players in the drama. Overall it is a wonderful representation of a complete formal wedding party of that time. The dresses are silk and depending on the extent of embroidery are valued at $500-1,000. The boy's suit is valued at $125-195.

22

1880 dress. Black and white characteristic of the second Victorian bustle period. Black velvet fitted bustle jacket, lace dress trimmed with velvet. Black ebony handled parasol trimmed with Spanish lace. Wool hat with cock feathers. Dress, value $1,200-2,000 (with jacket). Hat $200-250.

Late 1870's style dress. Made of light blue wool, trimmed with brown velvet. It is accented by a high collared silk blouse. Undergarments consist of a corset and wired bustle. This dress, as shown, is a 1979 copy of an authentic dress in the collection of the State Historical Society of Wisconsin and patterns may be obtained from them. The original pattern has been altered to add the collar, wide cuffs and an extra ruffle to the skirt. Hat is of brown velvet with tinted feathers. Hatbox from Dobbs, Fifth Avenue, NY. Purse is of brown velvet to match the dress.

Costume appraised in 1985 at $2,000, value norm. Approximate cost of materials $170.

Dark green and amber silk short jacket, high banded neckline of lace over silk, lace bodice. c. 1880-1885. Value $400-500.

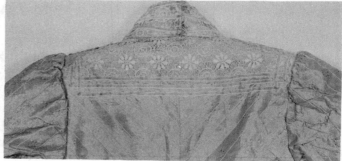

Back detail of above photo.

Typical well-dressed couple of the early 1890's. This shoulder and waistline was not just every woman's dream; with boning and lacing it was for many an actuality. Fainting was common in those days.

Late Victorian white crocheted house jacket, princess type seams create a beautifully fitted garment. This is photographed on a 1909 patented dress form by Hallborchert Dress Form Co. NY, Chicago. Value of jacket $400-500.

Worth of Paris gown, tussah silk, with train, c. 1898. Known to have been worn in 1900. Value $5,000-8000.

Victorian blouse with silk corde applique which is different from most blouses of the time. Probably worn with a full skirt with bustle in back. Notice how blouse is cut in back to accomodate the bustle. Tied at waist to form pigeon breasted look. All hand made. Value $500-650.

Victorian combing jacket, machine made lace, silk satin ribbon insets, lined with blue silk. Value $500-750.

See-through lace over rust colored taffeta underdress. Known to have been worn about 1890. Value $750-1,000.

White cambric nightgown, crocheted straps and bodice, tucked and ruffled nightcap. c. 1885.
Nightgown value $195-200. Nightcap value $45-50.

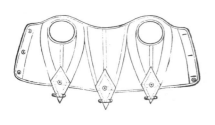  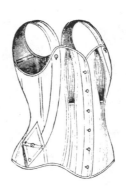 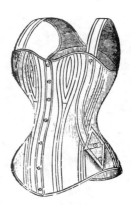

These undergarments of 1893 were called 'waists'. They are rare and make a great sociological comment on the way children were dressed in those years. Left to right, baby's waist worn by infants 1 year old, double V model, ages 1 to 3 years wore this type which in a slightly longer version was worn by boys and girls up to 10 – young ladies ('growing girls') wore this kind until they were 16 – and the ladies wore the extra long waist. This was covered in sateen. These waists supported stockings and underclothes from the shoulder, it supposedly allowed for more freedom of movement. Value $250-300 each.

Left to right

Princess slip or 'foundation dress'. Shaped to the shoulder by seams to the shoulders front and back. Circular flounce gives round length. This is of lawn but most often these were made of Chinese silk or dimity, worn under the lingerie dresses in vogue in 1910. $200-275 1910-11. Another princess slip with three ruffles for support of the outer garment. The kind of dresses worn dictated this style of slip. The lower support of flounces gave the dress what was called "the sweep". Value $250-350.   Drawers 1910. Despite the popularity of the combination lingerie, drawers and corset covers continued to be used especially when a 'sheath effect' was not desired. These drawers show a 'yoke belt' finished at the bottom with a deep ruffle which may be either straight or circular. It could be tucked or trimmed with beading or inserted lace. Tape is run through a casing formed by a row of stitching. Embroidery was often used for dainty effect and this affects price. These were an important fashion item at the time and they are most often found in cambric or batiste but they can be found in all qualities some boasting magnificent laces and handwork. Regulation length of these drawers was usually 24" at the side. Price dependent upon materials and trims. Types shown valued at $125-250.

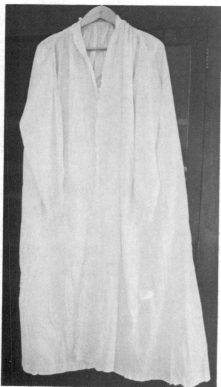

Gentleman's nightshirt, cotton, button front, small pearl buttons, crocheted edging at front and sleeves. c.1880. Value $175-225.

Elaborate nightdress, c. 1880. Muslin with crochet trim. Value $195-250.

Above

1909. Apron. In 1908-1910 an apron was considered a necessity. "Suitable clothes for the kitchen are as indispensible as the street garb" was the fashion dictate. This apron has a gored skirt to eliminate 'bunching' at the top. It is joined to a waistband and bib portion which fastens at the back by two extensions which button onto the belt. Nurses and housemaids also wore this type apron well into the century. Usually found in gingham, percale, muslin or lawn. Shown in lawn. Value $195-250. As with most everyday type clothing these aprons were often discarded when they showed wear so they are now scarce and still overlooked.

OUR IMPORTATIONS FOR THIS Season comprise all the latest and most attractive Novelties in Fans and HOLIDAY GOODS, including Clocks, Bronzes, Art Porcelains, Terra-Cotta Figures, Pedestals, etc., etc.

THE JEWELRY TRADE ARE SPECIALLY INVITED TO VISIT AND FAVOR US WITH THEIR TRIAL ORDERS.

THE MOST ELEGANT AND EX-tensive Line of Fans in the World to select from. SUPERB FANS with Artist proof Paintings.

Fans with elegant mountings in Oriental Pearl, real Tortoise-Shell, with beautiful combinations of Gauze, Laces, Ostrich and Fancy Feathers, etc., etc.

THE "TRIANON."

HECHT BROTHERS,

IMPORTERS OF

FANS

— AND —

Fancy Goods,

483 and 485 BROADWAY,

NEW YORK.

Fans typical of the 1890's. Feather fans range between $195-450, lace fans of the type shown $175-350, gauze in combination with other decorative accents $150-195.

Straw hat, with long taffeta ribbons, floral, ribbon and net trim. c. 1890. Value $175-250.

Parasols, linen, c. 1880. Left, cream linen with blue trim, embroidery. Folding wood handle, still in original box. Value $200-250. Right, tan linen, plain, long wooden handle. Value $125-175.

Millinery trade card of Willis and Dunham of Minneapolis, c. 1870's. This type bonnet was worn for a fairly long period of time. Trade cards are an instructive, very definitive tool in any area of collecting and should always be sought after. The hats are valued at $300-400 in their wonderful shapes and soft straw and floral trim. The trade card cost $24 some years ago.

WILLIS & DUNHAM,
WHOLESALE & RETAIL MILLINERY,
323 Nicollet Ave., MINNEAPOLIS.

1898. Girls dresses, cotton, belted, scalloped hems and sleeve edges. Value $165-250.

This adorable child of the 1890s wears a velvet coat with white piping and many buttons over a white cambric ruffled dress. The pockets on the coat are quite distinctive. Her soft bonnet ties under the chin and is composed of rows of ruffles with a large velvet center. A coat such as this in good condition is valued at $200-300; the bonnet $50-65.

A general overview of children's and young peoples clothing of 1870. It is almost impossible to buy this vintage for collections unless one happens on a long forgotten trunk. It was a period of fine velvets, fringes, flowing sleeves, mantles 'for old ladies', slashed skirts and sleeves, loops of scotch braid, button ornaments often of jet, all sorts of unusual collars, ruffles and black, black, black. Some of the mourning costumes of this period are still available since so many were made and worn for so long but the 1870s is not an era from which we collectors can expect to acquire too much. We should always be alert however and any gown from the 1860s to the mid 1870s in excellent condition and depending on trim should be valued at a beginning price of $2,000. Childrens clothing should start at $850.

Infant's high necked robe; these are now considered precious heirlooms and the family which owns one should consider itself very fortunate. Many people actually have dresses of this type framed and if properly done they make a beautiful sight. These back and front views show a robe with a high neck made of fine lawn and elaborated with Valenciennes lace, Hamburg edging and insertion. The cost of duplicating such a gown today would be astronomical. These were usually quite long and about 36" wide 1881. Value $600-800.

The girls' petticoat shown here both back and front is cambric, with **Hamburg** edging but many of this type may have an edging of commonly used lace. This was intended for a girl up to nine years old and the fact that the back of the petticoat is more elaborate than the front is dictated by the style of the dress she would put over it. These are charming, and still available, often in simpler styling. 1880. Value $150-195.

Girls' apron. Early 1880s. White muslin it was considered an ornamental way to cover the good clothing and in many cases was more elaborate than the dress it was protecting. Value of this type is $145-195.

Although in the early 1880s this was called a 'slip' it was actually a day negligee dress suitable for a girl to wear either for morning or afternoon occasions. It is in the style of a loose slip and is crossed across the hips with a sash of the same material as the dress, lightweight wool. Front and back views. Value $400-600.

This was called a girls' 'cap'. White pique trimmed with plaitings of the same pique and bows of ribbon. Girls hats are difficult to find in good condition but all collectors should be looking. 1880-1881. Value $85-150.

This baby reflects the attitude in 1893 that chubby was better. This darling was one year old and is wearing the uniform for infants those days, essentially a dress, in this case a jumper over a blouse with an elaborate collar and long sleeves. These little jumpers, often of cotton, have largely disappeared from the collecting scene but are simple and should be inexpensive unless trimmed with lace or hand made edging. Value $35-50.

The little girl on the left top wears an all encompassing fancy cotton apron. 1895 Value $100-150. Right: A nine or ten year old girl would wear this gingham dress with its fancy bows and trim for casual everyday occasions. 1895 Value $250-300. Boy at left wears the very distinctive clothing for a 12 year old in the year 1895. No mistaking this is if you find one. Value $250-350.

Front and back views of 1882 trade card of Bronner & Co.'s catalogue of Fashions for Spring and Summer. Clothing of this type is almost unobtainable but the price ranges for the garments worn only by the young children in the cart are $50-75 for the hats, boys suit $175-200, girl's dress, $175-200. Older children's outfits, girl's long jacketed suit, value $350-450. Boy's two piece suit, $350-450. High shoes worn by both. Each pair, $100-150. Straw hats, each $50-65.

Boy's fashions, 1867. Courtesy of Butterick Archives.

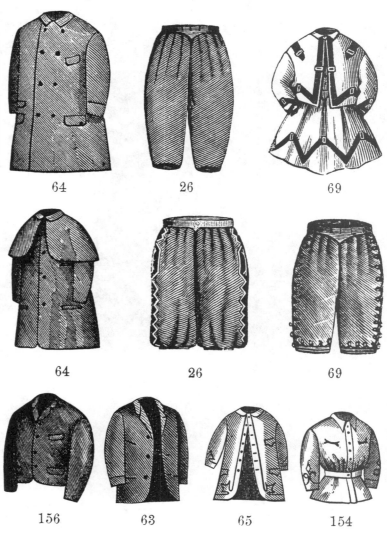

BUTTERICK'S PATTERNS FOR BOYS.

64   26   69

64   26   69

156   63   65   154

33

A formal family portrait of the 1912-1915 period. Everyone is neatly dressed, none of the extremes of that time, although both the mother and son look uncomfortable in their high, rigid collars and the younger boy and girl are also encased in high necklines. Father does seem to have opted for comfort over fashion. This is an instructive and almost historic fashion photograph since it displays the Sunday best of an ordinary family of those days.

This gentleman looks remarkably comfortable in his rather fashionable clothes, seemingly oblivious to the dictum which even then decreed that all photographic subjects should look stiff and posed. His full length coat has a velvet collar, his trousers fit well, his vest has a row of pearl buttons, and his collar is not too rigid. He seems to have been more prosperous than the photographer, whose chair desperately needs re-caning.
Value of coat $195-250.

Hat, straw with satin trim, c. 1898.   Value $195-225

New York fashions of 1871. Courtesy of Butterick Archives.

The hats of 1870 were beautifully made and great attention was paid to detail. They were rather flattering since their bonnet shapes frame the face so well. The black velvet hat is a mass of pretty ribbons, flowers, lace and since it does not tie under the chin was considered a hat, not a bonnet which was still the prevailing mode at that time. The hat on the right is chestnut velvet and again is highly ornamented. It can be seen from the trimming under the satin underbrim that these hats and bonnets were made to highlight the face and usually in colors that matched the coloring of the wearer. The black crepe bonnet on the bottom shows an entirely different approach to decoration, no bright flowers, it is ultra conservative but not plain. It is black crepe with satin trim. Any hat of this era and quality, again depending on condition, material and trim should have a starting price of $350.

CHAPTER TWO
1900-1920

The Edwardian era was a long one. It began at the turn of the century and continued until 1910. So the collector can appreciate that although there were modifications of dress and accessories during these years, the tendency is to label all clothing of the period "Edwardian". It has a lovely ring to it and much of the clothing was as elegant and attractive as the classification.

Paris was still the center of fashion and at this fountainhead the wealthy still worshipped.

Actually the clothes of the Edwardian years did not differ significantly from those of the preceding Victorian era.

Frock coats were still correct formal day wear for men, the female waists were still as small as could be managed, and the 'S bend' shape was achieved by tightly laced corsets. There was fullness at the front of the bodice and the skirt was long and bell-shaped. This is one time when emphasis was not on youth, many of the fashion photos and paintings show a mature, full-blown woman.

Although the designation "Edwardian" derived from the years of rule of King Edward of England, the term has become one which encompasses the age of that particular style. The years before 'the war to end all wars' were opulent ones for those who could afford it. The characteristics of the clothing took on the characteristics of the lifestyle; the very large, highly ornamented hats, the high built up hairdo, the standing collar on gowns, feathers, laces and anything else which was thought to enhance the female figure.

Some of the accessories to men's wear, the separate collars in their charming boxes, cuff links and their boxes, collar buttons and their receptacle, all make delightful collectibles.

The whole of fashion was dictated by the way people lived and while lifestyles may alter, fabrics may gain and lose favor, hemlines may go up or down, human habits die hard.

In the early years of the new century, a woman's magazine was noting the carelessness of some women's dress, and complaining about "those careless Cinderellas who go about in curl papers, flappy old wrappers and decrepit shoes through half the day and blossom out in belated splendor toward evening." Today there are those who decry hair rollers in the supermarket and the eternal, uniform tight jeans. Indeed the amusing list of worst-dressed women circulated each year is simply a commentary on one man's opinion of the way celebrities fail the accepted norms of dress. It is always difficult to argue with personal taste and preference is everyone's right, but 'Good Taste Costs No More' as Mr. Gump said and it is interesting that even in today's permissive society you hear echoes of notions of taste which prevailed in the 1900's.

This was a time when the house gown or wrapper became a major part of the average woman's daily life, and very often these were the product of home sewing, or were homemade as the more affluent were wont to label them. These wrappers were so widely used because they were a respite from the torturous corsets, and were loose and comfortable. The less expensive ones were made of calico, percale or flannelette and were made in the same way as the gowns, standing or small collar, cape effects over the sleeves and usually flounced at the bottom of the skirt. These inexpensive items sold for less than a dollar, and now if they can be found they cost $125 and up.

Nineteen hundred was a fairly enlightened fashion time in that it recognized the reality of women's figures, notably that "stout women" were a large segment of the buying public and needed flattering garments. They were frankly referred to in literature of the day as 'plump' and 'stout.' Nowadays there is a distinct trend to satisfying the "large woman" or man. This is a departure for general fashion, some advertisements are featuring size 38 or 40 models, not merely in the abstract to suggest the full figure, but with photographs. Sighs of appreciation can be heard not only from women themselves but from some men who have always found the broomstick silhouette less than inspiring. The 1900's woman had no problems, the 'pigeon breast' was a requirement in clothing.

In the early 1900's America was welcoming immigrants by the thousands, and all were filled with hope. In some ways this cheerful outlook transferred itself to fashion.

The covert skirt and shirtwaist which was a carry over from the 1890's could be worn again and again and interchanged. The mail order catalogues of the 1900's were filled with types of lady's waists, some of them in practical wool flannel. We tend to want to collect the things of rare beauty in clothing and much of what we have left to us is just that, but the ordinary day wear has a homey, well made look and often tells us more about the people and their lifestyles than the more lavish examples. While prices are rising astronomically on the elaborate dresses and gowns, they are going up more slowly on the lesser examples, but going up they are.

The average woman was a practical soul and oftentimes had a real need to buy garments which would give long service. The small standing collar introduced in the 1890's was an integral part of the 1900's scene. 'Wool tricot' was a newly introduced fabric in 1902, the summer dresses were two piece white lawn and were very attractive with their lace, embroidery and ribbon trim. Prices ranged from $3.75 to $6.75, not inexpensive for the time. We tend to think of that period as always incorporating the high banded neckline but the summer frocks were just as apt to be off the shoulder. With the popular bouffant hairdo tied at the nape with the large bows, these styles were quite alluring. Silk waists were expertly made and considered an absolutely necessary part of the wardrobe.

The young children and girls wore carbon copies of the adult clothing except for length which could vary from 20 to 28 inches in children one to five years old. Sailor type waists were in vogue for girls up to 14 years but the wide collar over the shoulder was prevalent.

Men were encased in one or three button cutaway frock coats or the single or double breasted sack which is a straight-lined jacket, and the average width of the pants leg was 22 inches at bottom. It was a neat look, a dandified look, worn with a bowler hat and high collar with bow tie. Surprisingly, many heavy overcoats from that period survive.

They can be found in differing lengths from 42 inches to 52 inches, depending on the height of the wearer, but the 42 inch coat was generally worn short, at knee length.

The cane was standard, and today we see an occasional good cane collection, but overall there are relatively few people collecting them. The umbrellas and canes of the 1900's are quite neglected by the general collecting public. The variety is vast and can keep a collector busy for years. The various material with which the handles were made are endlessly intriguing and often outlasted the cane or umbrella itself. Today we see these relics in the jewelry cases of dealers, and the sterling silver tops are already the subject of serious consideration.

Boys and younger men wore three piece suits for dress, consisting of coat, vest and knee pants which were tight fitting and usually made with 'double knees'. These met high stockings at the knee.

It should be remembered that men's clothing can be striking and expertly made, but currently it is largely the province of museums and costume departments of colleges and theatrical companies. Boys' and men's clothing beautifully round out a diorama or a family scene of mannequins. Not too many collectors have ventured into this field, except for some of the accessories like hats and caps, and this market is bound to make serious price gains.

One of the most important things a serious collector of Vintage Clothing must consider is display. Toward this, it is important to buy older dress forms if possible. If collecting before 1940 is your main focus, buy any dress form you see. In a one dimensional setting the bustle or the train, for example, do not show to advantage but on a dress form all these details are immediately apparent. Here, of course, you compete with many small retailers who are also looking for these forms as elegant display pieces.

The older forms are usually marked with the manufacturer's name and dated, and these are greatly coveted, as are the old wicker which are a challenge to find, the type which can be made small or large, and the ones with iron bases. But buy any form you see until you can buy exactly what you want, so your wonderful old clothes will avoid creasing, folding, and general wear and tear when you take them out to show.

The old wooden hat forms make marvelous background for hats of the period. It is difficult to show a hat collection properly unless the shape and detail can be appreciated and for this you need a hat stand. Although I have uncovered no very large collections of stands, smaller ones abound, and since dealers themselves need them if they carry hats, they are not scarce but are getting harder to find.

Nothing is more beautiful than a hat collection nicely set out, it can be used instead of sculpture, in many ways that is what a well mounted hat resembles. Hats are colorful and different and are a surprising aid to decor.

Some of the hatstands shown in this guide have been found at flea markets and the smaller shops and for the clothing collector it is important to keep in touch with these sources. Some remarkably lovely clothing is turning up this way and recently I purchased a pair of 1920's silk lounging pajamas for much less than the going rate. Basically though, the collector in this field needs to have rapport with a dealer in fine vintage fashion who will supply the kinds of garments in which you are most interested, in good condition.

Decorators, in a sense, are also seeking clothing and accessories of earlier periods to be used to accent a room, and you will find competition from people who have no interest in vintage clothing but have an eye for the unusual. Such a couple has an old life-size corset form, out of a mid-western store, ornamenting their living room. As with all artifacts concerned with vintage clothing, it is a conversation piece. So the clothing collector needs to buy whatever is pertinent to the collection when it is available, this is such a fast-growing field the watchword is haste.

Recently, an exquisite Edwardian silk dress became available through an estate sale. In perfect condition, the price was high. The skirt consisted of much precious material which seemed to flow from a bodice which was boned, but the collector hesitated. After considering it for a few hours, she decided to buy it, but it had been sold. Not too long after, the gown which had the typically low decolletage was spotted at a downtown shop at an even higher price, and it was marked 'sold.'

This is becoming an increasing problem as well as a great boon to the private collector, as more and more shops devoted to Vintage Fashion open and competition becomes keener. It is to the dealer in fine old clothing that the collector should turn for fashions of the Edwardian period. Although the typical dresses and suits are easily recognized, some of the other apparel made between 1900 and 1910 is not so characteristic and it takes a trained eye to identify it. With enough experience, collectors will acquire the same skill.

The Edwardian age fostered a fashion which has never actually disappeared. The shirtwaist look in a modified way has continued to this very day, largely because it is a flattering and easy style. Fashion was still set by the wealthy in 1900-1910 and Paris reigned supreme.

At the turn of the century women wore sweeping skirts and since they did, literally, sweep the floor it must have been a monumental chore to keep clothing immaculate. Around the house, some women resorted to large bands of material folded over the hem and secured on both sides.

Crossing streets and climbing stairs called for lifting the skirt and it was important to do this correctly so as not to disturb the fit over hip and back.

Worth, the incomparable designer and trend setter, was still a famous name and for the fashionable a gown from Worth of Paris was elegance personified.

Furs and feathers, as well as umbrellas and parasols were part of the costume.

Magazines of that time show innumerable ads for underthings and corsets which were considered part of a bride's trousseau and were an important part of the fashionable life of the female. One of the adjuncts to fashion which should appeal to any collector is the boudoir cap which was worn to cover any less than perfect coiffure. These were made in a wide range of materials and trimmings, and are among the delightful fripperies one can search for. While still relatively inexpensive because they have been neglected for a long time, they are rising in price.

Since there are still not too many collectors of these delightful concoctions it is a relatively untapped field, but now their beauty and potential is recognized and a beginning collector should waste no time. About 9 years ago, I purchased a lovely little silk and crocheted cap for $6, several years later I saw a similar cap for almost 6 times that. From an investment standpoint, that is certainly appreciation.

During parts of the Edwardian years, shoes were not always visible, as time went on and skirts shortened, the shoe again became somewhat important. Vintage shoes are becoming expensive and any from this period, either high buttoned or high laced, are quickly sold. The more utilitarian shoes, which were high laced, are almost impossible to distinguish from a man's shoe. Before I began my consuming pursuit of vintage fashion, I bought a pair of what I thought must surely be a man's footwear. A little research showed this to be a woman's shoe, so beware if you are new to the period.

It is always wise to look for shoes of the same vintage as the garment, so that when you display you can accompany the dress or suit with the complementary accessories. This gives a sense of completeness, and a sense of history.

The Hobble skirt was prevalent in the years before the first World War, satin shoes for evening and high button shoes for day wear. The flippant "that went out with high button shoes" summed up the reaction of the following decades to that style and that may be why they are so difficult to find. But the shoe collector has a veritable bonanza of choices. Patent leather vamps paired with elegant uppers, sometimes silk or suede, are just waiting somewhere to be discovered.

Of all the collectibles in clothing, shoes seem to attract the fewest fans, although a New York Department store recently had a rather limited showing of vintage designer shoes. Shoes are one of the great indicators of prevailing fashions and often delineate a specific era even more than the garments. Home sewing became widely practiced in the early part of the 20th century and so some fashions could have been made in older styles or clothing could have been altered, but shoes would normally have to be purchased regularly and would thus have been made in the prevailing mode and each time had its typical footwear.

The collector hopes for a pair that is unworn, but this is not always possible, and even museums are now resigned to showing shoes that are in less than perfect condition. High button shoes, especially those belonging to small children have an endearing quality that shoes of other periods do not possess, and of course there are those shoe button hooks which come in several sizes and have attractive handles, often silver or mother-of-pearl. Try for a few of these to match the shoes. Try always to think of your collectible in the round; the shoe button for the right shoe style; the appropriate stand for the hat; the dress form to show off the gown; the correct handbag, all of these can give meaning to your clothing. Visit your local museum or an available Vintage Clothing Museum (such museums are proliferating rapidly) or even a fine Vintage Clothing shop to see how the professionals do it. Any collection benefits from being complete and it is the small things which lend interest. The Smithsonian Institution is now placing emphasis on the background of the First Ladies' gowns. As well as the gowns themselves, the display is moving to include period rooms and accessories.

The hats had to be spectacular to accommodate the coiffure, and a long hatpin was needed. Hatpins are an almost legendary collectible and are often classed with jewelry, but I feel that those who love the Edwardian era should collect a few representative hatpins. A simplistic rule of thumb has it that the older the hatpin the longer the shaft and this is usually true, after all it had to pierce hat, hair, rats, padding and heaven knows what else. Hatpins, which were costing only a few dollars a few years ago can now go for astronomical prices depending on age, the kind of metal used as well as the genuineness of the stones, and beauty.

Of special interest during the 1900-1910 period were the hats men wore. A man's hat, you may say, is just a hat. Not true, even today when hats are seldom worn, notice the caps men are donning with more frequency; baseball caps, caps with company logos, caps with club emblems, usually vented on top and back for summer comfort, and peaked. In warm areas of the country these caps are becoming commonplace. In 1900 the top hat went with the frock coat, the homburg was becoming necessary to the less formal day suit and the straw hat became the fancy of both men and women.

Just as the fashions of women have moved to the less formal, the coats and caps of the gentlemen who drove their motorcars were for those times, fairly informal. In fact, the motorcar was beginning to change America and Americans.

It was in 1913 that a revolutionary change altered women's clothing. It was the V-neck and we can only imagine the freedom that must have brought to the 1900's woman. It was avant-garde for the time and not everyone immediately rushed into it, and the shirtwaist and gored skirt persisted. Silk stockings were worn and on shirts of sheer batiste sparkled crystal or rhinestone buttons. Cotton voile was the choice for day dresses, it was dainty and figured, and lined in a "suitable color."

By 1915 skirts began to widen considerably at the hem but remained tight at the hips. The high waist, raised as much as 2½ inches above normal gave a long line to the skirt, and the voluptuous, mature ideal of the first decade of the 20th century was phasing out.

The years from 1900 to the outbreak of World War I were a time of extravagance and ostentation. The balloon sleeves of the 1890's disappeared and were now tight and extended halfway down the hand. The function of clothing was more practical, how could they have functioned in their overdone, elaborate clothing, as they left the home for shops and offices it was evident that clothing was going to have to adapt to the woman instead of woman adapting to the dictates of fashion.

It was this era that gave us the Gibson girl with the hour glass figure and we can probably forgive fashion arbiters for almost anything just for the pleasure of looking at her. Charles Dana Gibson's creation was the epitome of female beauty of her day, and so lovely that even now, with a few alterations, she can be considered the model for full-blown beauty. Her intricate pompadour coiffure, her gorgeous exposed shoulders by night and her trim fitting neckline by day, coupled with her hour glass figure and provocative poses, decorate more walls of nostalgia buffs than one can count even in this jeans and tee-shirt age. One of the world's best kept secrets is the 'Gibson Man' but attractive as he was, he obviously didn't have that special something.

The late years of the decade were geared toward making the 'World Safe for Democracy.' Simple lines had replaced the former constricting clothing and by the time the men returned home from the trenches they must have suffered a culture shock – they had left a nation of females mincing about in long hobble skirts and now found the vision of women in skirts just below the knee. Women who had participated in the war effort began to forsake the clothes which limited their activities. Realization had arrived that there were things to do, women could do them, but the garments had to fit the dream.

That war changed not only fashion, it changed the entire world forever.

What is fashion anyway? It is probably the ultimate manifestation of a basic need, to be warm, to impress, or as some anthropologists would have it, an early need to be better than the animals. Whatever it is, the clothing collector daily gives thanks.

The average woman has probably not often had the desire to be dressed by a great couturier. Indeed it would be superfluous to her way of life, so it has always been the leisured class which has made fashion. True, the designs filtered down so what we buy off the rack can certainly be traced to an original made in Paris, or Ireland, or Italy but there are hordes of women whose main aim is to look attractive and depending on the occasion, alluring or competent.

Men have been locked into the business type clothing for so long that today any changes taking place are influenced by television. Men's cosmetics, colognes, high heeled boots, brighter colors – Louis the XIV would be right at home with the coming revolution in men's fashions. Some women are no doubt as startled to see these alterations in men's fashions as the returning service men were to see the short skirts of 1919, men have taken to the sports shirt and jacket and in many circles, academia is one, there is less emphasis on the tie; and the hat for purposes other than warmth, is a thing of the past.

Nineteen twenty marked more than the end of a decade, the coiffure was beginning to sport the permanent wave, shorter skirts and more slender figures with a less defined waistline had somehow evolved. Women had the vote, they were moving into the workforce in numbers and their clothes were becoming less restricted and more utilitarian. It was a far cry from Women's Lib, but the signs were there, and as usual fashion foreshadowed the future.

Lingerie dress, white, 2 piece. Waist has ruffles, sleeves have inset lace. Inserts on trim on skirt ruffles match those on waist. Value $1,000-1,800. 1910-1915. Parasol is small size silk with lace, velvet and flower trim. Value of parasol $195-225.

Lingerie dress, 1920's. White sheer cotton inset with wide bands of Irish crochet lace. $2,000-3,000. This beautiful garment is from the auction of actress Ruth Gordon's clothing held in New York in 1986 by William Doyle Galleries. The pre-auction estimate was $300-500, it not only went over estimate but it was a bargain at the price. Since clothing auctions are proliferating, do not neglect them.

Left to right: Tea gown, c. 1915, of black dotted white silk gauze with high-necked yoke of lace. Peacock blue silk sash, black velvet bow trimming in hobble skirt style. Value $600-850.
Two piece summer dress, white linen bodice and skirt with eyelet embroidery, c.1900. Value $500-850.
Summer dress of mauve and white striped cotton voile with square collar. Value $450-650.
Linen suit. Ecru and lace, two piece, linen, with matching embroidered parasol. Value of both $750-1,000.

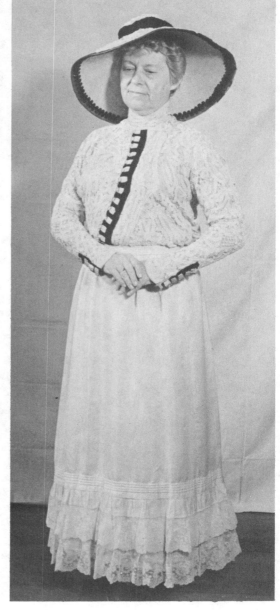

Silk ecru skirt with bustle in back drawn up with a ribbon. Ecru battenberg blouse trimmed in black velvet, rhinestone buttons. Hat is also battenberg with velvet and rhinestone (brilliants) trim. Skirt value $200-300. Waist $450-600. Hat $125-165.

Summer toilette, c. 1900. Black and white striped silk, chiffon and machine made Alencon lace fichu, lace engageantes (trim at sleeve ending), black satin trim. Label: Worth. Value of this striking ensemble $8,000-10,000.
Any Worth of Paris labeled dress should begin at a minimal $3,500, if in good condition.   Museum of the City of New York

42

Jacquard silk with French lace revers, appliqued embroidery, French rosettes, mauve with purple velvet sash, square buttons, C. 1910, value $650-1,000. Woman's straw hat, c. 1910, $95-125.

C. 1900 gown, brown handkerchief linen, inset lace. A magnificent dress. $1,400-2,000.

Dress from 1914-16 of fine lawn. Tiny tucks are used horizontally on the ¾ length fitted sleeves which also have lace insertions and have a tapered ruffle at the shoulder. The yoke is a combination of tiny lawn tucks and lace insertions, with a lace collar inserted at the neck. The full skirt is attached to a lace 3" wide waistband and trimmed with groupings of tucks. A 16" flounce with a wide hem finishes the bottom of the skirt which has tucks and lace insertions in its lower part. This is a lovely dress with much fine lace. Value $2,200-3,000.

This lovely dress is ecru cotton with black soft dots. The waist fullness is fitted at the center of both back and front. The yoke has ¼" horizontal tucks which continue into the high collar. Tucks also at the hipline, knees and just above the flounce at the bottom. A self braid is sewn down the center seam. Battenburg lace is applied defining the yoke edge and there are ornamental sections hanging from the yoke. Shepardess sleeves are tucked at the top. The cuff is flared and lined with net. This dress has a removable lining which is also tucked. A belt of ruby red velvet is fastened at the back with velvet roses. The sleeves are also trimmed with the red velvet. An outstanding dress of the early 1900s not only because it is good to look at but because it is a prime example of the way the clothes were ornamented, even over-ornamented, and yet retained their integrity. The dressmakers were certainly talented. Imagine trying to please the fancy of the women of those times with their demands for decorations on their clothing Coco Chanel would have blanched but each era has its pecadillos and now we treasure these excesses.

Left. Off-white linen, bodice and gored skirt with lavish braid trim. Worn with silk pumps with french heels, natural straw hat with tiger lilies. Sold at Butterfield's auction in 1989 for $288. Value today $500-750.
Center: Two piece, off the shoulder evening gown. Creamy silk satin brocade, swags of roses overprinted garlands of pink watered roses. Full lining of silk Sateen petticoat and chiffon scarf of 'watered' roses. Sold in 1989 for under $200. Value $400-500. Right: Pale brown walking suit lined with chintz. 2 petticoats, brocade jabot, fur hat, mink muff with tail trim, shoulder furs. Value of ensemble $1,000-1,500.

44

If is difficult for us in our casual levis to envision the ladies of the early 20th century functioning in these exquisite, totally feminine but fussy often delicate costumes. We really know not whereof we speak when we discuss layered clothing. These beauties must certainly have turned heads. The one on the left wears a deep amethyst polka dotted ribbon, faggoting and Tom Thumb fringe compose the decoration on the heliotrope twine voile.
Value of dress $2,000-2,800.

The gown on the right is of shaggy gray zibeline ornamented with black, gray and white silk bands. A vest of black velvet distinguishes this costume. Note how many fashions of the day, modified of course, have now returned to the fashion scene, the muff, the vest, the fringe. Value of dress $1,800-2,500.

In the genteel language of the early 1900s these two delightful confections are described as 'Ladies Toilettes'. Left: This is a round yoke waist. The detail work here makes this waist very effective. The body and sleeves are arranged in crosswise tucks in bayardere effect. The skirt has seven overlapping sections which form the outside, the skirt itself is five gored and each skirt has a habit back. This is what is known as the bayardere skirt and can have varying length sweep backs. This material is green peau de cygne with dark green velvet and white lace. The work which went into fine garments of this type was prodigious. Value $2,000-2,500.

A GORGEOUS ladies' waist and skirt of chiffon panama, white silk braid and figured tinted net. The long sleeves are shirred at the seam, Dark 'onion' chiffon with overall lace was used. It has an overblouse effect and bretelles were used at the shoulders. Brown was a very popular color in 1908. Value $1,800-2,500.

This ladies' waist and skirt is of dotted silk mull, Valenciennes lace and has a chiffon velvet girdle. The horizontal tucks in the bodice were often used in light weight fabrics at this time. The bertha with its lace trim complements the square neck nicely. Value $1,500-2,000.

Absolutely unbelievable as it sounds today, words such as 'fear' were used in connection with an evolving skirt shape. This ladies' Princess dress was a favored fashion. It has the waist panel forming the front gore of the skirt. The circular skirt is tucked to correspond with the waist. It is a very effective plaid silk, dark blue on gray with black braid and blue messaline girdle, Value of dress $1,200-1,700. Right: Ladies' shirt-waist dress with nine gored skirt in round length. This was an inexpensive summer dress made of cotton-wool mixture for easy washing. The waist has the 'Gibson plait' in front ¾ length sleeves, the skirt is plain nine gored. It has natural linen cuffs, collar and trimming fold. Dress $650-950.

These stunning creatures in their stunning outfits tempt you to go back in time for one day.

In 1907 certain style features on women's clothing were beginning to become standard. The Princess style for one and the circular skirt for another. This had originally been considered rather grotesque but in 1907 it found acceptance.

RIGHT:

A frock for the older woman. It is impressive to read of the older woman rather than 'senior citizen' it has a dignity which seems to match the clothing this model wears. It has long lines to slenderize and is cunningly designed with the collar extending into trimming tabs on the skirt which accentuates the slim line. The vest adds to this look by lengthening into a girdle. The dress has a definite waistline which was the style in 1919. The vest and girdle are of cathedral satin in the same rich shade of the trico-serge of the dress so as not to cut the figure in two. Skirts were also becoming wider in 1919 and this one falls in slender graceful folds without bulkiness. This dress valued at $1,200-1,700.

LEFT:

This lovely dress is a combination of batiste flouncing, embroidered in delicate colors, with deep flounces of lace. It has a softly draped girdle of satin ribbon which matches one of the shades in the embroidery. The blouse has a gathered vest and has deep bretelles and puffed sleeves. The skirt is cut in three gores with three gathered flounces. Spring of 1914. Value of dress $1,500-2,000.

A tailor made suit for Fall, 1919. The skirts that season were a bit shorter and somewhat fuller and the coat is longer at the sides and back than in the front. Suit $1,200-1,500.

These three summer frocks of 1914 are all of sheer fabrics. Top left, this is soft silk crepe which shows the Dolly Varden flowerings of tiny rosebuds. Trimmings of white mull and soft white lace and tiny bows of satin. The hat also features rosebuds. Dress $850-1,400.

Top right: Lavender lawn with insertions of Valenciennes lace are featured in this summer frock. The blouse is cut in kimono style, the skirt is cut in one piece and is set onto a two-piece yoke. Her reticule and hat are quite dashing. 1914. Value of the dress is $850-1,400.

Bottom center: The waist of this dress is white china silk, trimmed with Valenciennes lace, cut with kimono sleeves and a novel collar opening over a surplice chemisette. The skirt which is cut in 2 pieces has two tunics and an Obi sash. Her hat and parasol illustrate how best to display vintage clothing, always with appropriate accessories of the period. Value of dress $1,800-2,500.

47

Calico morning dress or wrapper, c. 1900. Square collar, rounded yoke, ruffles at shoulder. Skirt has wide flounce at ankle. Made from a contemporary pattern (no longer available). Value of original in period, $250-450. Photo courtesy of FOLKWEAR formerly of San Rafael, CA.

Afternoon dresses, 1913. Waistline at almost natural level. Left, satin dress with draped skirt and jacket effect over chiffon chemisette. Tight sleeves. Value 750-1,200. Afternoon dress. Draped skirt revealing underskirt of silk to match silk jacket and lining of dress. Dress has double line of buttons decorating front. Value $850-1,500

This is the stylish overblouse effect, 1916. The skirt is circular and the girdle is wide satin. Value $850-1,500. Chemise tunic dress, tunic is one unbroken piece from shoulder to hem. Neck has a turnover collar at back and sides. Value $750-1,200.

Left: One piece 'calling' gown. The blouses were by now fairly plain and this is typical. It has a front closing and plain sleeves. The neck is trimmed with a wide epaulette collar. The skirt is four gores and opens in front and is attached to the blouse. These rather simple dresses were considered appropriate for almost any time of day and released women from changing their clothing so often. This is very fine serge. Value $500-800. Notice the length of the bag strap. Right: Youthful frock has simple blouse made with drop shoulder and has a small full vest in front. Three gored skirt has a narrow front panel of contrasting material. This dress is wash-silk. 1912. Value $500-750.

Left, a dainty figured cotton voile dress worn over an underslip of contrasting color. In these sheer fabrics a contrasting colored undergarment was considered fashionable and "care should always be taken that the underwear does not show through". The blouse closes a little left of center, it has the drop shoulder and a plain sleeve. The neck has a small, shaped collar. The skirt is three gored with a high waistline and a soft girdle hides the joining of waist to skirt. Value $750-1,000.

Center, This dress reflects "the dignity of plainness." Although this shirtwaist 'waist' and five gored skirt which fastens in back does not seem too austere to our eyes it had none of the highly esteemed trims so favored. It was considered a good style for 'mourning' clothes of the period, in a suitably muted color, of course. Value $500-750.

This is a smart coat-costume. The coat is actually a blouse and forms the waist of the dress without the use of any other bodice beneath it. The deep neck opening accomodates a chemisette. The sleeves are cut in one with the body of the coat and the peplum below the belt gives the cutaway effect. The tailoring on much clothing of this period is quite sophisticated. Value of costume with skirt of linen and coat of satin and crepe, $750-1,000.

Above right:

1914. This Spring model is all wool French serge. This dress is designed with a detachable shadow lace yoke and collar. The collar is in a new shape embroidered and elaborated with Honiton effect braid. The vestee is trimmed with lace frill and small crystal buttons. The skirt is draped gracefully with self-covered buttons. Navy blue embroidered in white. Very attractive dress. Value $750-1,200.

Afternoon gowns. Left to right: C. 1910. Calling costume, 2 piece, blouse is gathered along the shoulder seam in the front and the fullness thus falls loosely about the figure. It is gathered at the belt. V-neck which could be filled with a small chemisette and standing collar. 2 piece skirt fits snugly but at the lower opening of the side seam there is a slit which displays the petticoat. Value $500-1,000. 2 pieces. The blouse is gathered along the shoulder seam in front and along the lower edge of a shoulder yoke in back, which gives a soft, droopy effect. The skirt is a plain peg top style with a little fullness in front but the back is flat in the upper part with a bulge below the hips then again flattens. Recommended for a slender or medium figure. $500-1,000. 3rd from left: For morning wear. Bodice built on shirtwaist lines but is given a decorative touch by the very low drop shoulder and the yoke which is straight and is used only in front. Sleeve is plain at the shoulder but wide at the armhole where it is set in and slightly full where it joins the cuff at the wrist. Narrow skirt with sash. Morning wear demanded simplicity. Value $450-750. 4th from left: For the Matinee or Afternoon Tea. Plain blouse opens in front, skirt has three gores which gives a seamless back and center-front closing. Value $500-1,000. Two models wear high button shoes, two wear pumps with buckles.

Early winter styles of 1912-1913. The coat blouse was popular and the model at left shows small V shaped opening at neck, single pointed revers; side and back have a wide ornamental collar, worn with a chemisette. Sleeve fits the arm snugly with no fullness at shoulder. The blouse has a peplum which hangs over front and sides of skirt. The skirt is narrow at the hem. Wool rep with small figures, trimmed with white. Value $500-1,000.

This model is 'dressy' and has the drop shoulder which by late 1913 was almost a fashion requirement. It also has the loose sleeve without any fullness at the shoulder. Sleeves are widely cuffed at the elbow, the neckline is a shallow V with which a chemisette was not strictly necessary. The edges of the neck opening are trimmed with small sharply pointed revers faced with brocaded velvet. The closing is in front. Five gore skirt opens to display a narrow panel of brocaded velvet which produces a slash effect without an actual opening. These fancy dresses show a remarkable sophistication and were intended for matinee, for calls, and for afternoon wear in general. Value $850-1,200.

The hats of 1913 can be safely described as overwhelming.

Left: Waist is of gray drap in the Directoire style. It has a silk lining, when joined to a skirt it forms a semi-princess line. 3/4 length sleeves. Satin and lace. Value $450-750.

Right: Intended for the larger woman this waist is of old-rose crepe meteor with a square neckline with tucked insert, ruff chemisette. Satin sash, chiffon sleeves. Value of chemisette $225-350. Value of waist $450-500.

2 piece dress, 1915. Overblouse and girdle with an underblouse of satin with frilled neckline. Velvet and satin. Value $650-1,000. Coat, loose sports coat or 'college coat.' Sacque cut (which means without a break from the shoulder to the hem.) Value $450-750.

A summer dress reflecting the popularity of bordered materials. The blouse has the then-new style kimono shoulder and closes in the back. Square neckline. The skirt is a one piece model with a straight lower edge and is laid in folds around the waistline. Silk. Value $800-1,200. Notice the distinctive standing feathers and bows on the hats. The parasol was carried as a regular accessory.

1914. The silhouette of 1914 was flattering and rather sensuous. This dress has a vestee effect, flat collar, drop shoulders, tunic over tighter skirt, pointed shoes just visible. Long sleeves with chiffon ruffles are very kind to the hands. Dress is of silk. Value $850-1,500.

Spring of 1915 was a flattering time for the female figure. The looser easier fashions were very feminine. These two dresses are typical and are good examples of the length of the clothes as well as the hats. Fashions such as these of good quality and in excellent condition are valued at $1,000-1,800.

A 'wash' dress for summer. In the period 1910-1911 the soft look for summer was considered modest and proper since petticoats could then be worn underneath. This skirt is batiste and is attached to a waist of the same material. Trim is Valenciennes lace which in those days was considered inferior to Cluny, Maltese or Irish laces. Skirt is five gored lengthened by a flounce. Dainty bag and hat with large silk roses complete the outfit. Value of dress in this very desirable material and the favored white $1,200-2,000.

53

The variety of skirts and blouses of this period is almost infinite yet not enough survive intact to satisfy demand. This waist indicates the beauty, femininity and marvelous design work in clothing of this period. A very jaunty style indeed is this waist which closes on the left side with buttons under a row of fancy braid. The lower round neck is complemented by the chemisette in ruff style. Tucked to waistline. Sleeves are one seam leg-o-mutton, trimmed at the wrist. Chemisette is organdy finished with lace. Often these chemisettes are found separately and not recognized. The skirt is striped cheviot, considered a walking skirt and might very well be worn under a coat similar to that shown in coat group. Value of chemisette $200-225, value of skirt $450-600, value of waist $450-650.

Waist and skirt outfits. Both waists are made to be adapted to either separate skirt or to be attached to a skirt and worn as one garment. Worn with belts, high round standing collars and appropriate hats. Entirely typical of the 1909-1910 era. Blouse on left is worn with contrasting colored skirt to make a shirt-skirt outfit, waist on the right worn with matching skirt to give the appearance of a dress. Both belt buckles would be highly collectible in themselves. Value of waists of this type $450-750. Value of skirts $400-600. Complete outfit value $1,500-2,000.

Often the skirt and waist combination was an elaborate affair but practical clothes were important for general use. This skirt was made for everyday use, its overall line is the sheath effect with a fullness at the lower edge. 7 gore skirt with tuck, close fitting in a 'clearing' or walking length. Broadcloth. Value of skirt $300-450.

Center: 1911. Blouse or waist with narrow tucks stitched in pointed yoke effect front and back, lined with silk, leg-o-mutton sleeves, simple flat collar, chiffon with satin bow. Waist value $195-250. Walking skirt, nine gores, seams lapped and doubly stitched. Has what was called the 'clearing length'. Graceful. Linen. Worn with belt. Value $300-450.

Right: 1911. Waist and skirt. By 1910 the new skirts were being made with a high waistline and shirts or waists were being made to be adaptable for the ordinary style or the newer Empire line. This waist shows the Empire influence with the bodice being made over a French lining which is faced for the chemisette and should the waist be attached to a skirt in high-waist effect this lining serves as a bodice stay. The waist is tucked in panel effect front and back, left side front closing. Soft silk, value of waist and skirt $1,500-2,000. Hat value $250-300. The skirt shows the lengthening of lines and softening of skirt lines and is semi-princess, six gores, sheath fitted having a panel in front and a seam on each hip. High waisted button closing. This kind of skirt could also be had with the then newest trailing effect, the short train.

Left: Misses' one piece dress for summer or travelling. This kind of dress was also considered correct for beach wear. This is of linen, hand embroidered, the coat is basically plain held in at the waist with a belt, neck has a small turnover collar, notice lack of fullness in the sleeves. This was intended for the teenager. Value $500-750. Right: Another dress for the young miss. This is a one piece garment combining comfort and style. The blouse has a tuck at the shoulders, wide collar, elbow length sleeves ending in a cuff. Three gore skirt opens in the center front. The usual buttons. Notice the towering decorations on the deep brim hats. Value of dress $500-750.

Left: Coat-suit for a young girl of 1912. The coat is quite long reaching near knee length. Resembles the Norfolk style with a deep yoke in front and back and below this the material is tucked or pleated leaving the center front plain. Notched collar with small revers faced in plaid. The sleeve is plain. Five gore skirt is adjusted snugly to the figure all around. It was considered more stylish to have this costume made in two different materials, the jacket for example would be plain and the skirt plaid. This was considered economical as well as fashionable for then the jacket could do extra duty.
Value of suit $850-1,500.

Right: Young girl's dress for general wear. The blouse has a square yoke which was coming into vogue in late 1912 with no yoke in back. This dress has a modified V neck with a turnover collar. This was termed the 'medici effect'. Sleeves are plain at the shoulder and gathered at wrist with a deep cuff. Skirt is three gored, cut to give a tunic effect. Chevior serge, value $350-500.

Left to right: The very fashionable vest in the summer dress of 1915. Three gore skirt has a yoke in front and on the sides. Ribbon trim runs in an unusual way through loops on the top of waist. Muslin. Value of these 'pretty' dresses is rising. $500-850. The waist of this dress buttons up the front to a wide flat collar. Frilled. The skirt is three gored and is joined to the yoke with a belt. Both skirt and waist are cotton. Value $450-750. The waist of this dress is made with the body and sleeve in one piece. It is worn over a guimpe. Skirt is in one piece and has scalloped outines for placing the ruffles. Figured lawn in a very soft, feminine style. Notice the continued use of the parasol which is making a comeback today to ward off the sun. Value of this dress is $750-1,000. These dresses are typical of 1915 with the increasing emphasis on the soft look and comfort. The dress on the right has the 'new' Quaker collar. Value of these types of dresses depends on materials, details and appeal. Range is $500-1,500.

In 1915 no dress was complete without the fancy collar which could be wide or narrow, high in the back for a long neck opening or shallow with the little collar. This is a cross section of various types of collars popular in the summer of 1915. Occasionally these collar and cuff sets are found intact.

Left to right: Some of the very attractive fashions of 1915. A 4 gore model skirt has attached suspender trim made of straight pieces of velvet ribbon. Worn with a simple blouse. Skirt value $350-450. The blouse of this dress has an open neck with small collar and long tapering revers. Front forms a panel passing over the belt. Three gore skirt attached to the blouse without fullness. Pongee. Value $450-500. Popular middy blouse (which is still a legitimate fashion). Lacing on sides, sailor collar. Cotton. Value $195-275. Shirtwaist dress, loose untrimmed blouse closes in surplice style. These pieces which can be considered 'separates' are valued separately. Blouse $195-300. skirt $350-450. This blouse has the bolero effect. The skirt is gathered at the top. Figured lawn. Value $400-500. This is one of those dresses every collector tries for. Silk with the soft feminine look. Shorter hair, attractive shoes, 1915 was a good year for fashion. Value of this dress is $850-1,500.

Left to right: 1915 afternoon wear. The waist on the left is considered to be in the 'military style.' The sleeve is the 'bishop' which is simply a sleeve plain at the shoulder and slightly full at the wrist. The skirt is circular. The dress value is .$500-750.

A good example of the surplice-style waist. This is made of lace flouncing with a guimpe (underblouse) of chiffon which has the high collar although this was no longer so popular. Long loose sleeves. Skirt is a one piece model, tucked. A very wide girdle. Value $950-1,800.

A jumper type dress with a one piece circular skirt. The jumper-like top is considered an 'overblouse'. The underblouse is messaline, the dress is silk with an extremely wide girdle sash. Value 950-1,800.

Left: Directoire Princess dress, foulard silk, the waist has square yoke of net with a band of embroidered net, four large self-covered buttons, entire sleeve is made of net, a rather usual thing in that period, shaped net collar. The skirt reflected the new mode which was to hang gracefully from the hips, stitched belt attaches the skirt to the waist. Silk was not an unusual material in the most popular dresses of that day. Value $1,000-2,000.

Right: 1909. Princess jumper dress, taffeta silk in wisteria color, front of waist is trimmed with soutache braid which gives panel effect, skirt designed in the new style and is trimmed down the center with a row of taffeta silk covered buttons, braid trimmed belt attaches skirt to waist and fastens in back.
Value $1,000-2,000.

1915. Lustrous silk was widely used for evening dresses as well as dresses for the house. This is a waist and skirt dress made of silk with the drop shoulder and small standing collar. Value $650-850.

Typical shirtwaist styles of the first decade of the 1900's. Value of each of the blouses. $500-750. Value of each of this type skirt, $350-500. Price depends on quality and trim.

Right: 1910. Dressy waist of fine quality ecru net over Japanese silk; front is embroidered in floral design and trimmed with tucks, rows of wide and narrow lace insertion and lace edging, rows of lace insertion give a short round yoke effect in back. Full length tucked sleeves with pointed cuffs, trimmed with lace insertions, tucked with trimmed collar, fastens in back. Notice the buckled belt. Value $500-650.

Left: Another waist of the period, dressy style in messaline silk trimmed in front with Venise and Valenciennes lace edging, lace collar, full length shaped sleeves trimmed with lace insertions and edging. Value $500-700.

1912. A soft, graceful afternoon gown. The blouse is scarcely fitted at the shoulders and the balance of the front and back is soft and loose. The sleeve is attached without fullness and makes a soft puff at the wrist where there is a frill. At the neck is a square collar and joining the lower edges of this are two scarf-like insertions forming a fichu effect. The drape of the skirt is called the 'Turkish style' and suggests harem wear. Raised waistline and drapery over the hips. The front small skirt opening is filled in with chiffon, the gown is crepe de chine. Satin sash. An outstanding dress, value $1,200-2,000. Notice the buckles on the shoes.

A high waisted semi-princess dress. This style was prevalent during the 1909-1911 period. Made of sateen with velvet trim and soutache braid. Value $1,500-2,200.

1909 House dress, sometimes called 'morning dress'. Tucked blouse-waist closes down front side on left making it easier to put on or take off, band facing on the waist is made with high neckline, long sleeves. Linen with striped band trimming. Value $950-1,200.

Semi-princess dress with normal waistline. A basic lingerie dress in soft linen with satin trim. Bodice not lined, button trim. Simple construction of deep V neck shirt, skirt has short train. Value $650-950

1905 Gibson Girl silhouette and coiffure. **Outfit, $1,800-2,500.**

1905 Young ladies' outfit, $1,200-1800.

Semi-princess lingerie dress. These dresses had no blouse lining. This is fine lawn trimmed with Valenciennes insertions and edgings. In buying dresses of this type it is important to note the compatibility between the openings of the waist and skirt which must be at the same point either center back or side. White lawn. Value $650-900.

Cream serge dress, 1913. Bodice is deep U filled in with yoke of lace and moire taffeta. Skirt narrows at ankle. Value $650-950. Young girl's dress; 2 piece skirt with tunic overdress. Wide panels front and back and belted. Linen, value $225-350. Plain waist skirt, shirtwaist type. Neckline trimmed with notched collar and is closed in the duchesse style in the center front. Skirt closes in the front. Waist is Japanese silk with satin trim. Value $750-1,000. Another shirtwaist dress, 1913. Plain waist, striped, unusual sleeve which continues in a point to the edge of the collar. Skirt is four gore, closing at the left side of the back, belted. Usually these waists are made of pongee silk and skirts of light woolen goods, serge or cheviot. Value $750-1,000.

Left to right: Everyday dresses, winter. 1915. Shirtwaist dress, printed crepe de chine, high neck with gathers. Skirt is of mixed cheviot. Value $650-950. Raglan sleeve blouse with tunic skirt. Matching underskirt. Value $750-1,000. The popular overblouse, worn with long sleeved waist. Tunic skirt, Chiffon, silk and satin trim. Value $1,000-1,500.

Left to right: Sports coat worn with 3 piece skirt for every day wear. Wool plaid skirt, solid color cheviot jacket with wide belt and self-covered buttons. Two large pockets. Skirt buttons down front. Skirt $95-125 in excellent condition without moth holes, coat which can be buttoned to neck is valued at $275-450, again in excellent condition.

This dress exhibits the 'drop shoulder'. It closes in the front. The skirt is 2 pieces with a 3 piece yoke. Skirt narrows considerably at the hem. An easier style becoming evident in 1914. Value in silk $750-1,000.

Semi-fitting, full length coat with broad revers and velvet collar and cuffs. Cheviot. Leather handbags were popular at this time. Coat $450-550. Coats are not widely collected and still undervalued.

Vests were extremely fashionable at this time and in this dress the vest which is of the same material as the collar, extends below the belt. The 3 piece skirt is topped with a satin sash. This dress is worn with a lace chemisette. The sashes are not usually found with these dresses unless they were attached. Value of dress in silk $750-1,000.

Easy to slip on dress for everyday wear in 1914. Skirt is six gores, blouse is simply styled with side buttoning and flat collar in contrasting color. Chiffon ruffle at wrists. Value $550-950.

Misses' dresses, 1915. Considered a youthful style, this blouse and skirt has a bordered skirt and a blouse whose collar can be worn flat or arranged to close in high necked style. Sleeve fullness is gathered into the band cuff. Skirt has a deep round at the front. Serge. Value $650-950. Right: Overblouse worn with a plain waist, which again has a convertible neck. Bishop sleeves with wide cuff. Skirt, 2 piece, circular cut. Usually found in fine serge with chiffon or net, or velvet and wool. Value $500-750. Today it is difficult to determine that these were worn by young women since the sizes are large.

Home garments: left to right: 1912. Semiprincess style, for home wear, sateen. $550-850. Child's apron. Sacque style, fastens in back, has ties extending from side seam, roll collar and long sleeves. Figured lawn. Value $65-85. House dress, morning wear. Has patch pocket and some sleeve fullness at shoulder. Cotton crepe. Value $250-350. Russian suit for young boy. Coat closes over at side standing collar, sleeves have little fullness and band cuff. Pants are made without a fly. Linen. Value $300-450. Maternity dress. This is attached to a lining which is adjustable. Drop shoulders and plain sleeves. Lightweight silk. Value $650-950.

Afternoon dresses, 1913. Frock for young girl. Light and dark fabric, buttons down front, five gored skirt. Value $285-300. One piece Empire dress. Striped silk. Value $300-325. Shirtwaist costume of tan cotton pongee with white linen collar and cuffs. Value $285-300. White serge afternoon dress, black satin trim, value $325-350.

Right: Shirtwaist design with four gored skirt of 1913. Box pleated with collar and cuffs of contrasting material. Front closure, buttons from collar to hem. Tan pongee with green and white satin trim, green glass buttons. Value in silk with original buttons $300-350.

Left: 1913. This is a morning dress in a simple style. Gingham with collar and cuffs of dotted lawn. The blouse is ornamented with a fancy collar and cuffs. No sleeve fullness at the shoulder. The three piece skirt fits snugly and has left side opening, pocket. Value $250-275.

Left to right: Ladies' House dresses, 1916. Simple style, button front, small collar, bishop sleeves (plain at the shoulder and gathered into a cuff at the wrist). Usually found in washable fabric. Value $145-185. Apron, serviceable work apron, front panel fitted, gingham, value $40-60. House dress, side closing waist, 7 gore skirt. Cotton. Value $145-185.

Costumes for home wear: 1915. Left: ladies' bath robe, flannel or wool. Not too many robes of this type survive. Value $100-125. Right: House dress, 2 piece, plain blouse with center front closing. Skirt has 3 gores and is gathered at the top, the sides and the back. These were usually made of washable material, and occasionally in wool. Value $145-185.

An overview of the fashions of 1919, top left is a cotton, one-piece house dress $125-150; two variants of the waist, value ranges $150-225; three dresses typical of the daywear which range in value from $500-700 depending on material, trimmings and overall appeal. A good example of the skirts which were made in 2, 3, or 4 pieces. Value range $300-450 because these are difficult to find.

Misses' Silk Gowns

Advance Spring Models

Women's Silk Gowns

Advance Spring Models

1916. Misses' taffeta silk and georgette gown in old rose, with hand embroidered bodice and sleeves in self color, vestee of georgette crepe, tunic skirt with panel front of taffeta and georgette crepe which is hand embroidered, crushed girdle of taffeta silk. Gorgeous dress $1,200-1,500. Shoes are tan Russian calf laced boots. 1916. Misses' changeable armure taffeta silk gown in blue, bodice and standing collar embroidered in self color, sleeves and vestee of georgette crepe, full flare skirt with peplum and girdle of silk. Both high shoes and pumps were fashionable. Dress $1,200-1,500. Model wears white buckskin pumps with self bows. For the more mature woman a taffeta silk gown in black, vestee of lace and embroidered georgette crepe, georgette crepe sleeves with gauntlet cuffs of taffeta, pointed tunic skirt with bands of velvet ribbon. Value $1,000-1,200. White kid boots with Havana brown kid backs. Women's taffeta silk gown in navy blue with georgette crepe sleeves finished with taffeta cuff, the then-new 'Spanish collar' and vestee of white net, girdle of georgette crepe with bands of taffeta silk. Value $1,200-1,500. She wears patent kid slippers with hand-sewed shell ornament.

Beaded black lace evening gown, c. 1915, in tunic style with long sleeves, black furred trained hem, cream satin underslip, the lower tunic bodice and sleeves decorated with crystal and jet beading the central bodice panel has rhinestone and coral decoration, later applied, some renovation to interior. Even with these deficiencies the gown sold at the recent Butterfield auction for $425 and restored is worth $750-1,000.

Cream and Black Lace Evening Gown, c. 1905, black Chantilly lace bodice and short sleeves appliqued with black and cream sequined design, the full trained skirt similarly embroidered, cream taffeta underslip later replaced. The estimated pre-sale auction value was $300-500. This gown sold for $1,200 and given its quality is worth much more. Value $2,000-3,000.

Center, c. 1915 silk evening gown of orchid satin, the trained skirt with center chiffon panel, gold lace and velvet trim, crossover bodice and sleeves of pale blue chiffon similarly trimmed, taffeta lining. Shows some wear but a gorgeous gown. Value $2,000-2,800.

Left: c. 1915 powder blue satin evening gown, the skirt has two front flying panels, short black net sleeves are trimmed with black jet beads, flying side panels of black net are similary trimmed, black, blue and rhinestone beaded, appliqued central front panel decoration, cream taffeta lining, which is a replacement. Value $750-950.

Right: c. 1915-16 deep burgundy velvet skirt, bodice of pleated chiffon and gold lace, ornate rhinestone decoration on the bodice, burgundy pleated underslip. Value $850-1,000.

Formal gold dress with train. Trimmed with lace and jet beads and completely lined except for train. Yellow pearl buttons. Worn about 1900. Black lace ball fan. Value, dress $650-950.

1906. Formal gown of black velvet. Overskirt drapes in front and back with tassels of sterling silver and velvet. Sleeves and bodice are heavy but fine Continental lace. Value $1,000-1,500. Black velvet hat with large ostrich plumes and with pin which matches belt buckle on dress. Marcasite. Value of hat $175-225.

Typical gowns of 1909-1910. Meticulous attention to detail, fitted with trims of laces, satin insets and chiffon and other expensive, elaborate materials. These gowns were considered to be all that the well-dressed woman could want – the total costume reflected the finished product of cosmopolitan progress. The clinging, trailing gowns were described as a "beautiful vase holding one perfect flower." What woman could resist that image? Gowns of this quality, beauty and workmanship are scarce and desirable. Value $2,500-4,000.

73

Typical waist and skirt outfits of the 1909-1911 period. Worn with round high collars they are Empire style, with semi-princess lines. The skirt falls softly and has a train. The skirt on the right has 'clearing' for walking. Costumes of this type are valued at $1,000-2,000 with the 'train' models usually commanding more.

Evening gown of pink chiffon trimmed with pink ribbon and silk Teneriffe wheels. High neck, deep bertha forms cape over sleeves. 1904. Value $1,500-3,000.

Walking suit of ecru linen c. 1910. Skirt has long yoke and wide pleats. Long pocket. $1,000-1,200. Straw hat with plaid ribbons $75-100.

Two piece black afternoon suit of wool with train. Revers trimmed with braid, ribbed dickey is satin. Top is boned with small stand-up collar. Early 1900's. The wool in this suit is very fine. Value $1,500-2,000. Victorian flat hat of sealskin with ribbons down back and chin strap. Value $200-300; ostrich boa of Victorian vintage. Value $275-300.

Brown wool, 2 piece dress with braid worked into the waist, the sleeves are decorated with very dainty, pretty old glass buttons. 1890-1900. The yoke of the dress snaps into the jacket which also has matching buttons. Value $1,500-2,000. Brown straw hat with pale coral silk flowers.

This skirt is not gored but is circular. The skirt is worn with a coat for a suit effect. Closure is buttoned to hem. Medium sweep in 'clearing length' for walking. Serge. Value of skirt with jacket, $1,500-2,000. Parasol of linen, value $195-250. Parasol values continue to rise.

1910. Tailored suit intended for Spring wear. The ultimate daytime wear for the Howard Chandler Christy girl. Not only is her suit in the latest mode with the long cutaway jacket, her hat is a masterpiece of the milliner's art and her handbag is the silver mesh with chain handle so collectible today. Buckles on her pointed toe shoes, the dress shows enough ankle to be tantalizing. Suit $1,800-2,500, hat $300-350, bag $100-125.

1913 poplin walking suit. Worn for travelling, visiting, shopping, etc. Trimmed with lighter colored poplin, glass buttons. Made in the one piece Empire style. The blouse has shaped revers, the skirt opens at front side. Value $1,000-1,500.

Afternoon 'frock' of white linen, piped in blue. The blouse is plain except for ornamental closing and embroidered collar. The sleeves are set in a plain way at the shoulders, and are cuffed at the elbow. The linen was heavy in this dress, the buttons of imitation lapis luzuli to match the piping. The four gore skirt is attached to the waist. Although this is a simple dress, it was considered fashionable and dressy. Value $1,000-1,500.

For afternoon wear linen was often preferred and in this dress the material is ramie linen, an imitation of real linen, but very soft and is half cotton. The waist is made in the Gibson style with a wide tuck extending over the shoulders and down the front and back of the waist. The closing is double breasted style the right side lapping well over the left. Flat turnover collar and in this model, still worn in 1913, the modified leg-o-mutton sleeve is evident. Seven gore skirt is joined at the waist. Value $1,000-1,500.

In 1913 the craze for Bulgarian embroidery was at its height, it was considered rich looking and effective. In a dress such as this which showed much attention to detail the owner was advised to wear it for several seasons. Pale blue linen with white trim embroidered in shades of blue and pink and white. The bodice has a yoke made without seams at the shoulder and quite shallow. Five gore skirt has a small inset panel showing embroidery which matches the yoke and cuffs as well as the belt. Value $1,200-1,800.

Fall, 1913. L. to R., Box coat, cut on raglan lines, worn with simple, tailored skirt. Coat, value $300-400. Walking dress; Plain blouse opens over a vest insert. Skirt is four gore. A walking dress was considered utilitarian, ideal for marketing, shopping or exercise. 1913. Value $950-1,500. Street dress to be worn without a coat. The dress has a coat-blouse effect with a 2 gore skirt. 1913. Value $950-1,500.

Suits from 1913. Three quarter length coat, 2 piece skirt. Sleeves have a little fullness at the shoulder. 2 piece skirt is plain at top and can be found in raised or regulation waistline. These suits are difficult to find. Value $950-1,500.

2nd from left: a semi-tailored calling gown, popular in Paris when something "plain" was called for. The coat which is cutaway in front discloses a vest, and has a little fullness at each side. Skirt has 3 gores. Value $950-1,500. For hard usage, including "business" this was the type preferred. The coat falls well below the hips and fastens below the waistline. 2 piece skirt absolutely plain. Value $800-1,000.

Ladies suits, 1915. This coat-suit boasts a jacket of the latest 1915 style. It extends over the hips, and has a front center closing. Revers and small collar, patch pockets, under the lap of these passes the narrow belt. Skirt is four gored and quite a bit of ankle showing is permitted with this style. Corduroy. $1,200-2,000. Ladies' dress. High standing collar, overblouse has yoke effect, skirt in circular cut which is closed in center front. Satin and net $1,400-1,800. Furs were often worn with this type garment, either around the neck or a muff as shown.

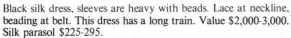

Black silk dress, sleeves are heavy with beads. Lace at neckline, beading at belt. This dress has a long train. Value $2,000-3,000. Silk parasol $225-295.

1917-1918 maternity wear. In today's money these suits would cost $250 or more, so if found in good condition they are usually a bargain. For some reason maternity wear is found infrequently. Norfolk style suit with convertible collar, which is inlaid with silk velvet, fancy bone buttons, short skirt has full sweep with adjustable belt. Wool. Value $1,000-$1,500.

1917-1918. All wool serge maternity suit. Loose lines held with adjustable belt, back slightly fitted to the waistline. Belt is trimmed with bone buttons and velvet. Large fancy collar trimmed with fold of velvet and buttons. Large patch pockets. Warmly interlined and lined. Skirt hangs in simple long line effect with inverted pleats at the front. Both of these have the self adjusting maternity waistband. The tailoring of these suits is so clever that pregnancy is well concealed. Large fur muff. Suit $1,000-1,500.

1918 Maternity wear, suits, each $1,000-1,200 if furred $1,200-1,500. Hats $250-350.
Notice the footwear.

1916 morning trousers $75-100. Jacket with tails, black, dated 1933 in pocket. $125-175; shown with Battenberg lace jabot from the 1920's $75-150; 1930's black and rhinestone pin in jabot, $45-55. The outfit is displayed to emphasize the fact that it can be worn by a woman.

The rather plain jackets should range between $300-350. The wrap with its extra large armholes for the large sleeve is a very desirable item. Wraps of this type range between $1,500-2,200 again depending on materials, condition and trim.

Waist in the surplice effect, pretty much a rounded style. Tucks on both sides in front, button trim. The chemisette is removable because by 1910 the chemisette had displaced the guimpe. This waist is gray linen with soutache braid and linen buttons and was intended for the 'robust figure'. Value $275-350.

1906. Blouses of this type, depending on condition, fabric and detail range $350-500, hats of this year should cost between $300-400, again depending on material and trim.

Two blouses from the 1910-1911 period. This is a tucked blouse-waist which was considered rather-plain for its time. Chiffon, round high collar. Closed at the back. This kind of blouse could easily be attached to a skirt to form a semi-princess gown. These blouses are much sought after for wearing today. Value $350-400.

Waist of embroidered Japanese crepe. Cluster of tucks at the shoulders give breadth to the shoulders. Standing collar. Value $350-400.

Left: The bodice of this waist is made over a French lining which is faced for the chemisette. The chemisette is in pointed outline. The waist is tucked in panel effect, closes left side of front. Wide tucks over each shoulder reach to waistline. Antique green satin waist, value $350-400.

Right: Gray cashmere waist with soutache trim joined to skirt of the same material. Chemisette is lace faced to a French lining and the bodice is cut in a rounded neckline. Waist value $300-350.

Although we tend to think of ladies of long ago as constantly having the vapors it is obvious that tennis and golf were very popular. This 1913 tennis outfit would certainly demand great skill of any female player just to run while wearing it. Gingham with a tunic over a long skirt. Value $300-400.

The garment on the left is a 'bungalow apron' of pink percale, edged with rick-rack braid around the square neck and side front opening. It buttons from shoulder to hem and has white binding on the sleeve, belt and pocket. Finding this today a novice collector would be hard put to identify it. Value $100-200.

The garment on the right is a 'house dress' or 'porch dress' and although it is a practical striped chambray gingham intended for hard wear, it is quite good looking. Collar, cuffs and belt are banded in plain chambray to match the stripes and the plain material is found again on the revers and the turned down corners of the pockets. Button trimmed. Lavender and brown striped. Both of these date from 1916. Value $150-200.

Stripes have always been considered an effective design in clothing. The early teen years of the 20th century were rife with stripes as a fashion statement. This cool, practical summer dress features very bold striped navy blue and white voile. The modish collar is embroidered white organdy as are the turned-back cuffs. Waist has white pearl buttons and is lined with white net. Deep tucks trim the skirt where the plain and striped materials are joined. The white sash ends with pendant buttons. Value $350-450.

Left: White dotted swiss waist, simple and cool, round flat collar, thin silk, lined. For the most part waists were elaborate so these simpler types are great additions to a collection. Value $200-250. Right: Waist of the same period. Linen with lace insertions. High standing collar. Value depends on quality and amount of lace but in general all waists of this type should fall into the $300-450 range.

Left: 'Utility shirt waist' in a conservative styling, simply made and yet fashionable. Front has tucks, high standing collar and tie. It is made of filet net which is very difficult to find in good condition. Value $350-450. Right: Shirtwaist is of checked madras, another 'utility' good, everyday type waist. Value $200-250.

Although one piece dresses were becoming stylish blouses were still popular. This 1908 blouse is of satin messaline trimmed with ribbon roses, bowknots and lace. Also called a 'waist' the blouse was usually worn with the skirt of the same color and made of the same material in many cases. To be fashionable, at the very least the same color would have to be picked up somewhere on the skirt. Yoke is of tucked chiffon, reticella squares and a heavy applique form the motifs and scalloped effect. Exquisite. $350-500.

Handmade blouse, c. 1900. Four varieties of hand made lace, ¾ sleeves, tight wrists, handkerchief linen. $1,000-1,200.

A more efficient looking waist of tucked crepe de Chine with strips of Valenciennes lace set between the tucks. A fold of soft satin edged with little silk balls forms a deep square yoke effect and little straps of satin finish the outer edges of the sleeves. Value $350-500.

'Armistice Blouse.' Lightly gathered front with long collar falling softly over a center panel or 'vestee.' Made from a contemporary pattern by Folkwear. Value of original $300-350. Photo courtesy Folkwear, San Raphael.

1918 Blouse. The back of the blouse extends over the shoulders to meet the lightly gathered front and gathers at the back center waist into a self-tie or ribbon which encircles the waist to tie in front. Deep rectangular neckline. Made from contemporary pattern. Value of original, $300-350. Folkwear photo.

Jacket, c. 1900. Faille with passementerie and lace edged sleeves lined and neckline decorated with stemmed flowers and leaves. Value $400-500.

Above: short jacket, white silk with black applique, standing collar c.1900. Value $400-500.

Right: Blouse - jacket, taffeta, blue, cream and black stripes, worn in 1900. Value $400-500.

Shirtwaists of this type should range between $350-500 depending on materials, workmanship and trim.

1905. All dresses and suits in this period and of these styles, unless they have some unusual features are priced at $1,000-2,000, but prices at this time vary from shop to shop and area to area. All prices on clothing of this period are rising very rapidly.

89

Left: This type garment is called a coat-suit and every woman was advised to have one in her wardrobe. The coat is a one-piece model with the seamless shoulder and a double breasted effect where the front closes. Belt across the front. Skirt is a four gore design closed at left side of back. Lower left side has tab extension where buttons are placed, Brocaded silk coat, plain silk skirt. Value $950-1,200. Right. Ladies' full length coat, soft cheviot, small collar and revers notched to form lapels. The sleeve is inserted without fullness at the shoulder and is cuffed. Satin trim. In 1912-1913 coats came in three lengths – full-length, seven-eighths length or three-quarter length. These are scarce. Value $850-1,000.

A stunning coat dress in light wool. An unusual burgundy color, it has a full length front panel of brocade. The gown has a long train and satin ribbon tie. Beautifully constructed gown. Value $1,800-2,200. Very early 1900's. Hat is straw with ostrich plumes. velvet and flowers. $200-250.

A fashionable Spring coat of 1910-1911. All the rage were the picturesque broad collars and flaring cuffs with unusual outlines. This is of satin in the Empire style. The coat has only two seams – under arm and shoulder and this gives the coat a graceful look and also only hints at the figure underneath. The collar is in contrasting satin braided in soutache and it nearly reaches the high waistline. The sash is attached to the coat. The sleeves have moderate fullness, cuffed in the same manner as the collar. This is not a typical style of the period and would be a tremendous find. Value $1,700-2,200.

Coat for very young lady. Matching skirt. Suit is of broadcloth with wide flaring cuffs of velvet with matching collar and pockets trimmed with velvet. Material trim on skirt is of contrasting color in broadcloth. Value of complete outfit $1,000-1,500.
Overblouse of linen, guimpe chiffon, skirt of linen with pleat and buttom trim on side. Belt is buckled. Value $750-950.

Figure on right in above photo is back view of suit on left.

91

Ecru light wool 'duster' coat with ornate braid trim. Lined in wool flannel. These are somewhat scarce and eagerly sought after by members of Vintage Automobile clubs. Value $600-1,000.

Coats for younger women. The style at left is known as 'Norfolk.' Made of serge, in a tailored design it has a velvet collar and is semi-fitted to accentuate the hipless, bustless ideal which was being emphasized in up-to-date coats of 1910 for this age group. The cutaway effect was also prominent, buttons still highly visible as trimming. The coat in the center is of broadcloth showing large buttons and button holes and velvet trim in a straight, loose fashion. Cutaway on right is made of herringbone suiting material, tailored in a princess style. Coats of this type, depending on material and trim are valued at $600-950.

Charles Stevens & Bros. advertisement, 1905. Coats of this kind, large sleeves and 50 inches long should range between $600-850. Hat on left, $200-225 in excellent condition. Hat on right, $200-225 in excellent condition.

Left to right: 1915. This dress has overtones of the shirtwaist, the extension of the sleeves forming a deep shoulder-yoke. The neck is soft and open with a flare collar. Two piece circular skirt which closes in the front. Oversized muff. Dress value $650-950. 1915. The coat is long waisted with double breasted closing, small roll collar. Wool with velvet trim. Coats are difficult to find especially with this interesting hemline. Value $700-900.

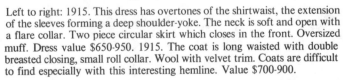

Ladies coats. These coats were worn over the skirts and waists and the general design is more or less the same. The differences lie in the way the coats were cut and how they are fastened. All have pockets and front fastenings and the cut determined whether the coat would have a round or square outline. Lapels on the two right coats are wide, the one on the left has narrow lapels. All are worn with elaborate hats. Coats of this type and quality without the matching skirt have a value of $650-950 depending on the trim. They can be found most often in broadcloth, cheviot or serge. If found with matching skirt value is $1,200-1,500. Almost all of these garments show magnificent tailoring.

LEFT to RIGHT:

A lady's wrap or coat with a large collar which can close across top. Lace trim on collar, cuffs and revers, fine, lightweight wool. Full length 1913. Value $1,000-1,700.

This cape is lined with satin, has a hood and a straight closing with frogs. Shorter length. Value $1,200-1,500.
This is an evening cape.

A two piece wrap, longer at the back. Embroidered broche silk. The sleeves fall free, it has very wide revers. A jeweled closure. Value $1,500-2,000.

This draped coat is full length with full length sleeves. It is satin with flowered taffeta trim, and tasseled closing. Dark blue. Value $1,000-1,500. All coats date from 1913.

Capes are very dramatic which may be why so few are worn and thus so few are around to be collected. Even now a cape does not hang in every woman's wardrobe. The Cape shown here is stunning but would take some panache to wear. It is made of Jersey and has a very deep yoke, 3 oversize buttons, red wool, checked lining which is visible when the cape is worn and it is cut high in front to show the dress. This is unusual even for a cape. 1919. Value $500-850.

Worth of Paris wedding dress. 1917. Silk illusion embroidered with genuine seed pearls in floral motif and trimmed with orange blossoms. Worth label.
Value $8,000-12,000.
Courtesy Museum of the City of New York

Betty Luther modeling beige sheer wedding dress, 1910 – at Gold Diggers' Fashion Show, Oct. 1977, Medford, Or. Kenn Knackstedt, photographer.
Courtesy: Southern Oregon Historical Society

Brides of 1913. Center, the satin skirt is a two piece draped tunic gathered at the top; three piece foundation skirt, the blouse is satin, open neck, full length sleeves, duchess lace collar and chemisette, and a one shoulder trimming band. The vest and frill cuffs are lace. Outstanding clothing of this era is somewhat difficult to find. Value of this bridal gown $1,700-2,500.

Left: Waist and skirt. Broche silk for side portions, cap, sleeves and tunic, satin plain vest, center back and front of skirt and back sections of waist. Lace collar, yoke, facing full length sleeves, full vest and insertion in skirt. An elaborate, complicated gown. Value $2,000-2,800.

Dress at right has a 60" train. The dress is satin with a lace blouse and lace frills at end of sleeves. The waist and skirt have a chiffon frill. The over blouse is lined, and it is worn with a three piece foundation skirt. Value $2,000-2,500.

Silk wedding dress. Gowns of this type and quality are almost timeless in their wearability and style. Extensive, magnificent bead work, draped sleeves, heavy silver thread used in the trim. Magnificent yet entirely comfortable to wear. Value $2,000-3,000.

Close up of bride and groom, 1912 wedding.

1912 wedding. Bride wears satin, lace and traditional veil with orange blossom headpiece and net train. Small ball fringe on dress yoke and sleeve edge. Chemisette of chiffon with high neck banded at top with small seed pearls. Dress, $1,500-1,800. Veil, $400-500. Bridesmaid, standing, satin dress, v-neck with lace insert, pearl and lace edging on cape. Dress, $650-750. Both wear long kid gloves, $40-55 pair. Boy wears linen jacket and pants (white) $300-400. Mens' suits, wool, value $250-450.

Wedding photo. 1903. Bride wears sheer voile, pleated bodice with lace yoke. High banded collar. Fullness and small cape at top of sleeves. Bride's dress had three ruffles and lace inset in skirt. Dress $2,000-2,500. Bridesmaid, left, sheer voile with ruffled skirt, large sleeve fullness and small cape effect at shoulder. Dress, $1,500-1,800. Mens' suits, with vests, wool, value, $250-400.

1913 house dress, wide collar on blouse, sleeve is cuffed at elbow. Three gore skirt opens in front over a small panel and is slightly gathered at the waist. This garment is without the small train whch was sometimes used at that time even in housedresses. The sash and little front panel is chiffon which was a new fancy in 1913. The cap is called a 'Charlotte Corday' cap and is made to match the dress. Figured cotton voile. These caps were adapted from the caps used by the servant class. Value of dress $500-750; cap $100-150.

Left: Japanese crepe kimono, satin trim, high shirred waistline, value $600-800.
Right: Tea gown of black China silk and net with satin trim. Both garments beautifully detailed and intended for informal wear at home. Tea gown value $1,500-1,800.

Kimono wrapper, shirred at the shoulders to fall in loose, straight folds to the hem. Sleeves are finished with a cuff and are flowing. Bands of plain material in green trim this kimono of lighter green dimity. Value of these kimonos is rising $350-500.

Tea gown or negligee. This is a lounging robe made of challis with shirring at waist. Value $500-600.

Morning wear. Left: one piece apron. Single piece, long seams at the sides, neck is a simple round, large arm holes. Usually found in calico or cambric or gingham. 1914. Value $40-50. Right: Ladies Kimono. Slender lines, panel front closing on its left side without fullness. Satin trim. 1914. Value $300-400.

1916. On left is a negligee gown. Plain sacque cut from shoulder to hem, apron front and back, hand scalloped trim. Found in various materials. Value $275-350. Maternity gown. Laced in front with darts which makes it adjustable. Skirt is one piece gathered at top with small frill. Found in various materials. Value $300-350. Combination corset-cover and short petticoat. Corset cover fastens in back. Short petticoat fits tightly. Lawn. Value corset cover, $75-100. Garment intact, $175-250. Petticoat, short, $55-75.

The negligee dainty and enticing then is dainty and enticing now. The one on the left even in sophisticated 1995 would do Victoria's Secret proud. It is crepe etoile with filet lace and black velvet ribbon bows and lacings. In good condition it is valued at $2,500-3,000. If a lucky collector should find such a garment you know the gods love you.

The serviceable robe at right is attractive and well-made with interesting accents. It is of violet eider-down, and its only decoration is heavy cord which also forms a girdle. Value $350-450.

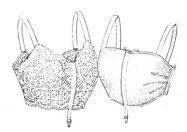

On the left is a serviceable but pretty white brassiere of Cluny pattern lace with filet mesh. The lace is quite strong and 'substantial'. Narrow tape straps, lightly boned at the sides. Value $65-85.

Right:
Lightweight close mesh bust confined with a rubber strip at the center back and 'comfortable' boning at the sides. Fastens in the front with hook and eye. Narrow tape straps. Draw string at the top. 1917. Value $40-50.

A poignant Mother and child. The mother's nightdress of white lawn, with a drawstring waist and a skirt flounce covered with a light white wool shawl with deep fringe kept for nocturnal infant emergencies no doubt. The baby wears a long white batiste gown with tucks and ruffles at the sleeve ends. 1900. The shawl is valued at $150-195 if in excellent condition, the nightgown $250-350, the baby's dress $125-200.

The chemise is probably the ultimate in seductive underclothing, although often they were advertised in large sizes. Size 44 was not uncommon. The model on left seated provocatively on the pillow and wearing a dainty bed cap is also wearing an envelope chemise of French embroidery which has floral spray decorations and front cluster tucks. It has a straight upper edge and tucked sleeve straps finished with buttonhole scallops, and the entire lower edge is scalloped to match, Satin baby ribbon runs through eyelets at top. Because of the materials and workmanship used on the chemises and *their overall beauty they are still much undervalued and underpriced.* 1916-1917. Value in good condition and depending on trim, $175-250.

Top, envelope chemise made of nainsook and trimmed with Val lace insertions, alternating with rows of white satin ribbon. Narrow satin ribbon is inserted at the neck and both neck and armholes are finished with edging.

A very dainty envelope chemise of fine nainsook trimmed front and back with insets of Valenciennes lace and embroidered organdy. Val insertions, and neck and armholes are also finished with the lace. Two rosettes of satin ribbon trim in front and satin baby ribbon finishes the top. *A good example of fine workmanship, elegant detail and lovely materials which often characterized these chemises. Look for them.*

Hot weather lingerie. Crepe de chine with filet lace combines to make this attractive camisole. Rosette of satin ribbon at neck, Elastic waistband. Flesh color 1918. Camisole only, $95-145.

The white muslin petticoat worn with the camisole is trimmed in white filet lace. The flounce is also ornamented with a cluster of fine tucks. It is protected by an underlay of the material. 1918. Value $150-200.

At top right is a fine nainsook corset cover prettily trimmed with embroidered organdy banding, Val lace insertion and edging, 'run' with baby ribbon. $100-175.

Crepe de chine camisole with straight upper edge daintily finished with embroidery beading and Val lace in 'fisheye' pattern. Shoulder straps of beading and lace. Satin ribbon runs through beading ties and front and forms rosettes on sleeve straps. Elastic waistband. Flesh color. 1918. Value $125-195.

Lady at bottom right wears a cool negligee of white dotted swiss. Collar and cuffs are finished with Val lace. The front of the collar is gracefully draped and the skirt joins the waist with a shirred heading finished in front with a rosette of satin ribbon. Elastic waistband. 1918. Value $250-300.

In any age corsets had to follow the dictates of fashion in order to showcase the particular lines being emphasized by designers at the time. These models show the 1913 silhouette 'the modish low bust, the very low hip and back' and after having struggled into one of these, 'the altogether uncorseted effect'. These were guaranteed not to rust, and not to break or tear with reasonable wear. Imagine worrying about your corset rusting or breaking? The boning was reasonably flexible and they all had hose supporters. Values vary depending on condition and trim, $65-150.

In 1913 mothers were advised to put their children into these waists which were supposed to be essential to the physical development of their offspring. These would 'protect the abdomen and strengthen the back' which would result in erect posture, grace of carriage, and better health in later years . Value of child's waist $35-45, Woman's $95-125.

Camisole, c. 1900, the bodice of the camisole boasts tucks and lace inserts. Fitted in back, bloused in front, closes with drawstrings at neckline and waist. $95-115 value of original.

Photo courtesy FOLKWEAR, formerly of San Rafael, CA.

Gored petticoat has dust ruffle at hemline, drawstring waist ties at back. Value of original $150-250.

Knee length drawers gathered at the curved waistband, front gusset and 2 buttoned side plackets. Ruffles at knee. **Value of original $150-195.**

Bloomers attached to camisole top c. 1915-1919. Value $150-195.

Women's underthings: Left, c. 1915-1916 silk 'teddy.' A 'teddy is a camisole top and loose panties, combined in one garment. The 'teddy' shown is hand made and hand embroidered. Value $175-225.
Right: slip, c. 1920, hand embroidered. Value $95-135.

1914. Combination corset cover and drawers, embroidered with Irish crochet, value $250-350. The fine tucks at the waistline and at the edge of the drawers are hand-run. Batiste.

A combination garment of 1912-1913. 'Open drawers' and corset cover. Cotton. The slight fullness in front is regulated at the top by a ribbon running through the eyelet. The drawers are darted and fit snugly over the hips. This is hand embroidered but garments of this type can be lavishly trimmed with expensive laces. Depending on the trim the combination garment value is $250-350.

Tea gown or negligee. This is a lounging robe or 'demi-toilette'. Made of challis and worn with a fichu edged with ruffles of chiffon draped around the shoulders. Value $425-650.

Woman's undergarment, corset cover and drawers combined. Semi-princess style, made of cambric and ruffled. Value depends on trim but these are enjoying great popularity now. Value $200-300.

All clothing seems to have been categorized into time segments depending on function. This grouping presents 'morning wear' for all ages, a lady's dressing sacque and cap; lady's negligee, empire style; corset cover; apron which covers only front of the dress, the back is a deep yoke; boy's rompers cut in a single piece; child's dress with bloomers, simple sack shape; house dress of cotton. All of these are worthwhile additions to a collection and should be diligently sought after. Values follow general guidelines listed elsewhere in the book.

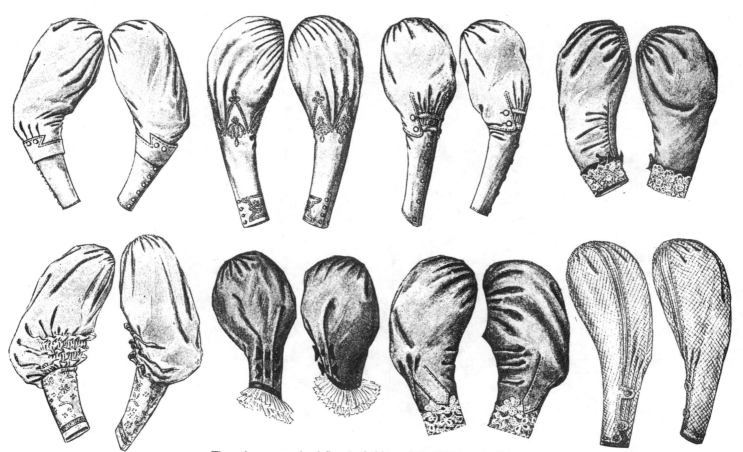

These sleeve examples define the fashions of the 1906 period. Often, even more than hem length or waistline, the sleeves can date your garment more precisely. Although these are varied in interpretation, the basic line remains the same, puffed at the shoulder, either three quarter or full sleeve length, usually trimmed at the tight wrist with fancy work and/or buttons. Collectors should study the sleeve shape, length, and trim as well as material and tailoring in assessing any vintage garment.

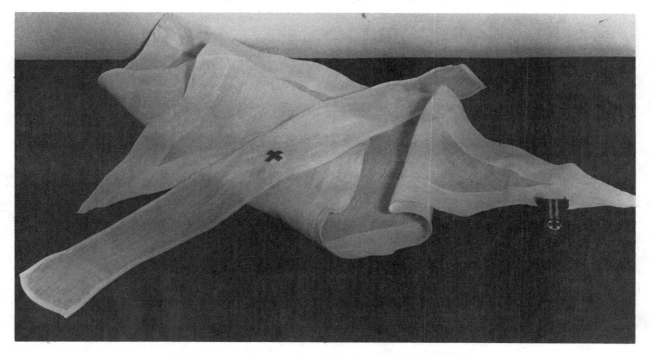

Red Cross cap and apron with official pin. c.1915. Value $95-110.

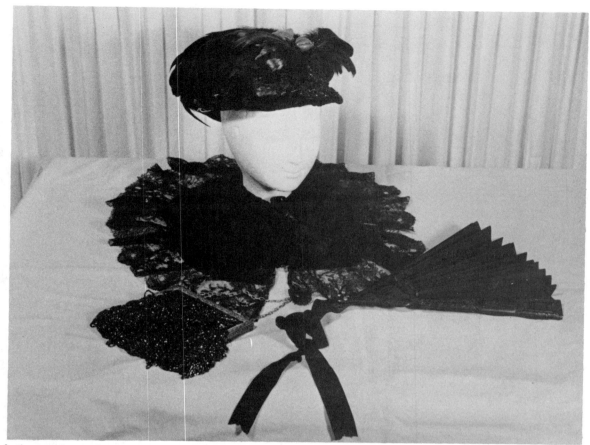

Bird body feathers swirl around red cherries on this Victorian hat. Black velvet with beading 1890-1905. Value $250-350 Victorian collar, overall beading with black lace, value $175-250. Black ebony wood fan, black silk, black ribbon. End sticks covered with lace. Value $175-235. Black beaded bag, silver frame. Value $195-325.

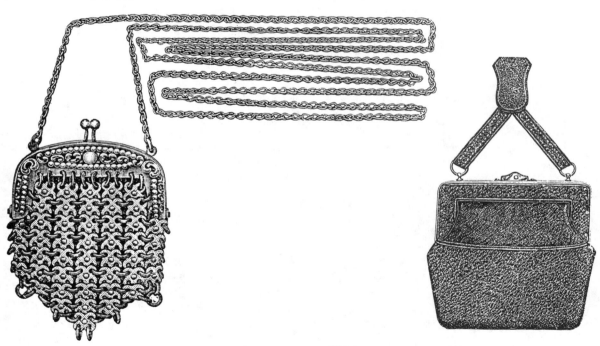

A silver plated purse and guard chain of 1900-1901. This metal purse' is composed of many small ornamental pieces joined together by rings. The frame is richly decorated. The purse is 2-3/4" by 3" and is meant to be worn suspended from the neck by the chain which is 44" long. Ornamental and useful. Charming. Value $175-225. Purse collecting has reached epidemic proportions.

This is one type of Chatelaine bag (about which there seems to be confusion). This is much larger than the photograph indicates, is made of Morocco leather, the interior is leather lined. The trimmings are of high polished nickel. It boasts an outside pocket, still the desire of every traveller. This was a type of carryall, for shopping, travelling, for carrying papers, this was it. Women used these in place of a handbag. 1900. Value $150-175.

These wonderful hats of the early Edwardian era are a revelation. They are decorated with flower-like rosettes of soft silk, often the whole hat or covering one side; they are made of fine or coarse straw, fancy braid and silk were used for the new Spring toques and turbans then coming into style again. The hats were becoming smaller in 1909 although by our standards they still seem oversized. Wings of feathers were often seen on hats of moderate size. Quilled ribbon is an indication of the age of these hats. The hair at this time was worn well over the brow and 'bangs' were having another revival. Value of hats depends on material and trim, as well as size in some cases, in good condition all should fall into the $250-500 range.

111

The truly magnificent hats of the years 1909-1910 are complementary to the equally impressive coiffeur of the ladies. Left hat features ribbons and full feather trim, right shows different kinds of feathers. Both are straw. Hats of this type are valued at $250-500.

Three different versions of the crocheted boudoir cap and different varieties of the hat stand. Each cap $45-65.

1916. Boudoir cap of hairpin crochet, ribbon runs through loops and ties at the front. Value $45-65.

In 1904 this cap-headgear was called a shawl/fascinator, a term which has never really left the fashion lexicon but has taken on slightly different meanings over the years. The one shown here is knitted with a knitted lace edging. These can be found in many variations since often they were made at home. Value in good condition $50-65.

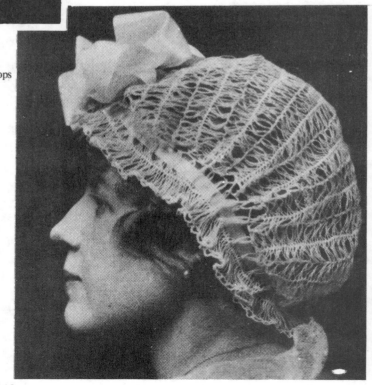

Boudoir caps in various styles and fabrics: satin, net, lace, ribbon and crochet work were the materials most used and many were made at home. Values clockwise, from center top: $60-95. c.1900. $75-100, satin and crochet, $60-95; silk and lace $50-65; $50-65; silk and lace $50-65.

Fans: various periods. Back feather ball fan, c.1900 dyed lavender with matching bow and ribbon on handle. $95-185. Left: cardboard fan, ornate. with scenes on each panel, sentimental and among the most collectible of fans. $150-195. Center: child's fan, feather with pink rosettes. Difficult to find $125-175. Right: feather fan from China, pre-1920 wooden handle. Peking glass bead and enamel decoration $50-60.

Parasols, c.1880-1910. Parasols have risen steeply in price. White lace with handmade black lace overall, value $300-350; beige silk and cerise silk in a handkerchief point design with a silk braided tassel on the wooden handle, value $225-275; child's black typically Victorian parasol, silk with ruffled edging, folding handle, value $200-250, high laced shoes in tan and brown leather.

Accessories: various periods. Combs resting on 1920's silk handkerchief. Backcomb set with small stones, c.1908, $75-135. Side comb c.1900, $50-65. Right: unusual tortoise shell comb set with rhinestone eagle $250-300. Umbrella handle, sterling silver. Cameos, all shell, all set in 14K gold: l to r: $400-600, $225. Locket, gold filled set with brilliants, $125-150.

Part of a large beaded bag collection assembled over a relatively short period of time. The collector was paying about $55 to $175 for those shown. Most of those purchased within the last five years have at least doubled in price and prices continue to rise. The bags are hung from fancy hooks on a plain white wall to highlight their colors and shapes and designs. Any beaded bag collection (aside from its intrinsic worth and the delight of knowing one owns these treasures) can only be appreciated when displayed properly, but care must be taken.

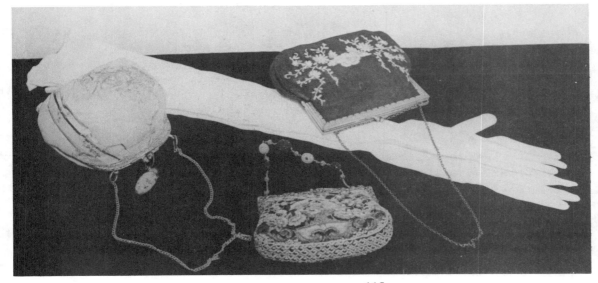

Fine French bags, all with chain handles. Left: French silk $175-225. Right: $100-150: Bottom: $200-225.

Selection of shoes from the early 1900's to 1920's. Black leather oxford, spool heel, ties, pointed toe, value $75-125, white canvas with spool heel. This type shoe was worn through the early 1920's and they seem to fit more people than other types, value $55-95; white leather, front lace $95-145; black leather, button strap, utilitarian wear of the 1920's, value $60-85. One problem with collectible shoes is the difficulty of finding a correct fit. Nevertheless, shoes of bygone days in good condition are not easily found and should be purchased whenever they present themselves.

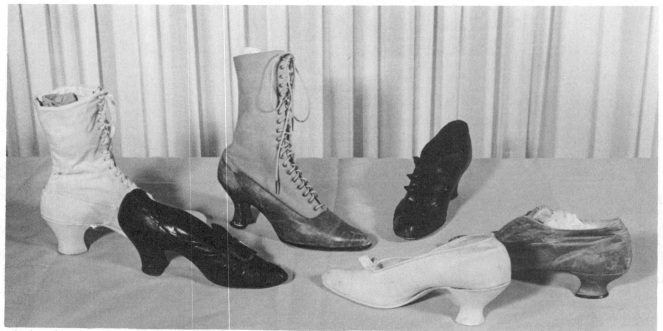

A selection of womens' shoes. Early 1900's white canvas hi tops, spool heel, cotton laces. Value $75-125; low cut black leather with beaded buckle, value $85-95; soft beige leather, lighter wool top, all lined, spool heel. For dress wear, value $175-195; low cut white canvas summer shoe, slip-on, bow of grosgrain ribbon, spool heel, hard rubber heel, value $85-100. Soft blue leather beaded 3 strap button shoe, spool heel. Value $100-135; silk lined heavy cotton shoe with spool heel, very pointed toe (partially hidden) burnt orange color. Value $100-125. Stuffing wadded tissue paper into the toes of these shoes can help them retain their shape.

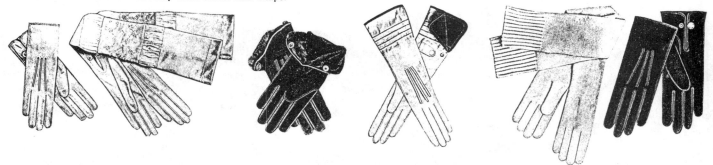

Gloves were considered tasteful and practical gifts, or tasteful and elegant gifts in the pre-World War I years. This selection is a typical array of the gloves of the 1916-1919 years. Top left and clockwise: Long white wool gloves for women, excellent for automobile wear; men's mocha leather gloves, unlined gray; Women's strap wrist white gloves for afternoon or evening wear. Long white silk gloves for women for evening wear. Women's lace gloves in white with embroidered backs; Men's fur lined mocha gloves. Gloves of this quality were not inexpensive when new.
The gloves shown here are all fine quality, prices of any pair of gloves depends on materials, lining, condition, trim and type since some types are much more common than others. Glove collecting can result in a beautiful display.

Graduation dress of 1908. White, elaborately detailed with embroidered netting.   Value $650-1,000.
Photo by Douglas R. Smith
Courtesy of Southern Oregon Historical Society

1914. Demure young high school graduate in the easy styling of lace and silk. Modest neckline. Very large corsage attached to belt. Value of dress $500-950.

117

Left: Suit for a young girl of 1909-1910. Reseda-green venetian, 2 piece semi-fitted coat which has cutaway effect, sleeve has moderate fullness but plain fitting sleeves were also popular. Turn back cuffs of velvet. Velvet faced collar. Seven gore skirt fits closely at hips and flares at lower edge. This is of serge and was the latest thing for the teenager in 1909. Value $600-950.

1908-1909. Center: Fitted dress, double row of front buttons, square neckline banded in velvet, buttons down sleeves which come to a point over the hands. Linen. Value $750-1,000.

Right: Teen-ager's dress or a dress for the 'young miss' of 1908-1909. White lawn with lace insertions, one of the most desirable types to collectors. Deep ruffle, tucks at bodice, moderately full sleeves gathered into armhole. Value $650-1,000.

Left: Dress for young miss. Simple design with fullness depending on the clusters of small tucks below the shaped yoke. The skirt is five gored with a large flounce. Linen with hand embroidery trimmed with bands of nainsook. It is often difficult to determine the age bracket into which some of the period clothing fits since size is not always a factor. Generally younger girls wore dresses of figured lawn, organdy or light weight woolens. The very small older woman has until recently had to go to these girlish styles. Value of dress $600-1,000.

Right: This young girl's gown was an exact copy of a dress intended for older women. It is semi-princess in sheath effect with a simple look. Slight fullness to the blouse-waist at the sides by single tucks at the shoulder, panel front and back are continued in the skirt which is joined to the blouse for the high waistline. Fancy neckline and short sleeves are provided for wear with a guimpe. This is old-rose cashmere. Value if material is in excellent condition $600-1,000.

1905 golfing and tennis costumes. The woman's outfit would probably be found as separates today and would fall into the price range quoted previously for 1900's blouses and skirts. This is also true of the gentleman's outfit, the pants would fall into the $40-50 range.

Misses' dresses, 1912. Left to right: Designed for the high school girl, this frock is rose cashmere. Middy style with sailor collar. Unusual lacing. Value $700-950. Middy dress, blouse is joined to a 6 gored skirt. Belt and sailor collar. Serge. Value $700-950. This dress closes at the left side of the front and has a 2 piece skirt. Cashmere, value $700-950. Lingerie dress. Embroidered flouncing with the yoke formed of rows of insertion with fine lawn. Organdy. Value $650-1,000.

Young ladies' wear is often sold as adult clothing even though it was shorter and the skirt was more boxy than the preferred ladies' gored type. Sizes were ordinarily 14 to 18 so again the waistline could have rivaled an adult waist. The look is different, much less fitted and looser. This sort of costume is very difficult to find, the range for the dresses would be $500-900 and the suits $600-1,200. The coats are again indentifiable by the sleeve at the shoulder, and the rather high back strap. $500-750.

A sports costume with hat for the young miss. Especially recommended for that special vacation, the dress consists of a 'smart linene' blouse in rose color and a striped poplin skirt, in rose and white. Striped material is also used to make the broad collar and to edge the cuffs. The blouse has a deep band at the lower edge and the button trimmed pockets are formed by the band. Pearl buttons and a patent leather belt ornamented with rings of white kid. The girdle top skirt closes in front. The hat is milan straw matching the color of the dress and trimmed with white grosgrain ribbon and a tailored bow. This was considered an ultra smart outfit in 1917. Complete dress $200-275, hat $75-150.

Gymnasium suits for young misses in 1913. Left, regulation type, plain blouse with round neck and small collar. Bloomers are separate and of moderate fullness. Lighweight flannel. Set value, $250-350. Blouse, $50-75. Bloomers, $145-175. Right: Same suit for the older girl, v-neck and pocket with striped sailor collar and sleeve edges. Value, set $350-450. Blouse, $75-100. Bloomers, $145-175.

Bathing Beauty of 1917. In spite of the modesty of this bathing outfit this beauty does manage to look provocative. This was considered the complete outfit-bathing suit, tights, cap and shoes. The suit is made of firm quality brilliantine, trimmed with white soutache braid. It has a V neck and shield sleeves. This garment slips easily over the head and the soutache braid holds the waistline in check. Navy blue. The tights are knee length cotton jersey and are made with low neck and wide armholes and button at the shoulder. The bathing cap is pure rubber, trimmed with a fancy rubber rosette. The boot high laced shoes are black sateen, are lined with canvas and have canvas covered soles. This is really a splendid outfit and could we find one intact it would be a treasure. The suit alone $150-175.

Red flannel swimsuit, c.1900. Fitted in back, bloused in front, which is decorated with large white buttons, white collar, sleeve and hem trim. Black cotton stockings, rubber bathing slippers. Bathing suit $95-150, slippers in perfect condition $45-65.

Two lady bowlers of 1901. Both wear two piece outfits of pantaloons and waists with ties. Loose comforatable action-oriented clothing which seems somewhat advanced for the first year of the century. Dark blue serge. Complete suit $145-175.

Winter of 1910. Young girl in typical clothing of the period, wool coat with low beltline and button trim with side closure. Large hat in the shape of a mob-cap with large feather wing trim. Coat value $300-450, hat $200-250.

1909. Young girl's dress of white pique with button-holed edges, box pleats from rounded neck to hem. Guimpe and one seam leg-o-mutton sleeves. Younger child's version has puffed sleeves. Older girl's dress is of tucked swiss, younger child's is of lawn. In either size, value $200-275.

A school dress of lawn trimmed with lace and embroidery. Fully lined. Small tucks in yoke effect. In a more elaborate material it could be considered a party dress. The shaped bertha gives the dress a certain elegance. Satin sash which bows in back. Large bows in hair. Value of dress $250-350.

1910. Young girl's cashmere dress trimmed with buttons. Front panel runs the entire length of the dress narrowing slightly from the neck to the waist then extending in a flare to the bottom of the skirt. Tucks over the shoulders back and front give fullness to the waist. Intended for a girl up to 14 years of age. This is pique. Value $350-400.

1910. White linen with embroidered bands. Dress closes at left front with 2 wide tucks over shoulders to waistline in front. Puff sleeves which were favored for younger girls up to about 9. Value $250-300.

For a girl up to 14 or 15 this navy blue repp dress was considered very fashionable in 1910. Buttons down side for trim, tucks extend into skirt, dutch collar, belted. Value $350-450. Large hair bows much in evidence.

Left: A 1909 boy's suit in the Russian style. Regulation knickerbockers attached to waist bands. The blouse has a wide sailor collar and a removable shield. The sleeves are gathered very slightly into the armhole and finished at the wrist with a band. There is a single pocket left front. Belted. Flannel. Boys suits of this era are among the most difficult clothing to find. Value $400-450.

Center: Little girls' dress of lawn. Considered a play dress or a party dress entirely dependent on the material and trim. Collectors of children's clothing need to be aware of the factors which separated the categories in this kind of clothing. Clusters here of tucks stitched from the neck and shoulders to yoke depth. This dress has a dutch round neck and short puff sleeves. Insertions of beading and ribbons at neck, sleeves and belt. $300-350.

Right: 1909 girl's dress intended for a child up to 8 or 9 years of age. Dotted swiss with high neck and long sleeves, tucked, green satin sash. Value $200-250.

Young girl of the early 1900's. Long wool, high waisted dress with hem ruffle. Emphasis on shoulder and sleeves which are long with puffed oversleeve, with an overall cape effect. Necklace and bar pin. Not much more clothing could possibly adorn such a small person. Dresses of this kind are scarce. Value $350-500.

1908 Child's playwear or play suit. Two wide tucks at the shoulder in front and an inverted plait at the back below the waistline afford fullness. This fastens down front left and has a standing collar. Bloomers are optional. This is of percale and intended for a little girl up to 10 years of age. These are often quite beautiful and are scarce. Value $350-500.

Party frock for the very young girl of the 1908-1910 period. Yoke of embroidery, high neck, full length sleeves. This is of batiste. Children's clothing continues to be popular. $200-300.

Same basic dress with added sash and different neckline. For older child. Girls wear shoes with straps and bows. Value of dress $250-350.

Left: 1909 Wrap intended for young girl. Cold or rainy day covering. It is basically a 4 piece cape which fits smoothly about the neck and shoulders and widens below the hips. Rolling collar. Fastens in front with opening for hands. Waterproof serge which lends itself perfectly to this military style. Scarce. Value $350-450. Sometimes found with a hood.

Box coat for little girl, also worn by older girls. Wide square collar with braid effect which is repeated on sleeves. Broadcloth. Shown as worn by both ages. Value $300-400. These young girls are wearing the huge hats decreed as fashionable by their mothers but seem overwhelming on the children.

A winsome 17 year old wears this white lawn, lace trimmed graduation dress in 1903. The big bow atop the one artfully arranged curl was a popular coiffure in those days. A beautiful soft, feminine dress. Value $1,200-1,500.

It is interesting that in 1903 children of these ages should be called 'young people' for it not only signifies a certain dignity but also explains the fashions these children wore. The clothing here is not special, it was designated 'standard fashion' for young people and is beautifully tailored, fitted and although we would consider it much too old for the wearers, it is quite flattering. The coat the girl wears (left) is full length with bishop sleeves with a bertha cape. It is marine blue in color with white lace trim. Matching hat. Coat is $50-195, hat $65-125.

The teenager (center right) wears a gray-green blouse with shoulder capes with a two piece circular skirt of the same color with an inverted box pleat at the back. The material is homespun with velvet trim and applique. Value $225-295.

A younger teenager wears a costume that could be adapted for wear by a child. A Monte Carlo jacket with a sailor collar and a pleated skirt attached to an under waist or belt which was sometimes called the NEWPORT. The bright orange with Navy blue trim is a lovely outfit. Value $225-300.

Children from six months to seven years were considered the correct ages to wear this coat. A very stylish garment in the early years of the century it is full length, double breasted, caped and cuffed. Dark green with a patent leather belt. So while asexual clothing hadn't yet invaded the teenage market younger children's clothing was often interchangeable. Value $200-295.

A child as young as six months could wear this but the girl shown is about 6 years. The lovely coat is champagne colored with a collar of all-over lace applique trim. It is charming. The exaggerated mob cap accentuates the dainty look. $200-295.

A wonderfully representative pair of children dressed typically in the fashions of the early years of the century. The boy wears a coat and trousers of mixed cheviot, coat is double breasted and the pants are knee length, his high collar looks uncomfortable but the excellent fit of the suit and the collar give him the proper look so desired. Suit value in excellent condition $200-300.

In 1903 and for many years after the clothing young people wore was highly ornamented with lace. The girl at the left wears a dress elaborately decorated with Cluny overall lace, it also has Cluny lace insertions, ribbon bands and bows. It is made of pale blue henrietta, one can understand the treasures these old garments represent given the tailoring, the quality and extravagance of the materials used and the design work. Even into the 1930s little girls were wearing the large hairbows. Notice her shoes, which are the low oxford type. This dress is valued at $500-600.

The center young lady is also wearing the large bow but her hair is up not down, a significant milestone in a young lady's life in those days. Her dress has a yoke of Irish lace, the basic material is reseda green voile with braid over black velvet trim. Irish lace has become something of a status symbol to collectors and when incorporated into a lovely costume such as this raises the value. Value of this dress $600-1,000.

The dress at right is pale blue albatross with narrow braid trim and applique lace, a stylish ornamentation of the day. Handmade lace adds considerably to the value of any vintage clothing. Value of dress $350-450.

From top left: A soft white nainsook dress trimmed with fisheye lace and fine embroidery. Ruffle edged with lace. This was intended for a child about 1 to 2 years. 1916. Value $100-200.

A play dress of black and white gingham (how avant garde) piped in red, white collar and cuffs finished with red piping, full 'plaited' skirt. A child from 3 to 6 years could wear this. 1917. Value $100-150.

The girl with the top and delightful high button shoes wears a plaid tan gingham dress with plain collars, cuffs and belt in matching colors. A yoke with pearl buttons, white piping and a full 'plaited' skirt complete the outfit. 1917.
Value $100-150.

The white gala tea dress is trimmed effectively with bands of red printed in a green and black conventional design. Black velvet tailored bow at the neck, full pleated skirt and pearl buttons. 1917. Value $100-150.

What the children were wearing in 1907. The girl at left wears a plaid dress with velvet trimming, the boy is in a Russian box-plaited dress with bloomers, the girl with the bird in hand is in bloomer drawers buttoned to underwear, the girl with the huge bow is wearing a cover-up apron of cotton over her wool dress. One of the functions of the apron was to cover up stains already on the underclothing. It was a quick, crisp, clean changeover. The coat the child wears was used until about age 6 and the double breasted effect added to the longevity of the garment. It is gathered in a full yoke at back. Wool. All children's garments are dependent on condition, function, beauty, tailoring and trim. Any of these would have starting value of $50.

127

This is a good illustration of the clothing children of various ages wore in 1907. The girl wears a dress of wood-pink cashmere and white silk braid, Value $175-300, the 'little girl' at bottom wears a dress of white batiste and embroidery. Value $145-195, the young miss at top right has a coat of pominos cloth and black velvet, she is totally overwhelmed by the hat. Coat value $200-250. The girl at bottom right wears a coat of Atlantic blue kersey with a darker braid trim. $200-250.

Typical children's clothing of the 1912-1914 period. Left is little girls' empire dress. Gathered ruffles, edging, bretelles at the shoulders, batiste. Elaborate, Sunday dress. Value $150-225.

Little girls' tucked or gathered dress. Square neck, short sleeves, beautifully embroidered. Dotted swiss with satin sash. Value $125-175.

Child's empire coat has a full cape. Lots of embroidery on collar, cuffs and the body of the coat. Coat value $150-200.

This empire dress has an open neck with a fischu, short sleeves and a gathered skirt, insertion and edging. Very pretty. Value $150-185.

This lightweight coat is very pleasing with its plaid pattern, boxy look, patent leather belt and high collar. The big buttons also add interest. Intended for a 4 year old. Value $150-195.

This dress is rather unusual for such a young girl. It is bright blue linen with a laced front and bretelles. The yoke vest is applied to the lining. The back which closes with buttons is slightly flared. The skirt is five gored and flounced and is joined to the waist and belted. 1901. Value $150-200.

This dress is brown albatross with velvet collar and wristband. The fitted lining serves as a foundation and the skirt which hangs from the waist is gored and flounced. The dolls are equally fashionable. 1901.
Value of dress $150-200.

A group of young girls dressed for Confirmation. These dresses are beautifully feminine and prime collector's targets if in good condition. It is highly unusual, if not impossible to find the complete costume including veil and shoes although a few such complete outfits have turned up. It certainly would be a prize to add to a collection.
Top left: This dress consists of a yoke waist closed at the back with a high or Dutch round neck, full length sleeves and with a shirred Monte Carlo bertha with a five gored skirt. Most of these dresses boast the same design except for differing details. These are graceful and must have presented a picture of ethereal appeal when seen in a group. 1902-04. Most of these dresses are fine quality, these are of Sicilian white, oriental lace, white silk applique, nun's veiling. Value $400-500.

The children's costumes have become a very big collecting field. The gun the child holds is too realistic looking for comfort, but it was made to shoot caps. The soldier suit is well made of good quality khaki with regimental insignia pins and the cap has the patent leather peak. Red trim. 1917. $185-225.

This Indian playsuit is made of durable khaki and trimmed with a broad band in the colors of Indian wampum. Trim is a scalloped yellow felt and a narrow stripe of turkey red khaki. The neck laces with a narrow red cord. This suit originally came with a narrow string of red beads. The head band has a loose red feather, a Christmas gift in 1917. Value intact and in good condition, $200-250.

These outfits were worn by small boys in 1918. Top left - a one piece romper with envelope closing. This is strictly a boys romper suit, considered 'mannish'. It is tailored with the belt running through the pocket straps.

Top right: This is a boy's dress, the wide box pleats and severe style supposedly making it possible for the little boy to be a 'real man'. It has bloomers.

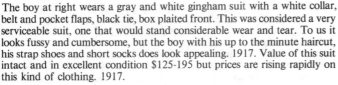

The boy at right wears a gray and white gingham suit with a white collar, belt and pocket flaps, black tie, box plaited front. This was considered a very serviceable suit, one that would stand considerable wear and tear. To us it looks fussy and cumbersome, but the boy with his up to the minute haircut, his strap shoes and short socks does look appealing. 1917. Value of this suit intact and in excellent condition $125-195 but prices are rising rapidly on this kind of clothing. 1917.

His friend on the left wears a suit of white linen, which was supposed to be easily laundered (but terms such as 'easily' are relative) and has a collar, cuffs and belt of blue, a white cord tie and pearl buttons. He too looks carefully coifed and tailored but adorable. Suit $125-195.

Center left: This suit has a detachable collar and cuffs, the center boy wears the still popular sailor suit, the boy on right wears an 'outing' shirt with a detachable collar, knickers with belt. Not a hair out of place. The boy at bottom wears a wool Mackinaw. All these clothes although quite the thing in 1918 do not seem all that dated. The top three valued at $40-50 each, center models $100-150, mackinaw in good condition (moths loved mackinaws) $125-295. The boy's cap is a very desirable collectible.

Rompers. Knickerbocker style. Blue and white galatea, white red and white collar. Value $45-65.

Little boy's double breasted sailor suit with overblouse effect and removable shield. Navy blue serge with red and white collar. Knickerbockers. 1913. Value of suit $65-100.

This boy wears a Norfolk styled jacket and slim knee length pants with three buttons on each side at the bottom. It is gray wool with a blue horizontal thread. A vertical pinstripe is black with white threads on each side. Two pocket flaps are buttoned down near the shoulders. The 3" side self belt is held in place by two more of these flaps. Jacket label reads STEEL FABRICS, SHEAHAN AND KOHN, CHICAGO, IL. c.1915-1920. Value of suit in good condition $200-250.

1913. Junior styles. Favorite yoke model dress in a plain sacque design which hangs straight from the shoulder to the hem and applied on this is the novel yoke which comes down almost to the waistline. Wide collar and cut off sleeves. Hand scalloping on edge of collar and sleeves. Linen. Quality of the material and handwork add greatly to the value of garments such as these. Value $250-300.

This apron resembles a dress. It is a coverall type which completely covers the dress beneath. It is a Mother Hubbard or Kate Greenaway style made with a yoke which extends well down on the chest and back. Full skirt, high neck with turnover collar. These were always made in washable fabrics. Cambric. Value $125-195.

Two piece dress, the skirt being attached to the underwaist which fasten in back. V neck. The blouse coat has a diagonal closing in front and a broad band in Balkan style at the lower edge. Poplin $250-295. 1912.

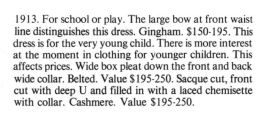

1913. For school or play. The large bow at front waist line distinguishes this dress. Gingham. $150-195. This dress is for the very young child. There is more interest at the moment in clothing for younger children. This affects prices. Wide box pleat down the front and back wide collar. Belted. Value $195-250. Sacque cut, front cut with deep U and filled in with a laced chemisette with collar. Cashmere. Value $195-250.

Child's sweater, cap and muff set of ostrich wool. Sweater and muff have cross stitching design, muff is satin lined. Cap has large satin ribbon bows. Worn over white linen cambric dress. Stockings are long and worn with high button shoes. Value of sweater, muff and hat as a set $300-400.

Top, girl's coat, high neck, small collar, circular skirt. Wool. Value $200-300. Left, made of different materials which was considered 'new' in 1916. Serge top with velvet skirt. Value $225-295. Separate skirt and blouse, which is long length. Satin with wool. Value $175-200.

Boy's Russian suit. This easy to launder suit has a front closing blouse. Made of chambray, these are endearing additions to a collection. Value $195-250. An 'Oliver Twist' suit which consists of shirt waist with pleats and straight trousers buttoning to the shirtwaist. Value of suit $195-250.
Girl's dress of 1914. A child's kimono dress slips over the head. Drawers are worn under the dress. Cotton. Value $100-150.
Teenaged girl's short jacket of plaid wool worn with plain colored wool skirt. Jacket $100-150. Notice large tam and high shoes.

1909 girl's reefer. Gray broadcloth, notched collar, cuffs and pockets finished with stitching. Close fitting sleeves with gathers at top. Worn by girls up to 14. Value $165-275. Right: same coat intended for younger child. Value same. Notice overwhelming hats on young children.
Center. 1909. Child's coat in the Empire style, following the adult fashion. Wide fancy collar and cuffs. Blue bengaline silk. $175-300. Button shoes.

Body and sleeves of this coat are one piece. Belted. Wool. Value $150-200. Girls' dress. Copied from a new fashion for women in the winter of 1913, the deep, straight yoke. A row of shirring at the waist, and over this a wide belt. Plaid silk with velvet trim. Value $175-225. School dress for winter. Serge, value $150-200.

Summer frocks, 1913. Diagonal front closing, wide shawl collar ending at belt which has buttons below, linen. Value $275-300. Seamless shoulder in drop style, ribbon threaded through for effect, cotton. Value $250-295. Bodice and skirt dress. Simple style with wide banding trim. Skirt joins waist beneath belt, cambric. Value $250-295.

Boy's single breasted overcoat. Well fitting collar and rolled lapels. Usually found in wool. 1913. $125-155.

1915. Girls' apron. One piece with a short dart below arm to adjust to figure. Closes in back. Gingham. $30-40. Girls' coat. Simple box type, raglan sleeves. Tweed. Value $150-200. Boy's overcoat, with long shouldercape which does not cover coat buttons in front. Detachable cape. Wool. Value with cape $225-275. Coat without cape, $95-125. Cap in child's size, $25-35.

For the small child, 1915. Top left: Garment is quite simple, front side closing. Square neck, can be worn by boy or girl. Serge but can be found in velveteen. Value, $145-195. Boy's Russian dress. Wool, high neck with banded collar, closing well over to side in front. $145-195. Simple dress with plain blouse with drop shoulder and wide collar. Diagonal closing across front and meets line of skirt closing. Value $200-250. Boy's suit. Coat of modified Eton type, edges meet at neck but hang apart to hem of jacket which ends below the hips. Vest and trousers made without a fly. Velveteen. Value $350-450. Slip type dress with guimpe. Small box pleats front and back. Dress with belt $195-225.

1915. Sacque cut, shirring at neck and waist for children up to 6 years of age. Challis. Value $165-200. Long waisted blouse with pleated skirt. Collars and cuffs match hem border. Belt, Value $195-250. Tunic over waist and skirt. Belt of leather at low waistline. Tunics were also popular with the ladies of 1915. Value $195-225. Sailor dress with collar which joins revers with notches. Pleated skirt. Cashmere. $175-230.

1915. Children's coat. Plain sacque coat with highly ornamental cape. Round neck is trimmed with a small collar and the full sleeves end in a cuff. Value $195-225. Often these children's coats were made in expensive materials such as ottoman silk, velvet, cashmere, fur. The bonnet, which went with this kind of coat was also usually silk or velvet, is round and full, finished with a flat band around the head. Value $50-60.

136

1913. Waist and skirt dress for young girl. Skirt attaches to waist beneath the sash. Cotton. Value $145-195. Russian dress worn by boy. Plain sacque cut, closes at side, sleeves now showing no fullness at shoulder. Usually worn by boys under three years of age. Value $195-250. Gingham dress in tan stripes. Value $125-175. Sacque cut, one piece. Hand embroidered collar and cuffs, belt passes through slots. Value $200-225. One piece, broad belt, hand embroidered. Linen. Value $225-300.

This is what the schoolboy was wearing in 1901. It is a sort of coverall or apron which was worn to protect the boy's clothes. This is made of linen although they can often be found in serge. It closes in the back under one of the pleats. This garment was worn only indoors and could be used by a boy until he was about 8 years old. Not easy to find. Value $125-175.

1913. Dresses for the small girl. Long bloused effect, pleated skirt, bow at neck, button front. Cotton. Value $150-200. One piece dress with attached bloomers. Green challis with rosette of blue satin at side. Value $145-175. One piece with front closing and separate guimpe. Value $150-200. School coat. Box style, circular front, contrasting trim. Value $175-200. Utility dress made in many washable materials as well as wool. Value $125-195. Embroidered flouncing on this one piece dress. Closes at back. Value $195-210. Large bows if original, $30-40.

In 1912 boys hats were fashionable when they were 'shapeless' and made of cloth. In typical style the crown fits over the head and the brim is stiffened by means of stitching. The jockey cap was also a favorite and is now making a minor comeback especially among girls. The cap with visor is flannel. Notice the variety of ties worn with the same collar. Value of boys hats of this kind and era $25-45.

C. 1916. Cotton with lace dress. $195-250.

1912. Baby's short dress in crochet. The flounce and upper part of the skirt was made separately and attached to the waist. Surprisingly durable for all its fragile look. This beautiful handwork is now eagerly sought after and a dress combining this beauty and marvelous crochet work would be of heirloom status if found in excellent condition. $500-600.

Boy's suit, blue serge, paneled front, 2 piece. Bow of linen. C. 1900. Value $200-250.

Child of the 1920's. Knitted suit with straps to hold pants over shoes, matching cap. Small sized ice cream chair. Value of suit $145-175.

138

A Joan Crawford evening ensemble. Pale green straight cut jersey under dress, net gilt embroidered separate overlay. No label noted. Part of a lot at Christies' auction in June, 1993. Estimated price was $800 -$1,200, actual sale price $978.

Assorted marabou feather boa wraps belonging to Joan Crawford and sold at Christies' for $748 in June, 1993, well above estimated of $150 - $200. Black and white, pink with gold and cream, solid black and solid white.

(left and right hand pages) An assortment of clothing and accessories from the estate of Joan Crawford. While Miss Crawford dressed in a rather severe, tailored way in public, her personal effects indicate a penchant for the frivolous. All of her personal things were auctioned, including gloves, scarves, even handkerchiefs. The piece de resistance of the Crawford auction was the Oscar she won in 1945 for her performance in" Mildred Pierce". The Oscar brought $68,500, more than $50,000 over estimate but everything went over estimate, an assortment of scarves, for example, estimated at $100 - $200 sold for $2,530. Many of Crawford's personal belongings were not particularly spectacular either in quality or style and the lesson here is if you are ever fortunate enough to find clothing or accessories belonging to a famous celebrity buy without a qualm, even if you have to eat peanut butter sandwiches for a month.

Four sweaters belonging to Joan Crawford. A black crocheted short jacket style sweater with hand applied black sequins, a cream colored lambs wool jacket style with raised panel embroidered flowers and pearl buttons; a hand beaded lambs wool sweater with pink beaded flowers, clear sequins and pearl buttons, and a hand beaded cream crocheted short jacket style sweater with iridescent sequins. The four sweaters were estimated at $100 - $200, actually sold for $690.

Four more sweaters belonging to Joan Crawford. A pink lambs wool Saks Fifth Avenue model, pink satin flowers applied on the front with pink pearl and gray bugle beading, a lined cream lambs wool sweater with white and pearl beading, a cream lambs wool-angora blend sweater with iridescent sequins and pearl buttons and a lambs wool blend cream sweater with gold sequins and matching gold buttons. Estimated at $100 - $200, these sold for $690.

The heirloom quality of vintage clothing is nowhere more apparent than in the christening gowns of bygone days. This long christening robe was first worn in 1879 by the grandfather of the infant pictured. It is cotton lawn with hand made lace. Victorian christening gowns are in such demand a British company makes them to order to exacting old standards guaranteed to fool everyone. The company which specialized in these garments charges $80 - $110. Originals command higher prices if they can be found. The beautifully made dress this baby wears is valued at $350 - $550.

Lavender silk dress with overskirt. Off-white dots. Permanent pleats in skirt, chiffon sleeves. Neckpiece ties in back in a low V. This is a gorgeous dress. Value $950 -$1000.

Blue silk-satin dress with gold thread design.
Silk chiffon sleeves. Lace collar.
Value $1,200 - $1,800.
Straw hat, black with blue ostrich feather
and decorative pin. Value $250 - $350.

Blue lingerie dress with lace inserts.
Bands of embroidery and lace inserts also on sleeves and
on skirt. Sewn down pleats on skirt flare out,
buttons down back. Value $1,200 - $1,500.

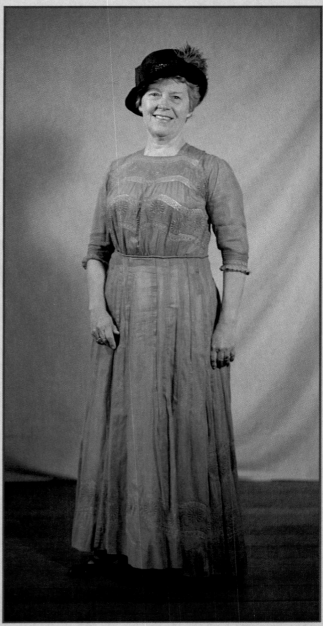

Black silk 1930's dress with pleated white silk collar.
Bottom cut on the bias. Value $750 - $950.
Black straw hat with large gold and black
velvet flowers. Value $65-$95.

Peach silk crepe 1940's dress.
Draped neckline, horizontally pleated skirt caught
up in a side drape. Value $195 - $225.
Open toe suede pump, needlepoint handbag
with celluloid clasp. Value $95 - $125.

Wedding dress and veil first worn in 1935.
Lace dress over silk slip. High ruffle at neck is fine net.
Veil is net with a lace cap trimmed with orange blossoms.
Dress and veil worn here at a 50th anniversary party in
1985 by the bride herself. It is very difficult to assess
the worth of these gowns since sentiment is often
the overriding interest. Excellent workmanship,
fabric and condition are important. 1930's
wedding dresses are becoming more valuable
as collectors realize their style and quality.
Value $500 - $850.

Wool gabardine taupe suit with padded shoulders. Suits were an absolute necessity to the well-dressed woman's wardrobe in the 1940's. This has a notched collar and closes at the waist with two buttons. Peplum flare to jacket. These suits can be very flattering to the figure. Value $195 - $250. The hat is wool tweed with brown feather, value $25 - $30; shoes are alligator with bow, value $50 - $60; handbag is also alligator, value, $95 - $195. Kid gloves. The scarf of stone-martens is valued at $250 - $300.

Late 1950's double knit two piece dress. These are very abundant and would be an easy, interesting way to begin a clothing collection. Value $40 - $50. They are undervalued. Mink stole, value $125 - $175.

Light lavender chiffon beaded dress with pearls around hemline. 1920's. Value $1000 - $1,500.

This brown velvet blouse has a detachable collar which is attached by hook and eye. 1880. The blouse measures 18" around the waist. Value $300 - $450. The hat is black velvet with gold ostrich feathers, hand tied to give extra strength. Value $195 - $225.

Selection of beaded bags. The two smaller bags are child size and were made specially for the author in 1938 when this was a popular, if somewhat tedious craft. The red and black were also made to order for family members but are somewhat earlier in the 1930's. All beaded bags are highly collectible and there are truly spectacular collections of such bags extant. Values of beaded bags vary greatly. Any good beaded bag should have a minimal value of $95, many reach into the many hundreds of dollars.

Off-white crepe dress of the 1940's. Draped front with beading. Mandarin neckline, mid-calf length. Value $200 - $225.

Selection of fans, not only a favorite fashion accessory but the favorite of multitudes of fan collectors. 1880's white feather fan, 1920's blue and gilt oriental fan with beaded handle, child's feather fan with French rosettes on the tip of each feather, and a pink Ball fan of the 1880's early 1900's.

1940's suit. Navy and white tweed, asymmetrical shawl collar,
3/4 length sleeve. Value $175 - $225. Necklace, matching bracelet and earrings are of red celluloid. Shoes are
black suede with small platforms, ankle strap closing, value $25 - $35; hat is small felt suit hat $20 - $22.

A sampling of baby shoes from the 1912-1914 period. Patent leather and kid; leather with an ankle strap, three strap red leather. Value of each pair $35-45.

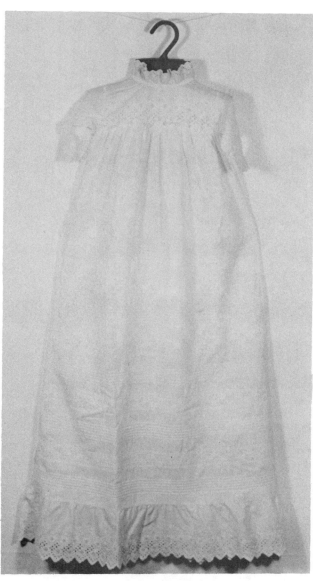

Long cambric infant's baptismal dress, worn first by boy, 1900, handmade, standing collar. Worn again recently. Value $450-650.

Baby bonnets are still inexpensive, often beautifully made with extravagent fabrics and trim and are still relatively easy to find. A truly wonderful rewarding collection could be made of these. Left is pink crepe with hand embroidery $35-45; pink silk with ruching and lace, value $65-75; Irish lace with pink silk lining $95-125; linen bib with white embroidery $30-35 (bibs are another underappreciated collectible): long linen bib with lace trim. Value $60-75.

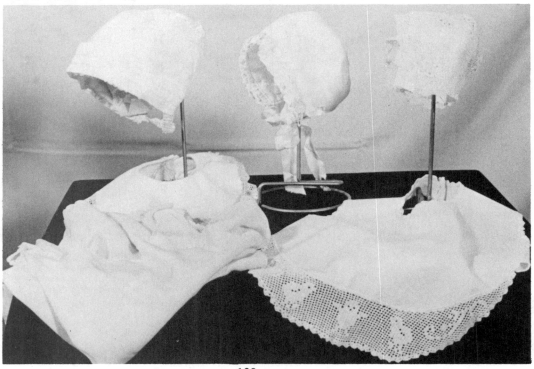

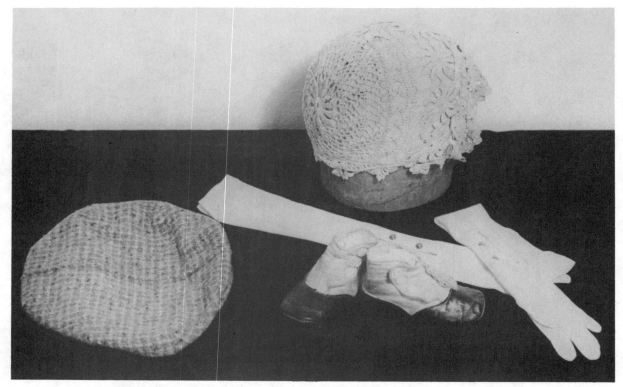

Children's accessories: various periods. Baby's cap, handmade, lined with silk, c.1917, $50-75. Boy's woolen cap, c.1930, value $22-25. Shoes, patent leather and kid, buttons and tassels, 1914. Value (worn condition) $20-25. Young girl's long gloves, silk and rayon, $18-22.

A baby saque or sack in material which could be laundered. This is of French flannel embroidered in silks with scallops forming the edges. Value $45-55. Another sack with a turn-over collar and scalloped edges. Crepe de chine but these are often found in linen or cashmere. Value $45-55.

The reason vintage baby clothes are so beautiful and expensive is the attitude toward their making, "all infants garments should be of the softest, finest materials, made by hand and never trimmed with coarse, cheap lace." These bonnets are hand made and embroidered. On left is a bonnet with wide strings and made of lawn; center is a hat made of corded silk with a 12 inch diameter; another bonnet embroidered and ribbon run through the soft linen. Value of baby bonnets and hats of this quality $45-65.

This baby clothing is most often found in nainsook, poplin, pique or soft linen. Dress is stamped Irish poplin. It was intended to be worn over a guimpe. Irish poplin is a lustrous mercerized cotton of good wearing quality. Embroidered. Value $65-95.

140

MAID UNIFORMS

What the Maids were wearing in 1916. This costume was called the 'La Mode' and was considered the 'service dress de luxe'. Black cotton pongee with white trim. Scarce. Value of dress, apron and cap $300-400.

Another of the LaMode line. This is of white cotton pongee. 1916. Value $325-425. Ankle length.

Sampling of clothing label collection. More common types $1-2. Designer type $10-15.

Another man's suit of 1910, wool and tailor made to specific measurements. Value $295-350. At this time suits 'off the rack' were becoming more available to men.

The well-dressed man of 1910, replete with pipe and bulldog. His striped wool suit with cuffed pants and very large buttons has wide revers. Suit with vest $350-400.

College graduating class, 1905. Woman's dress, $800-1,000. Gentlemen wear the high bottoned frock coat, vests with high rounded collars and importantly placed buttons, one wears striped trousers, notice the differing ties. Complete suits, $500-750.

Dandy of 1912, striped trousers, long jacket, pearl button vest, small, rounded collar. Vest, $95-110. Jacket $110-145. Trousers $55-100.

Couple of 1905. She wears a wool dress with lace chemisette and trim. His 3 piece wool suit is formalized by the collar and tie. Value of dress $750-1,000, man's suit $250-350.

This gentleman of 1911 obviously opted for comfort with his soft collar. His wide tie features a lovely, rather large, square cameo tie pin. His wool coat is bound in satin and the fancy buttons are self-covered. Value of tie pin $300-400; value of coat $200-250.

Formal wear of the early 1900's. Black cashmere, satin trim on lapels, jacket and sleeves. Vest has matching trim. Black and gray striped trousers with original suspenders. Coat labeled: Von Longerde & Antoine, Chicago, Ill. Value $300-400. There is a great demand for mens' clothing of this type. Gray top hat and a watch fob which is a family piece.

143

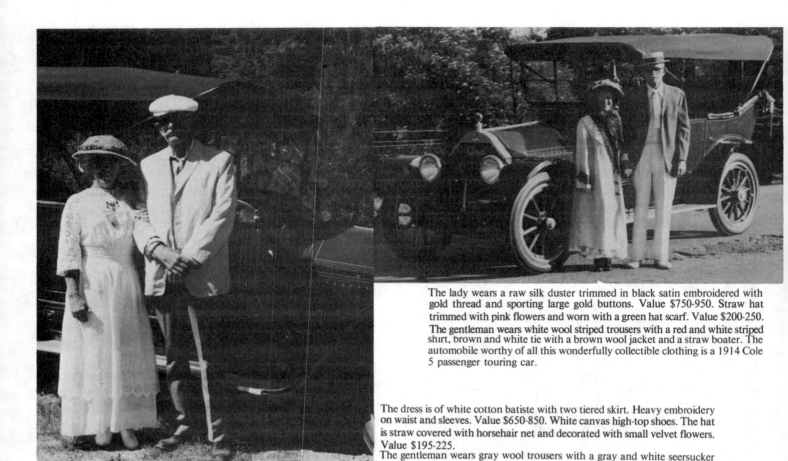

The lady wears a raw silk duster trimmed in black satin embroidered with gold thread and sporting large gold buttons. Value $750-950. Straw hat trimmed with pink flowers and worn with a green hat scarf. Value $200-250.

The gentleman wears white wool striped trousers with a red and white striped shirt, brown and white tie with a brown wool jacket and a straw boater. The automobile worthy of all this wonderfully collectible clothing is a 1914 Cole 5 passenger touring car.

The dress is of white cotton batiste with two tiered skirt. Heavy embroidery on waist and sleeves. Value $650-850. White canvas high-top shoes. The hat is straw covered with horsehair net and decorated with small velvet flowers. Value $195-225.

The gentleman wears gray wool trousers with a gray and white seersucker jacket, a white driving cap and black shoes.

Full dress suit of 1901. Watch fob prominent. High collar, vest. Fobs are now widely collected and valued according to material and stones. Full dress suit in excellent condition $500-600.

Business suit of 1901. Rounded effect, high collar, derby hat and prominent watch fob, all fashionable in the early 1900's. These suits are very difficult to find. Value $400-600. Derby hat $75-100.

'Outing suit' intended for a day at the shore or similar activity. Contrasting jacket and trousers. Almost impossible to find as a set. 'Boater' hat of straw $50-65.

Mens' shoes of the early 1900's. Black leather with felt top with buttons. Value $100-145; black leather oxford with tie laces $35-45; black leather with felt top and buttons, 'pull tab' showing. Value $100-145.

Man's cotton starched collar, white, c. 1900, $10-15; black neck scarf, knitted, one front snap closure at neck, value $20-25; white knitted man's scarf similar to the black, one front neck snap closure. These were worn under a coat to provide warmth in the popular touring cars. Value $20-25. Mens' socks, silk, 1930's $10-15; garters for silk socks which did not have elastic tops, 1930's $15-20; mens' ties, painted silk, 'tie yourself' $5-10. Crafts people are buying these for many other uses other than clothing collections. At top are mens' ties which were pre-shaped to fit $5-15.

The well dressed man of 1916-1917. Tie pin, stiff collar, cuff links and well brushed hair. The strong-jawed look promoted by Charles Dana Gibson. Value of these collars is $12-15, even more collectible is the delightful collar boxes which held them

145

CHAPTER III
1920-1940

No wonder we are dazzled by the 1920's. A time in the United States when triumphant post war fever swept the land, it was a time to release tension, a time to let go. Americans were having the last big fling, although they didn't know it. There was more freedom for women and the entire attitude was young. Women bobbed their hair, did the frenzied Charleston and listened to jazz. The evening clothes reflected the outlook, it was easy, it sparkled and it was a trifle bizarre.

The flapper leaped out of every page. Mention the word today and a vision of pencil thin, bobbed haired beauty, wearing her rather shapeless beaded dress and long colored beads comes instantly to mind. She also wore cloche hats, although later in the decade hats became large and lovely, and her waistline was only suggested by bands near the hip line. In truth many of the dresses of this period can be found in rather large sizes so not everyone was petite. The style was generally flattering to the figure, being basically straight line and loose.

The hair and the hats were prominent fashion features in the 20's. The cloche was it. Tightly moulded to the head, sometimes with a narrow brim, it was worn well down on the forehead. It was made of felt, silk, velvet, satin or crepe and it complemented the dresses beautifully. The individual touches on the hats were enchanting — "a brilliant pin placed on the right front side", or "a peaked cloche of capuchine crepe satin trimmed with long feathered bands which break into soft tufts at the apex".

"Millinery", said a prominent 1920's magazine, "is not just making hats, no indeed. Millinery in its creation is an art." It was, and is, true that the proper headpiece considers facial contours, skin and hair coloring, and the coiffure will frame the face in a flattering way. Also the proper hat can strike a master stroke for individuality. Coordinated properly with the dress or suit it is that last finishing touch.

Plain silk frocks decorated with colored silk flowers, or 3 sprays of silk roses with silver encrusted leaves and flexible stems on a rustling taffeta dress might match the spray of flowers on the hat. The flowers on the hats were made of silk or chiffon or sheer gauze. The lapel flower made an appearance at this time and has never entirely deserted the fashion scene since.

The cloche hat survived into the 1930's but it did not continue to dominate the 20's scene; by 1926 large brims were the rage. But time was running out on the hat industry. During the early 20's many thousands were employed in the hat industry in New York alone. What has happened to all those hats and elegant headgear of the 1920's? It seems to be one of the most difficult of periods from which to find good representative millinery but when such a piece is found it is usually a gem.

The beading on the evening dresses make these garments the goal of every 1920's vintage clothing collector, and often are sought by collectors of clothing of other periods. Not only is the workmanship superb, the beads glittering and worked into intricate designs, but the dresses are still eminently wearable if found in good condition.

Some are so heavily beaded that care must be taken in their display. Hangers are unsuitable and if a dress form is not available, the dress should be folded and stored carefully. Ready-made beaded panels could be bought separately and added to the basic slip-like dress.

Today, long after the heyday of these glamorous gowns, any collector of vintage fashion would be delighted to add one to a collection, and even non-collectors covet them. Today, everyone seems to love this fashion.

Displayed on a dress form the dresses seem to have a life of their own, they shimmer and change colors in different light and aside from their obvious beauty this may also be part of their appeal. The satins and chiffons move with every breeze. Sequins were also used generously in the late 20's as the curved and pointed irregular hemlines began to inch downward. Waist lines were still low on the hips, long dangling earrings were clearly visible with the short hair, and in evening wear the keynote was a kind of casual elegance.

In fact fashion arbiters were advising 'the studied, careless look'. "Avoid a dressy look, even in formal clothes," they said, and had some words of wisdom for the young college miss. "The college girl should wear felt hats, dented here and there nonchalantly, soft, pull-on gloves sufficiently large to crush generously, plain sandals or pumps, and all of this will create the well groomed but studied careless air that in this year of 1924 is really chic." Today's college girl would swoon at the thought, but when you find a 20's look hat that is dented here and there, it is more likely by design than accident.

Suits with matching frocks and a ¾ matching coat were fine for street wear or a ¾ length blouse of material to match the coat and worn with a tight skirt, was considered more than acceptable and the slightly mannish look of the earlier 20's was passing. The ensemble idea was stressed and capes were being worn again. Masculine type lounging robes were being worn by women and wide leather belts worn low on the hips were the big accessories.

The beaded bags which these lovelies carried already have so many devotees, it is probably sufficient to remark on their workmanship and beauty. It is rather late to begin such a collection because prices have risen steeply and continue upward. Already there exist many large collections of these, but if beaded bags are your fancy they are a beautiful investment.

The young people who danced all night in their fancy satin shoes were lively to the point of exhaustion. Our essential national innocence had been dissipated by the 'war to end all wars' and in the 20's the accent was on youth, 'flaming youth'. The flapper became a by-word.

John Held Jr. created her and named her 'flapper', so the story goes, because she often wore galoshes with the buckles undone and they flapped as she walked. Whatever the exact origin of the word, its two small syllables sum up an entire era.

Until recently the rental companies dealing in vintage clothing had few flapper types to loan. Not too long ago a college student friend sought in vain for a beaded dress, proper shoes and a feathered headband to wear to a school dance. Finally she borrowed the dress seen on page 151 (center) from a private collector. It was such a success and elicited so many inquires the collector now rents her clothing to selected customers. Business is brisk. She feels that she is educating the public, many of whom have never seen such clothing, especially the young people. Anyone with a good vintage clothing collection should definitely share it in some way with others, club meetings, junior groups of young people, convalescent homes, even schools. That is the ultimate joy of collecting; the sharing.

The girlish look of the early 1920's, reinforced by the soft materials used in the dresses, contrasted sharply with some of the movie stars of the day, personified by Pola Negri and her 'vamp' image. Other Hollywood stars held out against bobbing their hair, but the late Gloria Swanson was an early convert. This indecision about image was reflected in hem lengths which varied from knee length to calf length to almost ankle length.

Coco Chanel came along with her classic look that still retains a measure of popularity, and it is felt that in her the 20's spawned one of the great dress designers.

The short dresses of the early 20's led to more interest in the shoe. The Louis heeled, long pointed vamp, and T-strap pumps were entirely visible beneath the uneven hemlines of points or fringe.

For collectors shoes can show some wear if it does not affect the material of the uppers. Perfection is always the goal, but in the search for shoes this becomes very difficult. Proof of the fact that even some party clothes were worn often by the average person is the wear often found on the shoes of the 1920's. The shoes are intriguing though, and anyone collecting in the period needs at least one or two pairs to delineate the dress.

The shoe buckles are even more fun. Four years ago cut steel buckles could be bought for $4 or $5, and two years ago I paid $8 to $12 a pair. Recently prices have moved into the $30-$40 range. Although I have seen collections of buckles which are singles, it is wiser to search out the pairs. The values will hold and of course, it's necessary if they are to be worn unless you are a real trend setter and are willing to wear a different buckle on each shoe.

Although the cut steel are usually fine quality the rhinestone sets can be spectacular, but are somewhat more difficult to find. Often the backings are made of velvet, or satin, or patent leather, although some were made without any backing at all.

Shoe buckles can be traced to the Celts (600 B.C.) and since those ancient days their popularity has waxed and waned but never completely disappeared. There is tremendous variety in shoe buckles and their charm is a decided asset to a clothing collection. Recently at auction a pair of cut steel buckles in their original box sold for $75. We collectors are certainly on the right track.

And just what is happening in the auction market? Some larger auction houses are holding sales geared only to vintage clothing and interest is always high.

Furs seems to hold a special appeal for collectors who buy them not only to display but to wear. Recently a full length ocelet coat with a narrow mink trim sold for $4,000 at auction. This is a tremendous rise over a similar coat on which I had bid about 4 years ago.

Furs must be previewed very carefully since the small splits which develop as the fur dries out cannot always be noticed in a casual perusal.

The reason for this clamor for vintage furs is three-fold: 1. Their usefulness, 2. their scarcity, not only as vintage clothing but because many animals which were used to make those furs are now on endangered species lists and so the fur piece can never be duplicated. 3. luxury, the feeling that wearing an elegant fur coat imparts cannot be explained fully, but if you've never worn a vintage fur, try it, you'll like it. Another consideration is that the older fur coats are unusual bargains, often times many hundreds of dollars less expensive than they were originally.

The velvet shown on page 144 is a perfect example. Where today could a coat of such quality and beauty be bought for the price quoted, where today could one buy a coat with such style and flair? Made in the 1920s it is flattering to the figure, the color is exquisite and anyone lucky enough to own it could hardly avoid a feeling of glamour. Isadora Duncan may or may not have worn it, but it certainly brings her to life.

The vintage clothing collector of the 1920's period should follow the general advice of dating within a decade unless historical research demands pinpointing. However, quite specific changes makes some years easily definable.

1920 women wore deeply crowned hats, the skirt was at ankle length or a bit shorter, the beltline was at the hip, long sleeves were tight and wrist length. The exposed leg cried out for slinky silk stockings and the beaded necklace became almost a badge.

In 1923-24 the cloche hat vied with the large organza or 'garden party' type, dresses were mid-calf length and rising, shoes had the Louis heels which were used thoughout the 20's and the shoes themselves could be made of satin, kid or leather. The hip belt was still in fashion.

1925-1926. The big news was the hemline, now knee length. Women wore bust flatteners and girdles and fancy underwear. Petticoats or slips in beautifully detailed silk with narrow shoulder straps and lace and embroidered trim. These were worn short, well above the knee. It is mostly these slips and petticoats and the silk lounging pajamas which entice collectors today. The materials are fine, the workmanship exquisite and some are so elegant that they can be used today. At a recent party in New York a guest was wearing heavy silk lavender lounging pajamas under a silver fox jacket. The costume created a minor sensation. The undergarments should be a highly specialized collecting area. There are enough of them available to build a good collection without too much effort and they require less care than the gowns.

A minor revolution occured in the 1927-1929 period. The V-neckline was introduced and created controversy. The T strap shoe and cloche hat were still worn and generally there was a crossover of all styles.

By the 1920's it should be remembered that the made-to-order clothing catalogues were advertising ready to wear outfits for one and all. Now people could look beyond their Sunday best or 'company' outfit and indulge themselves with full wardrobes without too much expense and bother. This applied to the clothing of men and children as well as women. A large variety of styles and types were offered and the choices offered are reflected in the many 1920's garments we can now choose from.

Although all periods are reflected by the way people dress, the clothing of the 1920's is perhaps one of the most precise indicators of its time. It was an exciting decade, it had an air of forbidden fruit about it, it was a time of great changes and as the decade moved to its frantic close, economic barometers were predicting disaster.

If you are already a collector, or thinking of collecting clothes from the 20's try for a reputable dealer who handles only the best quality. Such a person will assure that your dress' beadwork is intact, the clothing clean, the hats have their original trim, appropriate shoes, and the furs soft and wearable; all the things that are important to the definitive collector who wishes to build a valuable, in depth collection.

Everybody today thinks back on the 1920's as a riotous time. For some, it surely was, but the millions who wore the ordinary clothing of the day are being neglected, their dresses and suits are interesting too. But everybody wants those beads.

Men of the 1920's were still in a conservative mood. The wide trousers were a change, sometimes they were as much as 22 to 24 inches at the bottom. Knickers or plus fours were big with sportsmen and were buckled four inches below the knee, hence the name 'plus fours'.

Lighter colors were favored in summer but cold weather called for another of those items which makes an age memorable — the raccoon coat. All the college boys had them and some of the co-eds too. I inherited a raccoon coat in perfect condition and wore it in the 1950's. Recently I saw a young man in San Francisco sporting just such a coat. It was like a one man fashion show. The raccoon coat, a great coat in every sense of the word, useful, stylish even now, and large, larger even than life.

That was the 1920's. . . .

If the 1920's prove one half of the adage that hemlines go up when the stock market goes up, the 1930's surely prove the other half, the hemlines go down when the stock market drops. By 1930 skirts were longer, and the waistline was again in its normal place, nothing else seemed normal though.

When historians refer to the 30's, we read about "the great depression", the songwriters were asking, "Brother can you Spare a Dime", but fashion dictators were advising longer hair, wider shoulders, narrow hips and in evening new emphasis on the back.

Many Americans can recall the time with great clarity. As children, the depression shaped their futures in all ways, and encouraged a sense of caution. Many, left with a sense of thrift born in those difficult days, never discarded the clothing of that period and so collectors today have an opportunity not always possible when dealing with other times; except for Art Deco fans, not too many collectors have taken advantage of the opportunity.

For years clothing of the period was neglected. People who had lived through the bleak years did not want to be reminded and the young had not yet begun to consider the rather shapeless day wear attractive. But as we continue to be more removed in time from the 30's we can focus on what was good rather than bad and can decide what a good collection should include.

The best of the clothing and the evening wear is only now attracting buyers in numbers. At no time, for example, has there been a more simple but classic design than the plain black velvet evening dress of the 30's. It is so characteristic that collectors simply refer to it as "the thirties black velvet". It is stark and beautiful, can be worn unadorned or with ornamentation equally well. That, in fact, may be a summation of the 30's fashion scene.

America's dress image became blurred — factories were manufacturing clothing by the ton — and anybody who could afford it could wear any clothes that appealed. This was the early period of homogenization and where once clothing defined social status and the role in life, now the rich continued to patronize the great design houses, the college students wanted to look like workers and began to adopt the Levis, and clothing no longer labeled the wearer.

Clothing was made for every conceivable use and wardrobes began expanding. There was a very wide range of fashions. Sportwear was a big item at this time, tennis was fashionable, but skating was geared more toward the average person and the costumes are pretty and available. In most of the feminine apparel at this time, in sportswear as well, the waistline was natural and bosoms were accentuated.

The 1930's brought dramatic changes to the fashion picture. The zipper came into wide use and it takes little imagination to realize what its convenience meant, and in 1939 — nylon. The zipper replaced all those buttons or other closures and nylon revolutionized the clothing industry.

Other surprising things came out of the thirties, Hollywood coined some memorable words — 'glamour' was one. It's hard to imagine how we ever lived without the word and harder still to realize it was part of the depression years.

Another faint shock can be felt when reading the women's magazines of 1930. They were devoting many pages to fashion. Perhaps as an antidote to the times. Ski clothes, if you can visualize that, were being touted, "winter sports are becoming more important each year and comfort is the first requisite. Smart women," they said, "are forsaking modernistic designs in favor of somber colors, such as black, navy or brown, the long trouser suits in serge or gabardine or waterproof whipcord with brightly colored accessories, and a heavy woolen shirt should be tucked into the trousers that fit tightly over the hips." It was a somewhat classic look, and while certainly not in tune with the ski clothes of today, could be worn without seeming out of place.

Another publication was promoting "Fashions for the South". These were beach attire which was becoming quite racy, backless, large armholes, no overskirts, with a deep decolletage. Also the one piece tennis dresses, casual lightweight jackets and the long, straight evening wear.

The clothing collector is perfectly justified in seeking out these garments which were worn, for the most part, by people of means, who bought the best and took care of it. The average person wore garments until necessity decreed a replacement and while these are often very easily found, it is a problem to get them in mint condition.

The House of Worth was showing "restaurant" or informal evening wear with low decolletage and low back edged with a band of green and white beads. The materials could be very rich, Worth used brocades and chiffons and velvets. While not everyone can own a Worth, the evening wear of the thirties is what many collectors are seeking. I have recently seen several gowns in excellent condition and prices on clothes of the type have only begun a rather steep rise.

Practical, though, was the word for most day wear. Belts were popular around the normal waistline, skirts flared from the knee down touches of white at the neck were considered a nice touch. Often you will see these little collars thrown in boxes of unknowing antique shop dealers and you should be alert to what they are.

Wool crepe, which wore well, was used for daytime clothes and velvet predominated at night. The jabot, which was a cascade of frills down the front of the dress or shirt, was high style.

Although collectors have somewhat neglected the 1930's, it was actually a time when fashion had much to commend it. The clothes were fairly simple and practical; bows at the chin, or on one shoulder, or attached low on one hip were a flattering device; the quality was excellent, both as to fabric and finish and they were comfortable. The beret, the cloche, and the 'large, garden-party' hats vied with soft felt, flat staw and the turban.

In our mind's eye, we consider the fashions of the 1930's somewhat dowdy. To those who remember the housedress, a plain, utilitarian garment if ever there was one, but oh, so comfortable and useful, or the everyday dresses of the less affluent, this is understandable, but the better clothing, well made and well designed, hung gracefully on the figure hats or turbans and overlaid with fascinating furs, it could be alluring. It was a style particularly suited to the person with an ingrained sense of elegance and yes, flair. It was essentially a streamlined fashion and much of it is mistaken for clothing of the 20's.

The cloche hats are almost impossible to tell apart, the strap shoes were worn into the thirties, the dresses themselves are often labeled incorrectly and this is where knowledge of waistlines and necklines can be important. This is why, too, anyone who is collecting should try to get any possible information from the dealer and why anyone who is scouring trunks and attics should get the family history.

It is indeed difficult for almost anyone to differentiate clothing made during transitional periods. The styles of the 1928-29 period were already showing the flared skirt, but were shorter, waistlines had risen by 1928-29 but were still lower than those found on the 30's clothes. It becomes increasingly important to the collector to know exactly what the collecting goal is. A lovely, general collection of old clothes, a certain kind of clothing, regardless of period, or, as is always advisable, the clothing of a given time segment. Buy what appeals and is affordable and fit your collection within an overall category of years. Buy what is typical of the period and do not worry overmuch whether the garment or hat was made in 1929 or 1931.

Mail order which really caught on in the 1920's was big business in the 30's and ready-made clothes prospered along with the catalogues. The first fashion illustration ever to appear in such a catalogue was published by Montgomery Ward in 1878. These old catalogues, many in reprint, are wonderful source materials for the collector. When I peruse these, I feel transported back in time and get the urge to pick up the phone and order what I see displayed.

Some of the favorite features of 1930's clothing are still popular, the jabot, the scarf collar which could be tied anyway you pleased, and the lovely deep fur trimmed coats which had the collar set back from the face and yet framed it.

These coats in good condition are bargains at any reasonable price. Well made and beautifully furred and usually wool, they oftentimes cost less than a gown or suit and are lovely to look at, or wear.

If there was one typical daytime style of the 30's it was the print dress. As yet, there are not too many of these available but they should be searched out. Women really loved these bright, cheerful prints, either in small closely spaced figures or medium sized, widely spaced. They often had cape effects or jackets, and for hot weather they were adapted to lighter materials and made sleeveless. This passion for print was one of the characteristics of this time.

Shoes were pumps with bows, or the plain walking pump, or the leather oxford, or the one strap. Kid was the most chosen material, but calf and patent leather were also in favor. Pumps were the favorites, but the reptile skinned shoes made an impact which carried over to later years. The toe could be elongated or pointed and a very attractive type for collectors were the evening shoes with buckle trim, the buckle was part of the shoe itself.

The notable shoe from the 30's was worn for sports activities. It was an oxford with the fringed, outside tongue. This covered the laces and is another of those immediately recognizable styles that can be dated at a glance. Interestingly enough, men's clothing is so scarce that in searching for a collection of men's clothing on any large scale, particularly a comprehensive shoe collection, I sought but did not find.

It was in the 30's that the idea of promoting sales of men's clothing could be based on snob appeal was advanced. Clothing designers and manufacturers have always known that if enough changes are made in garments to render them out of fashion in a short time, more sales will be made as women would rush out to refurbish but this concept had not been widely applied to men's clothes. It was also the time that men began to discard undershirts, supposedly because movie star Clark Gable took off his shirt and only bare chest was visible. Warm shirts in large plaids, and early in the decade the single breasted jacket was the male look. Later, jackets became double breasted and the front of the jacket was higher.

One of the radical changes in women's wear in America during the 30's was the latex girdle. It was flexible and moved with the body and became enormously popular. It was a far cry from the whalebone corset. It was lightweight and could be easily laundered. Even in those days there were obviously some fashion rebels for recently I happened upons several of these girdles unworn, but unfortunately not boxed. "Never were boxed," said the owner, they were bought off store counters and I never wore a girdle at all." These are interesting and if in pristine condition when found, should not yet cost much.

Another drastic change was the neckline. The halter neckline was introduced and caught on. This neckline has survived and prospered, and as with many earlier styles is now being revived by designers and shown on new clothing.

In the late 30's and early 40's traditional modesty was challenged with the introduction of the bare midriff. As with all clever clothing, it was simply an indication of things to come. Fashion always seems to anticipate events.

As net and lacy trifles began to replace hats, the industry quaked. The automobile contributed to the trend, a closed car required no head cover. The hat began to fade as a prime requisite of dress and the industry was further crushed when the Catholic Church announced that feminine head no longer needed to be covered in church. The hat has all but disappeared except for utiliitarian purposes, making the hats of the thirties fine collectibles. Almost the last hurrah of a fashion survivor.

The jewelry of the thirties should be considered just that and has already found a huge market. However, there are certain pieces, such as the dress clips, the belt buckles and the shoe clips of the late 30's which should be added to a clothing collection. The pairs of clips which attached to a dress neckline are particularly desirable. Often this type jewelry is chunky art deco rather than the rare platinum and diamond pieces from the same era. The everyday decorations that women wore have an appeal that is not easily defined, but appeal it does.

Schiaparelli was a product of the thirties and her chief contribution was color – shocking pink became a rage. She had a sense of fun and many of the things she designed seemed outrageous, but she influenced fashion and a Schiaparelli label is something to boast of in a collection. There is a whole new collecting area, not the clothing collector, but the collector of labels in the clothing.

It makes for a surprisingly beautiful collection, the labels are varying sizes and while the new ones are mostly machine woven the older ones are so lovely that the backs resemble needlepoint. The woven ones are much harder to find than they were a year or two ago, the owner of a large collection tells me and "most of them on cheaper clothing are stamped now." If this kind of collection catches on, and already I know of several fine collections, what will happen to the designer-identified gown?

Long beads were still worn at the end of the decade, but chokers lived happily with the V-neckline. The beret was a fitting companion to the slim fitting jackets of the suits, but it was but one of many of the diverse hat styles. America itself was diverse and diversifying, but soon had its course decided for it.

The 1930's were years of depression, then of hope, and finally of war. A stirring ten years, but regardless of other happenings the thirties proves that the influence of fashion goes on.

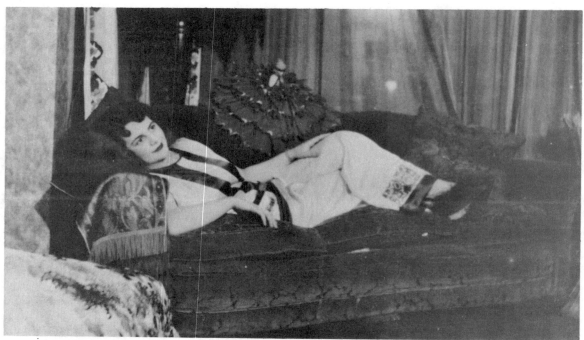

A real flapper of the 1920's in silk lounging pajamas then all the rage. Typical satin trim. Value $450-650.

1925 Black satin flapper dress with pink roses embroidered on the lowered waistline. Value $800-900, black felt cloche hat with rhinestone pin. Value $145-195. All contemporary flapper types are busily seeking the cloche. Automobile is a jazzy Reo Flying Cloud.

Knitwear was popular during the early 1920's. This dress is especially interesting because of its bead trim. The top (or blouse) has 100 or more beads which were strung on a ball of yarn and knit into place. The skirt was knitted first and then filled with a tiny wooden mold or other button which would fit. An unusual piece of knitwear. Value $600-900.

RIGHT:
The well-dressed tennis player of 1921. Long sweater over blouse and skirt. Since this clothing is difficult to pinpoint as to original use the collector should be guided by existing photographs and documented family history. Value of sweater and skirt which are pictured in shades of old rose $200-225.

Tricotine suit, braid trim, chinchilla standing collar. Value $1800-2500. Lustrous charmeuse in tunic effect. Attached sash acts as belt, V neck with wide flat collar in back. Scalloped edges. Value $750-950.

A richly beaded embroidered silk satin and silk georgette dress. Navy blue and right up to the minute in 1921. These materials as well as the era make dresses of this type much sought after. Value $600-700.

1924. All dresses of this year fall into the $500-650 range, unless beaded or unusually designed and decorated.

153

Left to right:

The straight lines of 1921. A one piece slip-on with an adjustable collar, draped at the underarm and has a tie back sash stitched onto the seams. Silk value $400-500.

This has a separate waist with long sleeves, camisole closing at left side front and is joined to a one-piece straight gathered skirt with side tunics. Value $250-350.

Intended for the younger woman, this dress has a separate draped waist closing at the shoulder. The 'Bramley' collar gives it a youthful look. This is jersey cloth with linen collar and cuffs. Value $300-400.

This dress has a kimono-sleeve waist and a 2-piece gathered skirt. Velvet with deep collar of lace. Value $600-700.

Serge. This dress has an embroidered motif on the skirt with collar facings in the same tones, and is a young miss' dress. Value $275-350.

One piece dress with front inset. Scalloped edges of the panel which also boasts braiding. Value of dress in silk is $400-600; Notice the differences in the shoe styles, all being worn in 1921.

If found in good condition, these dresses are all wearable today.

154

Typical fashions of 1921. Dress for afternoon entertaining, suit with long tunic jacket, wool coat with beaver trim. Dress value $185-225; suit $400-450; coat $800-1,000. Notice shoes.

Left to right: A selection of dresses typical of 1924. All are of linen suiting. Bands of embroidery trim the oval neck, sleeve and front of bodice and skirt. An exotic flower on left side gives the simple dress distinction. Value $400-500.

Lavender with French knot stitching, square neckline and kimono sleeves. Value $450-550. Rose, green and black embroidery on green runs from neck to hem on left side of dress. Value $450-500.

Greek key border on pongee material gives this dress a coat effect. Value $500-850.

Left: In 1922 Paris decreed a new silhouette. All garments had to be draped, coats, dresses and the new coat dress. Skirts were longer and in most cases fell straight from neck to hem. This coat is softly draped at the low waist with an ornament. Another innovation of that year is shown in this coat with its interlaced stuffed tubing rather than fur to collar and cuff these exclusive garments. Velvet. Value $2,000-2,800.
Center: This dress is of silk and georgette, draped and with lace at the neck and hem. Value $1,200-2,000
Right: Braided fabric girdles were considered 'interesting' in 1922 and so were the handmade motifs. The braid is evident in the belt and the soft draping makes this dress of softest wool very feminine. Value $1,000-1,800.

Linen suiting, the trim gives this dress a bolero jacket effect. Pockets and side pleats. Value $600-900.

Linen suiting, French knots in blue form the flowers with yellow centers, square neckline side belting, kimono sleeves. Rose linen. Value $600-900.

The Nancy Lopez of 1923 wears a sleeveless sport coat and skirt of cream homespun bordered with rows of yellow, orange and brown lustre wool. Model wears a deep crown wide brim straw hat and comfortable shoes. Value of coat and skirt $500-600.

A 1923 afternoon dress of black and blue chiffon adhering to the straight silhouette. The skirt is pleated at the side with a straight front panel. The intricate sash adds interest to the dress. A very good example of the accessories of the early 1920's. Value of dress $1,200-2,100.

A 1923 semi formal frock of faille with georgette. Pleated skirt and overblouse effect. Beautifully simple. Value $1,000-1,500.

157

A silk dress and matching coat. This set is reputed to have belonged to one of those proverbial early 1930s "movie stars". It is silk embroidery on beige silk, coat is corded, lined and is collarless.

The designers of the 30s were clever with their bold overall prints, their endless little capelets, their unusual, eye catching belts, the jabot, the scarves, the very bright accessories to distract the eye, the skirts which gave movement to the costume - it is all underrated. This is typical sheer print voile for afternoons, the capelet collar falls in a soft flare over the sleeveless arms which gives a youthful air. The scalloped treatment in a circular flaring skirt which is stitched to a snugly fitted hip yoke becomes more evident because of the slight blousing of the bodice. Tomato Red. A very subtle bit of designing for this relatively inexpensive dress. 1930. Value $200-350.

This jacket dress is of 'milk chocolate' chiffon with two belts for a slenderizing look and to create a peplum effect by holding in surplus material through the hips. The scallops add detail. This was considered an 'afternoon' or 'country club' outfit. Under the jacket, the dress is sleeveless wispy chiffon. The bodice is eggshell color, the skirt is circular. The cloche and handbag are orange. 1930. Dress $200-350. 1930s clothing is still underpriced.

Apron styles come and go but aprons have been around forever. Anyone who lived through the lean 1930s can probably visualize Mother wearing an apron similar to this. It was part of the everyday uniform and a constant in an uncertain world. These were colorful, veritable flower gardens, sturdy cotton, and exuded a certain cheer. They are great collectibles, still under priced and available because so many were brought and worn. Aprons were considered a welcome and appreciated gift. The most interesting feature of this apron is the circular skirt and the two little pockets formed by a pointed cut front. This apron was a one size fits all. If you are beginning a vintage clothing collection with a limited budget go for aprons. Value of this type $20-35, but often aprons can still be found for much less.

There is a serious movement today to phase out the emaciated models used by most advertisers to sell their wares. No one could ever achieve that pencil silhouette in a normal way is the complaint. But in 1926 the models were equally slim and the straight lines of the fashions accentuated the look. These seven evening dresses all have a definite waist line, and the tiers, godets and girdles are all arranged to accentuate that waist line. Trimmings such as flowers, fur and embroidery are all placed to bring out the position of the waist line. Some of these feature bouffant skirts but all are slim-line. These are dainty and intended for dinner and dancing. The beadwork and other accessories give a fascinating insight into the fashions of the 20s. Value of any dress of this era, of this beauty and quality would have a starting figure of $800.

1930s red satin formal dress. Loose lace collar fits under flat satin collar. Lace insertions in the shirt and sleeves. Lace insertions in the bias cut skirt. Large rhinestone pin at the typical 30s V-neck. Value $850-1,200.

A fabulous find. An Art Deco beaded dress of the 1920s or early 1930s, the hat is by Leslie Allen. The dress is bugle beaded on net over a taffeta slip. The evening cape is black silk.
Dress $1,500-2,500,
Cape $750-1,200.

Collectors often confuse fashions of the 1920s and 30s and indeed it is a legitimate confusion - because many of the fashions were worn years after they were decreed old hat by Paris, but old hat or not the headgear of the thirties, large or small was often spectacular and is often mistakenly considered to have originated in the 1920s. No matter, just keep buying hats in good condition when you find them. The three hats pictured here are totally characteristic of the period and it is uncanny how beautifully they coordinate with the dresses.

The dress on the left is exquisitely designed with the sleek, slender lines of the best of the 1930s. Black velvet with a white collar ending in a frilled jabot and a matching hat. The hat value is $150-200, the dress $450-650.

In the center the model wears an orange print crepe with the dipping back hem of the circular skirt which accentuates the slim line and gives exactly the right length the times called for. The milan straw hat is trimmed with orange ribbon. Hat $150-250; dress $450-650. 1930.

Right: A printed silk crepe in tan, orange and black with tapering 'plaited panels'. A large brimmed light felt orange hat with black trim. Hat $150-250; dress $450-650. 1930.

160

LEFT:
Custom made dress, 1930s. Large size French cut velvet in brown, red, and orange. Transparent mesh inserts. Hemline dips to a point in front and has a nicely finished edge. Value $400-500.

RIGHT:
The label in this lovely early 1930s beaded dress reads MADE IN FRANCE, RUE DE LA PAIX GOWN, PARIS. Black velvet with beautifully placed beads in colors of pink and black in the form of flowers, each flower centered with a rhinestone. A striking dress. Value $1,500-2,000.

Bottle green velvet with gold stencilling at the neck, sleeves and hemline. Small embroidered eyelets (six) at neckline. Includes two belts. Labeled MARIANO FORTUNY - VENICE. Sold in 1988 at auction at Butterfield and Butterfield, San Francisco, for $2,750. The estimate was $1,500-2,000. Value $4,500-6,000.

Right in photo: Blue and gold floral gorgette dress. Shown with a blue silk cloche. 1930s, in 1989 estimated auction price $20-30, sale price $120. Value $300-400.

Center: Lavender crepe underdress with an all-over floating panel of thin lavender silk. Worn with an evening wrap of creme velvet with black and white fur collar. Dress value $400-500. Wrap $400-450.

Left: Cafe-au-lait silk with blond lace summer day dress. 1930s. Value $200-250.

A MARIANO FORTUNY creation. Pale peach silk dress with a short tunic, hanging points at each side, edged with hand blown Venetian glass beads. Batwig sleeves with like beads. Dress and belt signed FORTUNY DSE. This gown sold at auction in 1988 for $1100. Its value now is $4500-7500.

MARIANO FORTUNY gown of sienna velveteen stenciled with gold in Renaissance fashion. enlarged TREE OF LIFE pattern. Under sleeves and side of dress gores of brown pleated silk, tied with silk cord and buttoned with hand blown Venetian glass beads. Fully lined with silk, slight train. Original label MARIANO FORTUNY VENISE. Auctioned in 1988, sale price $4,750. Value today, $8,000-12,000.

Right a Royal blue velvet coat dress with ivory satin bodice, cording trim. Feather hat. This was part of a small lot which sold for $121 in 1989 at a Butterfield and Butterfield Auction. Center - striped in shades of brown, a 2 piece suit from the 1940s. Value $55-75. Left, a side buttoned wool coat worn with a fur scarf. 1930s. Coat $125-175.

162

1927 tea frock. V-neck and cape sleeves. Skirt falls far below the knee. Made from contemporary pattern. Value of original $350-450. Courtesy of Folkwear, San Rafael, California.

Top: A slip-on dress of 1924 in Chinese design trim. Silk. Wide belt with buckle. Value $700-1,000. Cloche hat, long gloves, fur piece. Bottom: Afternoon dress of silk and chiffon. The cape-like collar extends down the back. Draped on side with bow. Value $800-$1,200. Cloche hat, long gloves, ever-popular pearls.

Flat crepe jumper dress is tailored for street wear and was considered 'serviceable,' a big plus in those years. Value $200-300.

Day dresses of 1926. Printed silk, button trim delineates lowered waistline on left, right dress is belted. Left $275-350. Right $275-350.

A shaded rose crepe evening gown is very simply molded at the front and is gathered into a mass of graceful folds which adorn the back from shoulder to hem. The fold is gathered into a pretty round buckle. Since the trailing fashions of this period were the real focus of the designs the models were often photographed from the back. These dresses are spectacular, and still the ultimate in glamour. 1930. Value $2,000-3,000.

Marion Davies wore this coat in 'Cain and Mabel'. It is ink blue with splendid lines. Hammered silver clips are used instead of buttons. An adaptation of a Russian Cossack overcoat. Value $2,500-4,200.

Typical formal day wear of the 1930s. She wears her cloche, her gloves, has her jabot in place, her fur neckpiece on her arm and generally looks rather stylish. 1930s clothing is still under appreciated.

Depression or no, the evening clothes of the mid-1930s reflect a little understood fact of American life - some people had money and bought lovely gowns and went out to enjoy themselves.
These gowns are often spectacular, copies of or adapted from the flamboyant movies stars costumes of the era.
The V neck and low back were two characteristics which make these gowns so truly marvelous. The top gown has winged shoulders and is made of crisp white pique with red design. The other gown is of satin with the low back and low bow which draws the eye. The winged shoulders here soften the sexy look.

Left to right: The clean, lean look of the year 1930. The dresses were essentially flattering to the figure. This has the rippling collar then coming into fashion. The pleating builds up the top of the silhouette and makes the hips slimmer by comparison. The gores in the skirt stress the slenderness and height. Sheer sleeves. Value of 30's clothing is increasing rapidly as collectors realize its clever tailoring and easy wearing qualities. Dress $300-450. The coat of this sheer frock and coat ensemble hangs in loose, easy lines because the dress has a cape collar trimmed with pleating and because the skirt has gores which contrive the new slight flare. Value $400-500. The Paris influence of 1930 is evident in this wool belted tunic. Under the coat the dress has enormous gathered sleeves. Slender shawl collar and again the restrained flare. Value $500-600. This ensemble with its contrasting colors and materials was known as "print and plain". The chic so evident in much 30's clothing is very apparent here. The confetti printed silk is used generously to liven the free-swinging wool coat and the wool is repeated in the sash to accent the frock. Value $600-700. The hat styles are typical of the period as are the pumps.

Young lady's prom dress of 1939. Pink taffeta with velvet trim, sweetheart neckline, puff sleeves. Value $165-195.

C. 1930 checked cotton in white, green, blue, with bottom of skirt cut on the bias and capelet sleeves, often a distinguishing feature of 30's clothing. Buttons in front, belted. Value $250-300; white crocheted gloves. navy blue straw cloche. The great cloche hunt is on, it is probably the most desired hat style which collectors are seeking.

1930's chiffon print dinner dress, purple, cerise print. Black lace bodice over a taffeta slip, removable bolero jacket which ends in lace and becomes the belt. Snap closure at the side, bias-cut skirt, it does not have a train but is made long to hang evenly on the floor. Value $500-750.

The remarkable low back dress of September, 1930 is a genuine classic. This is satin. Value $1,500-2,200.

These are 'Hoover dresses' of 1931. Linen and gingham, sleeveless, easy to slip on tying behind with long belt in a bow knot. They could also be worn over more formal wear if necessary to dash into the kitchen. They were usually one size, considered a 'house dress' or overall apron. These inexpensive items reflect the same styling as some more expensive dresses, the slight flare, the attention to detailing, and the flattering neckline. Value $65-95.

Pure silk pongee dress with dainty pipings on the cuffs, vestee and hipline. Crepe collar, full circular skirt, self material belt. One of the great attributes of silk pongee was its ability to launder well. The neat look of the thirties is evident here. Value $350-450.

Dresses of the 1930's were made in very fine materials. The dress on the left is of pure linen with a peplum at the waist, the cuffs of the short sleeves are piped in contrasting color. The skirt has large box pleats and 2 inverted pleats in the front. Loose belt with a composition buckle. The dress on the right was a very popular model. Patterned crepe with georgette collars and cuffs edged with lace. The skirt has box pleats both front and back and is piped with colors to match. The jumper skirt is made of all wool French spun non-sag jersey with a novelty box pleat in front. Loose belt with a metal buckle. Dresses of this quality and style are in the $300-400 range.

One of the charms of the clothing of the 1920's is its sculptured quality and purity of line which is very apparent in these dresses. The whole look was simple yet sexy. The lowered waistline, the side draping with large bows, the pleating, all lend an air of decoration without interfering with the basic line. Dresses of this type of the 1920 period are moving into the $850-1,200 price range depending on materials and trim. They are eminently wearable and are eagerly sought after. As beaded dresses of the period are disappearing into collections the more available fancy day dresses and less spectacular evening wear is moving up in price. 1928.

Left to right: 'Prints' were the rage in the 1930's. Left is 'print cloth' with organdy trim. Black bow tie, shirred waistline. Self belt ties in back. Value $150-195. Printed pongee with criss-cross collar, flare cuffs, belt has metal buckle, circular skirt with inverted pleats. Value $150-195. Printed broadcloth with Russian tunic effect, a wildly popular style, cuffs, collar, piping of white broadcloth. Grosgrain tie, trimmed with pearl buttons. Skirt pleated front and back, value $150-225. Two piece dress of linen. Silk streamer tie. Skirt has contrasting color piping around the hips and two inverted pleats. Pearl buttons. Value $165-245. Crepe dress has short puff sleeves for a youthful look. Embroidered and hemstitched organdy collar and plain rayon bow tie. Flared skirt with flounce at bottom. Value $150-195. These dresses run the gamut of materials and trims and are indicative of the often unusual combinations during these years.

A stunning creation of rayon canton crepe. This is the 'long' length and has lace in the sleeves which are puffed by elastics and shirred at the top. Neckline is softened by tucks in front melting into folds and heightened by a self flower. Skirt is seamed and flared in back with waist seamings at the front only. Incredible tailoring considering the price of the garments originally. Value $1,200-1,800.

All silk crepe-back satin, fine lace over an eggshell lining forming a rather ingenious drop-shouldered, star pointed yoke. Shirred sleeves held puffed by the lining. Covered buttons, rhinestone pins, belt has slide. Provocative. Value $1,500-2,000.

The capelet was another distinguishing feature of the 30's clothes. This dress is of silk crepe satin, which shimmered in the light. White undercapelets and flower trim set off the sleek simplicity of the gown. Another dramatic dress dress essentially languourous in feeling. Value $1,500-2,000.

All wool 'swagger suit' tweed, with an unlined jacket. Cartridge-tucked sleeves, drop shoulders, the usual Ascot throw with pin. Value $550-850.

Although these dresses of the 1933-34 period are made in a fitted style they are often found in large sizes, as is the case with this 2 piece ensemble of wool crepe. Shoulders were emphasized in this two tone dress with jacket with stitched epaulets. Attached 'throws' tie in ascot fashion. Dress is belted with the usual prominent buckle and has button trim. Value $550-850.

Clockwise from upper left: All rayon canton crepe in medium blue with lighter blue top. The material looks much like silk. Button trimmed collar, belt with typical 30's buckle. Value $145-195. Celanese taffeta party dress with detachable sleeves. Coral rose with self-colored embroidery on the scalloped collar. The sleeves were kept in place with elastics. This type dress can be remembered by anyone who lived through the 30's. Value $195-225. Center: Navy blue dress with military epaulets and shiny metal buttons is made of printed cotton 'tweedy' suiting material. Value $125-150.
Silk flat crepe in red with harmonious prints and eggshell trim. Self belt with bow. Value $125-175. Velveteen 'best' dress for a young child. Sleeves and picoted bud-trimmed collar of silk flat crepe. Contrasting hand smocking at front. Value $145-165. Brown wool and cotton flannel suit called a 'swagger suit' which in this case applies more to the swing of the skirt than the jacket. Jacket unlined, skirt plain at back and each can be worn with other garments. Value $150-195. Collectors of older garments all or partially made of wool need to check condition very carefully.

Top right two dresses: $155-275 value range.

Above two dresses: $155-275 value range.

These three right dresses: 1935. Cape effects were widely used in 1935-1936 and 1937. Dresses of this type as shown in this 1935 advertisement were designed for the woman who was "36 or more", on up to size 50. Dresses of this type range $155-275 if short, long gowns range $350-500. Dresses of this era are beginning to be avidly sought after.

Left to right: 1935. Cotton suits were chic for summer. Jackets of this type were generally about 25" long, the skirt about 32" long. White with black and white check was popular, as in this houndstooth example. Jacket unlined, skirt is plain in back. Value $300-350.

This suit is of woven nubbed cotton suiting, with slim line, unlined jacket featuring the ultra modish, almost mannish peak lapels. Patch pockets and fancy buttons. Value $300-350.

This is a coat and skirt ensemble. The coat is about 40" long. White and black check of cotton honeycomb suiting. The neck interest is evident in these fashions. Suits of this kind are still undervalued. Value $400-450.

Dresses were nicely detailed in 1939 and furs often carried for effect rather than warmth. 'Tubize' was a new fabric made of rayon yarn. If any clothing you own bears a label with this designation it can be dated exactly. Beautiful pleating and tucks are featured in these dresses. Both are belted and one is buttoned down the front. Both models sport fur hats, one carries a muff, the other a shoulder fur. Dresses such as these are valued at $95-125 and are finally coming into their own. Most flattering styles, and tailoring is superior in dresses of this era. Fur muff, mink, value $250-275, fur piece, mink, $175-200.

1920's evening coat, black, reversible satin and crepe with flaring cape sleeves. This 20's coat is shorter than the 30's dress the model is wearing. Value of coat $400-600.

1921, winter styles. All wool coat with wide belt, chinchilla trim and muff. Dashing military look. Value $1,500-2,000.

Early 1920's grey-blue silk velvet coat with chinchilla trim. Silk crepe lining. Weighted in hem. Value $3,000-3,500.

Fur trimmed coats were de rigueur in 1933-34. Often the fur was wolf-blended dog fur as in this case. Coat is dark brown with black fur. Value $300-350.

This coat is made of suede coating material which is about 2/3 wool and has an interesting diagonal weave and is trimmed with a profusion of rich looking fur-effect fabric resembling lapin fur. Lined and interlined. Belted. Value $250-300.

Short evening coat of 1938. Rose colored taffeta, rayon lining. Original rhinestone pin. Originally worn to a school dance in 1938, worn again recently with equal panache. Value $150-195.

Monkey coat, 1939-1940. Silk lining, corde collar. Value $2,500-3,000.

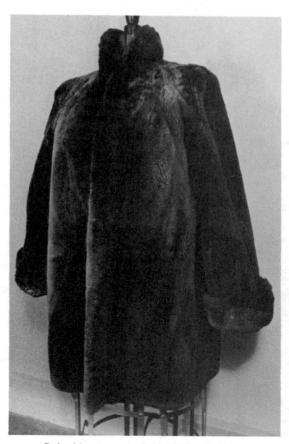

Ocelot jacket, 1939. Value $750-950.

Striped beaver coat of the 1930's. $1,000-1,500.

Woman's raccoon coat, full length. In excellent condition the value is $1,500-2,000.

1938. Hooded raincoat, processed cotton gabardine, double breasted, worn with high boots and fur lined kid gloves. Since these are still wearable, timeless and often found in excellent condition they are somewhat difficult to date. Value $65-125.

A particularly graceful chiffon beaded dress with large bow. 1923. Value $1,600-2,000.

A spectacular formal costume intended for an installation ceremony in 1924. Lace dress with side panels, scalloped hemline, narrow shoulder straps. Value $1,800-2,500. The headdress certainly commands attention. Value $125-150. Satin shoes, large bouquet.

The 1923 silhouette. An afternoon gown of black crepe Roma with sleeves set in from the waistline. The unusual drapery drops from the shoulder at the back on the right side, but from the waistline only on the left. Panels of embroidery. Dress $2,000-2,500. Wonderful hat.

Little soutache 'pancakes' of graduated sizes are the only decoration on this afternoon dress. The draped girdle is self material. Black crepe Roma. Value $1,500-1,800.

The design of this dress is most interesting. It is 'built' of wide brown satin ribbon combined with narrow bands of embroidery worked with antique gold thread in outline and single stitch. Fluted ribbons form the collar and cuffs and a big soft bow is used at the left front of the dress Value $1,600-2,000.

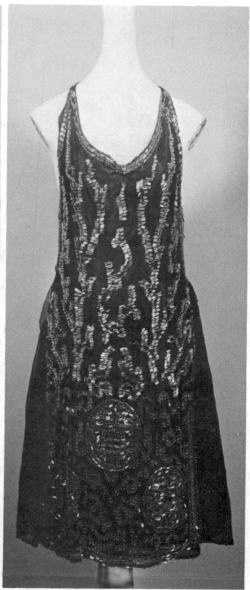

Black silk sateen 'dressy' dress, very early 1920's. Front and side gathers form drapes which not only catch the eye but form the dress to a flattering fit. Knee length. The long V shaped dickey snaps into place on the dress itself and when removed and the dress worn without it, the garment takes on an entirely different look. This dress, which does not have a label, exemplifies the fact that good tailoring recurs in every fashion cycle – it is made in much the same way as earlier clothing and this attention to detail is also found in surprising numbers of later dresses and coats. Value $650-950.

Evening dress of brown chiffon with fine lace and ribbon inserts. The skirt is cut on the bias, belted with a rhinestone buckle. This is a particularly interesting garment – the color, the way the lace is inserted and the sleeves are all of unusual interest. c. 1930. Value $1,600-2,000.

Large size bugle beaded dress of the 1920's. Black, silver and gold beads on black. Lined with black satin. A stunning dress, eminently wearable. $1,800-2,500.

182

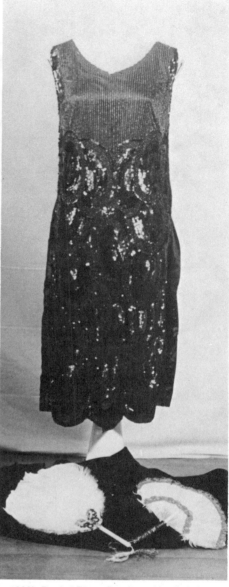

Black satin and pink chiffon 1920's beaded dress. Beading on front attached panel only. Value $1,000-1,500.

1920's satin beaded dress. Two piece, large size, skirt lined. Extremely heavy. $2,000-2,800.

1920's Beaded Dress. Sequin and beaded short dress, black and blue sequins form large swirls, tiny black beads fill in as well as forming the bodice which is chiffon. Net bottom and all lined. Side opens with snap, front and back panel lift so skirt can be raised to ensure no damage from sitting. Value $1,800-2,000.

Left to right: Silk crepe, c. 1930, chocolate brown long sleeve beaded dress worn with a fur neckpiece. Value of dress $800-1,200.

Royal blue chiffon cocktail dreess, c. 1929-31, the V-neck sleeveless gown with back and front rhinestone design, the lower skirt with multiple panels and uneven hemline. A striking dress. Value $1,200-1,800. The model is carrying a blue and gold evening coat with white fox collar, some renovation, labeled the HALLE BROTHERS COMPANY, CLEVELAND, OHIO. Value $250-350.

Iridescent green lace cocktail dress with brown underslip and chiffon sleeves, c.1920-1930. Value $400-650.

Cocktail dress, c.1930, black net lace with velvet trim. Worn with black velvet pearl-trimmed tiara, and a bead-bordered silk tulle stole. Value of dress $650-850.

This costume has an ecru silk skirt lined with lightweight wool. A ribbon draws the skirt to a bustle in the back. The waist is ecru crocheted with a high neck with pearl button trim. Draw string reticule and brown velvet hat with plume. Value of dress $2,000-2,200. The gentleman's very formal tails with black tie is contemporary. All mens' formal wear is highly collectible.

Lounging garments continued to be popular. In 1931 the kimono was high style. This was generally called a 'lounging robe' and is ornamented with little tufts of cotton. Slender tie belt. Value of robe $200-245. The pajama costume is decorated on only one leg and on the opposite side of the blouse front. The blouse could be worn inside or out. These lounging pajamas are rather difficult to find but well worth the effort. Value in silk $235-300.

Pongee pajamas, favorites in the early '20's. Value $195-235.

Left: French embroidered lingerie of 1923. A sleeveless nightgown of sheer, soft white batiste in the empire style with inset yoke sections at back and front. Embroidered with a dainty rose spray. Value $200-250.

Right: A brassiere and skirt combination of heavy white sateen. The brassiere is embroidered in white, shoulder straps of cotton tape. Skirt is gored, lightly gathered and joined to the brassiere. Value $150-200.

1931 rayon crepe pajamas, 'trousers' have pleated insets, V yoke front and elastic at back. Blouse has self bindings around neck and armholes. Embroidery. Value $150-175. Dress of good quality voile for little girl. Capelet sleeves, pleated down the front, embroidered with roses. 1931. Value $65-85.

186

Top, left to right: Lingerie was pretty and rather alluring in 1933. Girls up to 14 wore cotton broadcloth bloomers with nainsook slip, although even in lesser fabrics the construction was the same as in the more expensive silks. Value of bloomers $10-12; value of slip in girls' size $20-25. These are usually called lounging pajamas but were in fact worn around the house for general use, to do housework, to 'romp' in, or 'to exchange secrets with your girlfriend.' The butterfly sleeves were new in 1933 and the cotton broadcloth print attractive. One piece style. Value $155-195. The slip is crepe cut in fitted style, lace trim. Flesh color, value $35-40. All silk crepe chemise. Fitted style, trimmed with rosebuds and lace. Flesh pink or peach were the usual colors. Value $45-55.

Pajamas of soft finish longcloth, hand embroidered. Pink, peach or Nile green, Empire waist. Value $150-195. The gown hangs loose and has a sash, also hand embroidered. Value $95-135.

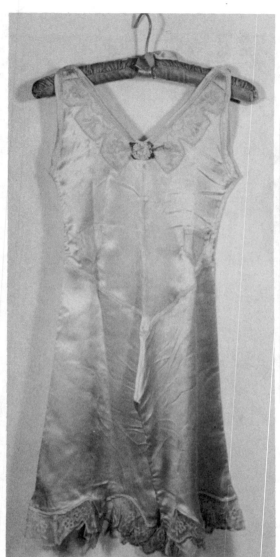

Child's French satin bed garment. Lace and satin, rosette at neckline. Made in Paris. Value $175-255.

Lounging pajamas, 1920's, 50 percent silk, 50 percent rayon, machine made lace sewn onto pajamas. Value $175-255.

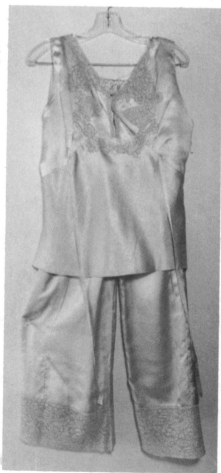

1930's 'Satin Dache' panties, buttoned on side. Darker lace trim. Unworn. $30-40.

188

Rayon jersey petticoat chemise. Fits snug to be worn under sheer frocks but is full below the hips. Value $35-50.

Underthings of 1924: Camisole tops: silk, $95-110; cotton, $55-65. Corsets of this period: $40-45. Combinations (bottom row) $45-50. These are characteristic of the 20's silhouette.

Below: An embroidered batiste camisole of 1923. Value $45-55.
Step-in panties which match the camisole. Value $35-50.

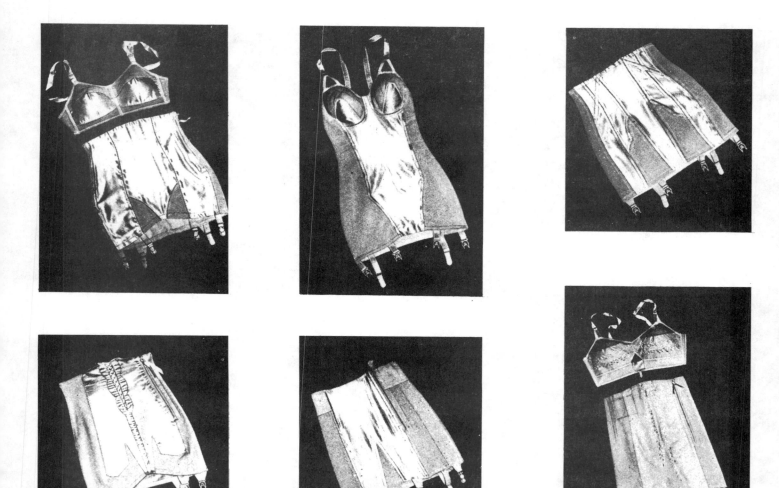

An array of corsets, 1939. Top left - 'high' corset with matching bra. The 'high' effect controls a 'roll'. Center top - corselette for half sizes; top right - this girdle controls the 'young' figure; bottom left - short front lacing decreases waistline; bottom center - softly boned elastic top nips waistline; bottom right - girdle with matching bra pulls in waist. All of these were used to nip in here and push in there but often they are found in their original boxes or bags indicating women were not so anxious to submit to these tortures. An untapped collecting field. Value $25-50.

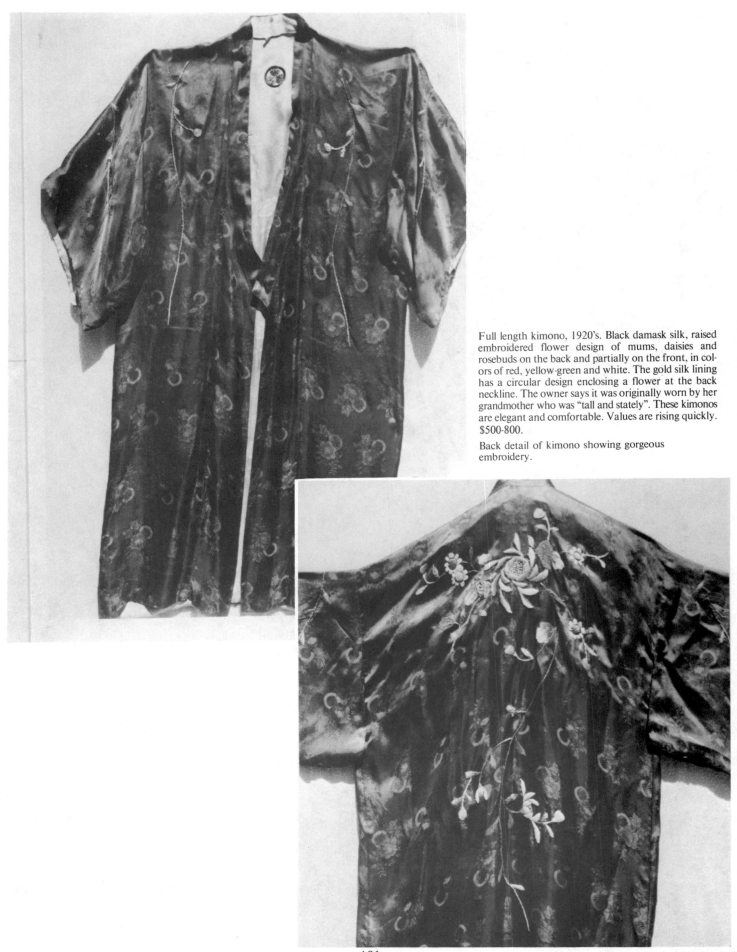

Full length kimono, 1920's. Black damask silk, raised embroidered flower design of mums, daisies and rosebuds on the back and partially on the front, in colors of red, yellow-green and white. The gold silk lining has a circular design enclosing a flower at the back neckline. The owner says it was originally worn by her grandmother who was "tall and stately". These kimonos are elegant and comfortable. Values are rising quickly. $500-800.

Back detail of kimono showing gorgeous embroidery.

191

Short kimono, very fine silk, black background with colorful floral and bird design 'mums' in orange, blue, green, tan, red and gold; daisies in pink and brown shades. Placking trim is flowered design. Both back and front have beautiful spray arrangements of flowers. Orange silk lining. Detachable sleeves. Probably from Franklin Simon's, New York. 1920's. Value $500-750.

Light blue rayon jacquard trimmed with lace. Child's christening coat, worn around 1925. Value $195-250.

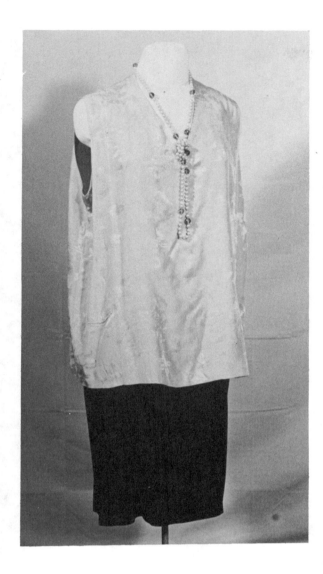

Black crepe underdress, sleeveless tunic of gold silk brocade, 1930's. Value $400-600. This dress has been worn recently with great success. Necklace of faux pearls and green glass beads is also 30's vintage.

Printed cotton smock, once a popular utility garment. This was worn in 1935. Three-quarter length, buttons down front, ties at the wrist. Value of these rather uncommon articles of clothing often stem from the interesting old printed fabrics from which they were made. Value $55-85.

Blouses have wide price variations. This type, $100-125.

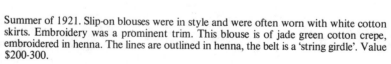

Summer of 1921. Slip-on blouses were in style and were often worn with white cotton skirts. Embroidery was a prominent trim. This blouse is of jade green cotton crepe, embroidered in henna. The lines are outlined in henna, the belt is a 'string girdle'. Value $200-300.

1921. A slip-on overblouse with long set-in sleeves, the fullness at the waist is confined with a ribbon drawn through button-holed eyelets under the embroidery. Scalloped edged. White voile. Beautiful addition to a collection. Value $350-500. The parasol is of white poplin with embroidery to match the blouse. Value $250-300. Matching hat $300-325.

Two hats of 1921, they are large and lacy. Left, cutwork over heavy linen with wide ribbon band and bow; right, white embroidered net over pink linen. These hats are not always dated correctly, but they were enormously popular in the early 20's. Value $250-295.

The little girls hats of the mid 1920s were attractive and in some cases actually flattered the child. Made of the finest materials, velvets, braided trims, floral trims, grosgrain and satin ribbons these are a find. In perfect condition they do not surface too often and many times are confused with hats of adult women. It takes searching but if you know what the girls were wearing it is somewhat easier to identify your goal. These are typical winter hats for the fashionable little girl. Value starting price (depending upon material, trim and condition) should be $145.

Clockwise starting top left: Hats of Spring, 1925. The large, flattering brim. A charming combination of hand embroidered silk with fine straw. Value $250-350. Fruit and flower appliques in vivid colors on straw. Value $225-300. Tailored straw hat of pedal straw trimmed with satin, and a jade motif. Value $250-350. Three tiers of little scarlet flowers on a velvet trimmed hat of cherry straw. Value $225-295. This hat has an interesting under-brim trimming of brilliant applique motifs subdued by a veiling of tulle. Value $250-350. The flapper hairdos, pearls, feather boas, the very poses are entirely representative of the period. No wonder every female is yearning for a collection of 20's clothing.

Counterclockwise, starting top left: Easter hats of 1925. Mata Hari could have worn this deep crowned straw trimmed with ribbon and lace. No one would have ever recognized her. Still it's a fantastic hat. Value $350-450. What was "ultra new" in 1925, a cluster of roses placed as to widen the brim of this straw hat. Value $250-350. 1925 version of the graceful Directoire poke with much maligned visor front. Women complained that this made it difficult to see around them. Value $300-400. A compact brim covering of flowers, widening into picturesque wing sections at the sides. Ribbon trim on top of crown. Value $350-450. Another poke, trimmed with flowers and crepe. Value $350-450. In 1925 the afternoon hat was a necessary accessory. This stunning creation has a hair crown and crepe brim in pastel tints, trimmed with a cluster of American beauty roses. Value $400-500.

An array of the most sought after type of hat of the 1920's, the toque. Counterclockwise: These are all of felt, although they can be found in straw, silk and other materials. Hat at top is a bolero toque with irregular brim revers laced with narrow ribbon; a life-sized poinsettia and torsades of felt add interest to the Pierrot shape with upturned brim; Two piece crown with slashed and folded brim; felt torsades and felt petals, petals in contrasting shade of green; collapsible toque with tailored trimming of felt; felt strips take the place of soutache and form a scroll design on a tall-crowned polo toque. Value of hats of this kind and of this period is rising and should begin at $195 and increase according to material, trim and general attractiveness.

Left: Hats of the 1933-35 period are wonderful additions to a collection and are quite neglected. Prices are 'right' and they are fairly easy to find. Rayon-faced velvet with a feather ornament and veil. This veil, like many of that time, is embroidered. Value $40-45. This adjusts to individual head size. Knitted cotton 'headhugging' turban and ascot scarf set. Rings decorate turban. These sets were popular and not often found together today. Value as a set $50-60. The turban is an enduring fashion note.

Right, top to bottom: Deep ridged crown of wool felt, two tone grosgrain ribbon trim, turned-down brim. Value $50-60. This hat was intended specifically for 'large heads.' Wool felt with ridged or creased crown. Two tone satin ribbons, a feather quill, tail coverts, veil. Value $50-60. Large head size model, this hat is of wool crepe, grosgrain ribbon, lacquered ornament simulates feathers. Value $40-50.

Accessories, 1920's, 1930's. Left to right: hat stand, top covered in velvet with rhinestones, c.1920, value $35-45. Hat form, painted with bobbed hair, c.1928, $45-65. Rhinestone necklace, hand set stones unsigned, $40-50. Rhinestone bag, chain handles, c.1930's. $175-195. Garters, 1920's each, $22-27. Satin shoes, ankle straps, buttons, c.1919, $70-80. Cigarette holder, $40-50.

The transitional influence of the late 1920's is shown in the hat worn by this elegant lady of 1930. The 'silver foxes' are still considered one of fashion's classic statements. Silver fox fur piece value $1,000-1,500; hat $100-145.

"Silver foxes" worn over 30's velvet dress. Net and velvet bow headpiece, c.1936-37. Fur piece, $1,000-1,500. Net 'hat'. This has no frame so is considered a veil. $20-25.

Accessories of the 1920's. Top - feather headpiece worn low on the forehead, perfect with a beaded dress. 1920's value $75-125; middle row, left - shoe buckles, cut steel, marked "France" $50-75; hand set rhinestone shoe buckles, 1930's $45-50; cut steel in an unusual shape, marked "made in France" value $65-125, lower line filagree metal of the 1930's $15-20; bottom row - art deco shoe clips, green and white $50-65; rhinestone and pearl shoe clips of the 1940's $12-15; bow shoe clips of metallic mesh of the early 1930's $25-35. All shoe buckles are rising in price. Shoe buckles are one of the most stunning collectibles, specialization is the key to a fine collection of these, but collecting can begin on any price level.

Fancy apron, 1930's, hand embroidered, $35-50.

1931. Long scarf, $25-40. Shorties scarves and ties, depending on material, pattern and label should have a beginning price of $35.

1928. This is an apron of the slip over the head type. It has a back to the waist and is seamed at the shoulders. Bias fold binding, two deep pockets. Aprons are still an untapped mine of interesting, unusual and often beautifully constructed clothing. Cotton, embroidered. Value $20-30.

Below: 'Smartest' shoe worn in the Fall and Winter of 1921. It has 'snap and pep.' Combination patent leather and kid finish. Uppers are soft black dull kid finished leather and are stitched in white. Patent leather tip, ball strap design. Patent leather front lace stay and 'wave' top. Concave military heel. Value $145-195. Shoes in perfect condition continue to be elusive.

1930's hat with rhinestone pin. Velvet and satin $35-45; peach colored nubby cotton, leather-trimmed shoes of the early 30's $50-60; 1920's black satin button strap shoes $45-55; black leather slipper, lined with satin, front bow $30-35, 1930's. In a short period of time I have put together a collection of women's house slippers (almost all unworn) which has proved quite pretty and rewarding and inexpensive. 1930's never worn light brown soft leather button strap shoes with a rather incongrous bow in front. Value $75-95, 1930's very collectible rhinestone slipper value $100-145. Rhinestones all hand set in deep wells to resist scuffing; snake skin handbag of the 1930's, leather lined with a black and gold art deco handle. These reptile handbags are one of the really rising collectibles. Value $195-295; evening bag of black velvet from the 1930's, self-handle on back, rhinestone clasp. Value $125-175.

The very characteristic pump and clocked hosiery of the early 1920s period. Hosiery, unworn $20-25. Shoes in excellent condition $75-125.

Silk satin shoes with cut steel buckles, c. 1928-29, known to have been worn in 1929. Often the shoes are being bought by collectors of buckles. Value $125-175.

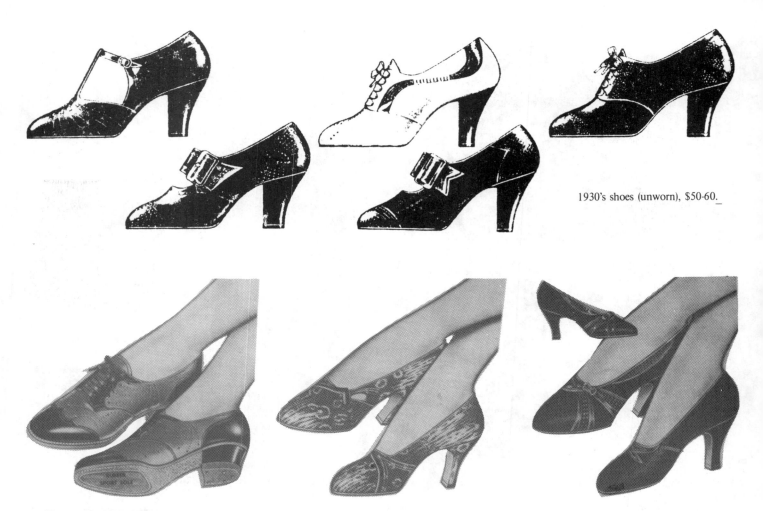

1930's shoes (unworn), $50-60.

Shoes present difficulties to the collector unless they are unworn or nearly so. These were the types popular in 1934-35. Heels were varied, the so-called spike was not the same as the heel we bring to mind at the use of that term, the 'Cuban' was also called 'continental Cuban' and flats were also popular. The same shoe could also be had in different heel types. Value of shoes of this era in excellent condition $50-95.

The shoe most identified with young girls during the 1930's. Soft, shiny patent with buckle. Rubber cushioned heels. Value $45-55.

Girls shoes, 1933. Black with gray and silver colored trim. Colonial styled slipper with slightly tapered toe and covered heel. Value $30-40.

Shiny patent leather with open cut outs and applique of black reptile effect and silver colored leather. Value $45-55.

Accessories, particularly shoes and hats often mark the period more definitely than do the major clothing pieces. A selection of shoes from 1931-1932 shown at top, brown suede tie with open lacy perforations, kid lined. Left, black suede with glistening patent appliques. Center: black suede, kid lined, right - high sides step-in of black suede. Bow of suede and kid. Shoes valued in excellent condition at $40-45 pair.

In 1924 word was that wherever one meets Dame Fashion she is carrying a beaded bag. Among the most popular were these knitted types entirely encrusted with beads. Beaded bag making was often a home project in these years and the first step was stringing the beads, often a complicated process in itself. The top left reticule is knit, lined with silk and covered with glass beads and crystal bugle beads. Value $150-250.
Top right: A different approach on this bag. Basically a light brown it is fringed with golden brown crystal beads and lined with brown silk. Value $175-300.
Bottom: This bag is also all done in brown. It is a fan pattern with overall bronze irridescent beads. All of these are beautiful. Beaded bag collecting is well established and is a costly hobby to begin now, although no doubt prices will continue to rise.

Fashion is nothing if not cyclical. For a long time the shoes of the 1930s were considered clunky and unflattering. Now the T-strap is everywhere, the sport shoes are back, the 'oxford', ghillies and kiltie ties would not be considered 'outre' on today's woman.
Top left: A kid walking shoe which is intricately cut out and stitched. The strap is fashioned to give a comfortable fit. Top right: This is an evening sandal in a range of brilliant colors, this is bright blue. It combines cut outs and straps to form a pleasing design. It was designed with a metatarsal steel shank and pad which was supposed to make for perfect comfort and correct posture.

Center left: Both these examples of sport shoes are firmly set on solid low heels. Meant to be worn with tweeds, the shoe on the left is a double kiltie strap in brown calf. Perfect for golf. On the center right is squat brown and white ghillie enhanced by stitching and perforations.
Although both these shoes were considered scientifically sound, they were also the newest thing and quite handsome. On the left is a one-eyelet tie oxford which has open work interlacing and a perky bow. It was well made with a steel arch support. It was constructed to clasp your instep "in a firm but unrelenting embrace". The oxford on the right has a solid leather built up heel and brown tip and wing with perforations. All of these are from 1935. Value of shoes of this vintage, in excellent condition and of this quality should begin at $95 each pair.

In 1927 the hairdo complemented the clothing and jewelry. Many of the hair styles would be appropriate today. Although some of these faces may not be familiar, the bobbed hair forever marks the era.

In 1932 when fur was not considered a plitically incorrect word, the fashionable woman inevitably had a small fur piece in her wardrobe. Paris was still ruling that world and it decreed that fur, capes and cape effects, short fur jackets, all had to be part of the scene. It is very interesting that in the midst of these luxurious garments ladies were admonished 'to buy quality for these days clothes must last'. In spite of the irony, it is still sound advice. Here we have silver fox, twisted silver and blue fox, the triangular cape of ermine, the short jacket of broadtail, and Schiaparellie's triple sables caught in a ring. There are many, many exquisite collectible furs available and since it is well after the fact we collectors can only hope the day will again dawn when all this beauty can be displayed without rancor. Since vintage furs are often not even publicly displayed today, prices are flexible.

To go with your hankies start looking for handkerchief cases. Three examples of unusual types, rising rapidly in price, but the plain ones are still around and still affordable. These were often given at holidays as the Santa one attests, with affection to a relative or friend as many of them are so marked, or the hankies were enclosed in cases which were themselves things of beauty as are the lace examples. The case intended for sister is in a startling purple satin and is valued at $20-25. The Christmas scene is pink satin and is valued at $15-20, the black lace over pink satin case is valued at $20-28.

1920 seashore fashions have always been sought after and collected. The exciting 1920s continue to appeal to collectors. These two bathers look surprisingly free in their wool suits, socks and bathing shoes. Men's bathing suits $45-65. Women $100-150.

A red wool swimsuit, belted and with star buttons, bra ties in back, top attached to bottom in front. Interesting design work, it does not look particularly dated in spite of its time frame, 1930s. This suit was sold by the owner to a famous contemporary designer, probably as a prototype.

These bathing suits, worn in 1935, were made for ease of actually swimming, but the hint of the future Bikini was certainly evident in the lady's two piecer. The gentleman's suit told us no similar story. Bathing suits are difficult to find in good condition, the early ones were often made of wool and many bathing suits were worn for a rather long period of time and discarded. Value of the two piece set $25-28, man's suit $30-35.

This one pice wool bathing suit could be extremely flattering to the right figure and is in total keeping with the designing flair of the 1930s. This suit dates from 1935, and is red wool. Wool suits did not survive in great numbers so are a real find for collectors when they do turn up. Value $50-60.

A two piece tennis outfit of the early 1930s. Surprisingly comfortable looking with a loose fitting top and pleated skirt of some width. It would probably be difficult to find such a costume intact and if found not easily identified. If Aunt Sophorina still has one in the attic it is valued, in good condision, at $45-65. The emphasis on sports clothes in this period was almost always accompanied by advice to keep fit and vigorous, so there is nothing new under the sun after all.

Sports attire for beach or tennis court in the Spring of 1922. The four bathing suits at top, replete with bathing caps or hats and bathing shoes make a remarkable picture.

The tennis blouse at bottom has a transfer print applique and actually looks roomy and comfortable. The bathing suits with their bloomers and overskirts, have fancy decorations, draw string waists and do not seem to be geared for championship swimming. Any of this type bathing suit is valued at $125-250. The tennis blouse at $45-55.

Bathing beauty of 1924. Wool bathing suit, one piece, skirted, bathing slippers of rubber, bathing socks. The accessories would be a tremendous find, the suit $125-165.

A couple of bathers in 1924. She wears a one piece wool suit with red and white check material at bodice and end of bloomers. Rubber bathing cap and shoes. Man wears one piece suit, wool, with black bottom and white top. Also wears shoes. Although early ads refers to the footwear as shoes, people who wore them tell me they were generally referred to as 'bathing slippers'. Bathing suits, each $125-165. Bathing slippers $30-50. Since both caps and slippers were of rubber, they are not readily available.

Black sateen bathing suit of 1923. It has an applique of orchid and purple and has purple piping around the sleeves, neck and cap. The cap matches and is of double sateen. A tight fitting rubber cap was worn under this headgear.

The bathing beauties of the 1920's exude sensuality in spite of the modesty of the garment itself. Some of the suits were belted, others were two piece with long tops without belts. They were made of cotton rib knit, 100% pure worsted wool, jersey knit and came in a variety of patterns and colors. Not too many of these seem to have survived and they are eminently collectible. Value of these types of adult suits $125-165. Child's value $50-60.

Elaborate formal wedding of 1928. The satin and lace concept was never more evident, the size of the bouquet, which was typical of those years, is not only eye catching but magnificent. Dozens of satin ribbons hang from the bouquet, the imported lace veil is worn low on the forehead and is trimmed with wax orange blossoms. The lace veil is worn over an underveil of fine net. The dress is chiffon and lace and tiered. Satin shoes. This truly ornate and beautiful costume has become a family heirloom, worn by other brides. Value of the veil is $750-1,000, the gown $1,200-1,800. The groom wears the requisite formal morning costume for such a wedding.

Clothing for children of the early 1930's, typical styles made of broadcloth, linen, wool spun jersey, cotton, crepe de chine, and pongee. The little boys' suits range in value from $50-75; the little girls' dresses $55-110; and the dresses for young teenagers (who never realized that was what they were back then) are valued at $125-175.

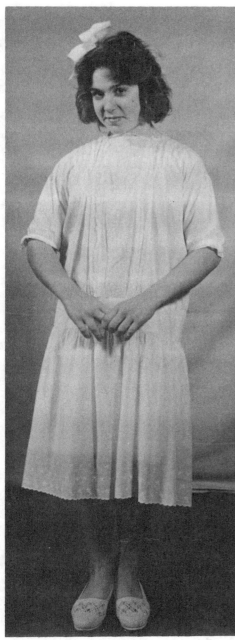

1936. Young girl's party dress. Taffeta with attached belt. Value $145-245.

Girl's batiste lingerie dress of the 1920's. Lace inserts, dropped waist and dropped shoulders. The great attribute of these 'lingerie' dresses was their ability to withstand many launderings. Value $100-145. Large white hair bow. Late 1920's, early 1930's. The dropped waistline can also be found on much earlier clothing.

A graduation frock, Spring 1921. Crisp white organdy. All edges except the bottom of the skirt are bound with bias binding and it has an organdy rose at the waist. Double apron panels are mounted over a plain foundation. The waist is attached to the skirt, has set-in sleeves and an outer panel to match the skirt. Embroidered. This is a very desirable dress. Value $850-1,200.

Girls' wear, 1924.
Dresses, $125-150.
Coat $150-185.

Spring of 1931 fashions for children. All of these are made of cotton so they could be laundered easily. Much of the decoration is the 'tucking' but in the 'ensemble' the skirt and blouse are joined together underneath the hip band. It is sleeveless and worn with the cloche hat. The dresses are short as is the hairstyle. Values of children's dresses of the early 1930's depends on the correct time attribution, often this is difficult. Some of these dresses were worn with matching bloomers and when the hipline is defined the dating becomes easier. Good quality with careful tailoring and good trim, dresses are valued at $125-175.

214

A girl's ivory flannel wool dress, jacket and cape. All are silk embroidered. 1930s. Sold at auction in 1989 for $66. Value today $150-225.

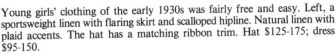

TOP RIGHT:

There is something essentially innocent about some of these 1920s fashions in spite of their calculated attempt to look daring and provocative. This costume is typical - she looks like a juene fille trying to look like a vamp. The middy blouse is still a very flattering fashion top, still used by designers at all levels in various guises, the tie has made a strong comeback, the knickers are "sports knickers" with lots of intriguing trim and high wool cuffed socks, oxfords in two-tone again a fashion being seen now. That hat is classic and complements the bobbed hair. Cotton Middle, cummerbund waistline, with tie $50-60. Knickers in wool not many of which have survived the moths, $35-45; Socks $15-20; Shoes $30-35.

TOP LEFT:

In the early 1920s young boys often wore long sleeves even at play. Although no one realized it at the time this was a sun safe fashion as this cotton striped shirt proves. This boy wears cotton shorts which have not changed much over the years in basic concept, with high socks tie oxfords he is easily garbed, comfortable and in tune with his age and ready to take off on his tricycle. This costume could probably not be recognized for what it is and would probably be found in separate pieces and would be inexpensive if found, but this is a good illustration of boys playwear in the 1920s.

Young girls' clothing of the early 1930s was fairly free and easy. Left, a sportsweight linen with flaring skirt and scalloped hipline. Natural linen with plaid accents. The hat has a matching ribbon trim. Hat $125-175; dress $95-150.

Center: An everyday 'ensemble'. The coat is slightly flaring the dress has inverted plaits at the side fronts and side-back of the skirt. Red and blue light wool for the coat, the dress is blue linen with red trim. The hat is also red and blue. Hat $125-175; dress and coat (Each) $145-185.

Right: This is a white pique bolero dress with a hip yoke and flaring circular skirt. The blue scallops on the jacket and collar are also carried over on the cuffs and skirt. In 1930 this would have been 'cute'. Hat $125-175; Dress $100-175.

A variety of clothing made for children. Clockwise: Child's rompers with waist. Suspenders attached. Waist closes at back. Trim on waist matches pants. Cotton value $65-95.

Bloomer dress. Embroidered puppy on band. Gingham with white banding. Value $85-125.

This girl's dress has kimono sleeves, a one piece gathered skirt and closing at left side of vest. Girls up to 14 years of age wore these. Value in voile. $150-185.

The wonderful middy dress which has never really gone out of style. The one piece pleated skirt is joined to an underwaist which closes at the back. Value with original tie $150-175.

Empire slip made for girls up to 12 years. Two piece skirt is joined to the Empire waist and slips over the head. Nainsook. Value $45-65. Notice polka dot socks.

Pleated bloomer for the miss up to 16 years old. Value $75-95.

Combination undergarment for young girls. Bloomer style. Cotton. Value $100-120.

One piece slip-on frock closing at the back with skirt gathered to long waist. Skirt panels are turned under. Value $125-155.

This girl's dress is made of blue suiting with white repp vest, collar and cuffs. Worn by girls 4 to 8 years of age. 1921. Value $175-195.

'Cherry Ripe' outfit for a little girl. White swiss with bright red dots, bound with scarlet bias binding which outlines the petal skirt panels and kimono sleeves. 'Dutchy' collar. Round hat with deep crown matches the dress. Red cherries dangling from waist give the costume its name. Value of set $200-250.

All wool beret and slip-over V-neck sweater. Hand embroidered boat and signal and flag design. All wool coat sweater, fancy striping and hand embroidered boat and birds. Sweaters of this vintage in good condition should be valued at $30-35.

Another romper suit of the early 1920's. Yellow Japanese crepe with a hand embroidered duck on front. It buttons down the back. The guimpe is of thin white cotton. These were worn by boys up to 6 years of age. $65-95.

1920 rompers. This is an 'Oliver Twist' romper suit of linen. Value $125-145. To find the scooter would be a bonus.

Boy's suit and cap, 1920. Tan soisette blouse, pique cuffs, collar and trousers. Cap is pique. Suit $125-195, cap $35-40.

The boys wear of 1922 seems remarkably dated. Boy at left wears a crochet slip-on sweater, worn with knickerbockers, bow tie and collar. The cap is shetland wool knit. Sweater $20-25. A coat sweater of wool worn with a peaked cap. Sweater buttons are oversized, boy-sized pockets. Value $25-35.

Boy's all wool single breasted suit, winter weight. The coat has a twill lining, knickerbockers are also lined. Brown. The cap matches the suit. Suit value is $125-175.

Girl's middy style dress, all wool serge. Pleated, trimmed with white braid and has silk embroidered emblem on the sleeve. Navy blue. Value of these which are scarce $195-250. Matching tam-o-shanter, value $30-40.

Dress 34B60

Boy's suit of 1930. Wool, knickerbockers, wool socks, oxfords, the cap was the popular headgear. Suit value $95-150.

1933. Everyday dress for children in the early 1930's. The boy wears woolen knickerbockers, short wool jacket and aviator cap. The girl's coat is wool with a small fur collar, beret and she carries a school bag with strap over the shoulder. Clothing of this ordinary kind is rather difficult to find and not yet widely collected. Values are dependent on condition, quality and desirability.

1926-1932. Men's knickers, wool, buckled at side of band below the knee. Golfers gave knickers a sporty image. Value $50-75.

Little boys in 1931. Suits of short pants with attached waists. The pants, even in this length, were generally referred to as 'trousers'. These are of flannel with a cotton waist. Suit $35-40. The romper suit was worn by boys up to 6 years of age. This is gingham and it is difficult to visualize a large 6 year old boy wearing such a costume. Value $45-50.

A variety of clothing made for children. From left: Children's wear 1924. Value of dress $50-75. Value of two-piece costume with white trim, $45-50. Little girl's coat with matching deep crowned hat. Value $95-110. Bloomer dress, gingham with white banding. Value $55-75. Value suit $55-75. Right boy wears cotton shirt with cotton belted short trousers. Value $50-75.

Kiddie clothes of 1933. For the 3 to 6 year old girl, dotted organdy party dress, value $35-45. Printed cotton broadcloth with a matching pocketbook dog. Value $35-45. Flowered summer organdy with matching hat and purse, value as a set $55-60. Dotted Swiss with matching hat, value of set $35-45. Voile dress with the attractive crinkle fabric called Plisse crepe at the collar and cuffs, value $30-40. Party dress rosette trimmed ruffled dress of all rayon taffeta, value $65-75.

During certain past eras children were dressed exactly as their elders, but during the 30's the clothing of youngsters was attractive, comfortable and appropriate. Little boys wore tailored suits of broadcloth such as the one on the left which has plain colored pants with a candy striped waist with white trim. Value $25-35; romper suit also made of broadcloth with picot edged organdy trim with embroidery and elastic at the legs. This suit opens at the bottom, Value $45-60; pique romper made in a double breasted style, collar and cuffs trimmed with organdy, opens at the bottom, pearl buttons. Value $35-45; little girl's dress of silk pongee. This is a party dress with a hand embroidered collar and hand smocked yoke, tiny capelet sleeves and a deep hem. Value $45-65; fine checked gingham print with organdy trim. Fastens down the front with colored buttons. The apron is white organdy with matching gingham print trim fastens under the collar and ties in the back. Set $45-60.

220

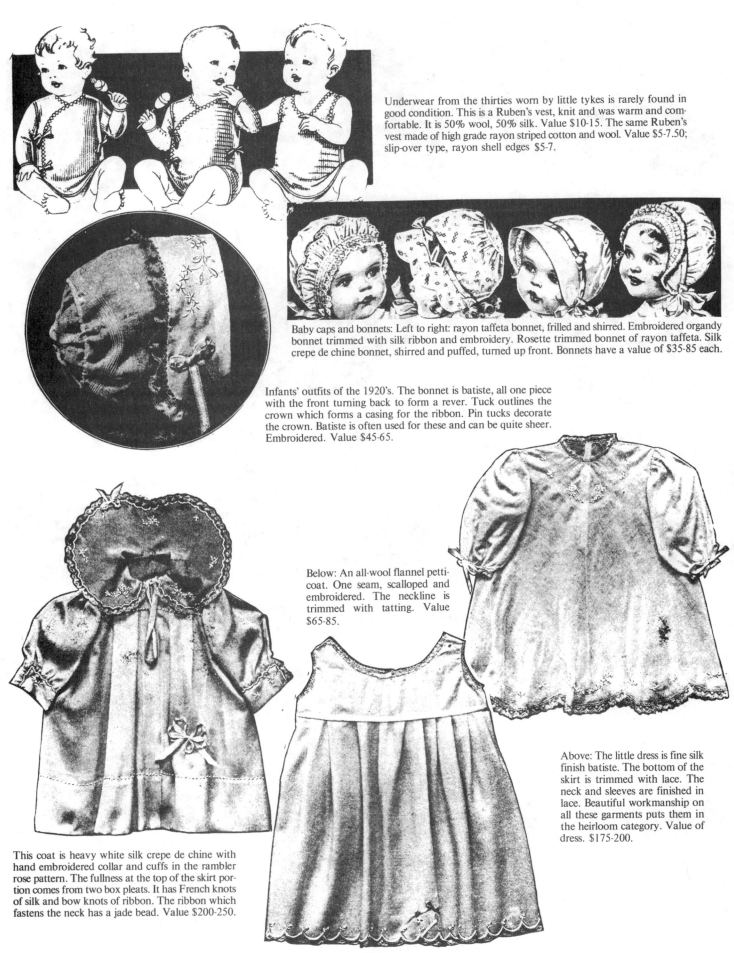

Underwear from the thirties worn by little tykes is rarely found in good condition. This is a Ruben's vest, knit and was warm and comfortable. It is 50% wool, 50% silk. Value $10-15. The same Ruben's vest made of high grade rayon striped cotton and wool. Value $5-7.50; slip-over type, rayon shell edges $5-7.

Baby caps and bonnets: Left to right: rayon taffeta bonnet, frilled and shirred. Embroidered organdy bonnet trimmed with silk ribbon and embroidery. Rosette trimmed bonnet of rayon taffeta. Silk crepe de chine bonnet, shirred and puffed, turned up front. Bonnets have a value of $35-85 each.

Infants' outfits of the 1920's. The bonnet is batiste, all one piece with the front turning back to form a rever. Tuck outlines the crown which forms a casing for the ribbon. Pin tucks decorate the crown. Batiste is often used for these and can be quite sheer. Embroidered. Value $45-65.

Below: An all-wool flannel petticoat. One seam, scalloped and embroidered. The neckline is trimmed with tatting. Value $65-85.

Above: The little dress is fine silk finish batiste. The bottom of the skirt is trimmed with lace. The neck and sleeves are finished in lace. Beautiful workmanship on all these garments puts them in the heirloom category. Value of dress. $175-200.

This coat is heavy white silk crepe de chine with hand embroidered collar and cuffs in the rambler rose pattern. The fullness at the top of the skirt portion comes from two box pleats. It has French knots of silk and bow knots of ribbon. The ribbon which fastens the neck has a jade bead. Value $200-250.

221

Childrens' shoes in 1933. Blucher oxford, white linen with open mesh vamp; strap pumps in patent leather; leather sandles; black elk leather for both boys and girls; patent leather swing strap; sturdy oxfords; dressy patent leather strap model. Children's shoes of this era are not yet widely collected. Value of these types $35-45.

The men's suits in keeping with the times project a macho image. Boys and mens suits valued $75-95.

Old fashion prints, photographs, and paintings are now all collectible on their own and such a series as this is a real find. Men's clothing has now arrived as a prime vintage collectible and the beautiful old prints of these fashions are rarely available... so a set such as this, each measuring approx. 12" x 14" and so beautifully done is a treasure. The clothing is from the 1920s and is clearly defined and pictured in striking color. The set is valued at $225.

Old Fashion prints, photographs, and paintings are now all collectible on their own and such a series as this is a real find. Men's clothing has now arrived as a prime vintage collectible and the beautiful old prints of these fashions are rarely available...so a set such as this, each measuring approx. 12" x 14" and so beautifully done is a treasure. The clothing is from the 1920s and is clearly defined and pictured in striking color. The set is valued at $225.

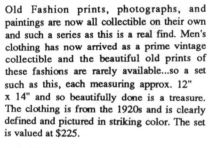

Old Fashion prints, photographs, and paintings are now all collectible on their own and such a series as this is a real find. Men's clothing has now arrived as a prime vintage collectible and the beautiful old prints of these fashions are rarely available...so a set such as this, each measuring approx. 12" x 14" and so beautifully done is a treasure. The clothing is from the 1920s and is clearly defined and pictured in striking color. The set is valued at $225.

226

Trench coat. A 'rain or shine' garment of double textured rubberized cotton gabardine with a plaid lining, two welt slant pockets and a belt finished with a ring fastener. Trench flap, leather covered buttons. Dashing then, dashing now. Value $150-175.

In 1933 the men were considered fashionable when their trouser bottoms measured 22 inches. The primary colors were dark blue, oxford gray, and medium brown. A 'nifty,' dapper style boasted one button closing, broad 'rope' shoulders and peak lapels. Wool with subdued small check two tone pattern with flecks. Value $150-195. 100% virgin wool suit of herringbone weave with harmonizing chalk-line stripes. Two button closing, tie and handkerchief match and were sold with the suit. Value $150-195.

1927. Knickers worn by college types with plaid knee socks and casual tie shoes. Wool knickerbockers, value $50-75.

1922. A knitted vest with a back and trimmings of tan. This golfer also wears a plaid cap, tie and long trousers. Vest value $65-85.
1922. The lightweight slip-on sweater in camel's hair was worn for sports under a coat. Since knit sweaters are still very much the same today this would be a difficult item to date exactly unless the provenance were known. $35-40. This tennis buff looks quite contemporary.

World War I doughboy uniform. P.F.C. tunic with two 6 month overseas chevrons. Includes breeches. No hat. $200-300.
Right: A blue-gray gabardine uniform tunic and trousers of the Culver Military Academy. Value $150-175.

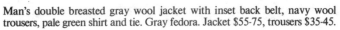

Man's double breasted gray wool jacket with inset back belt, navy wool trousers, pale green shirt and tie. Gray fedora. Jacket $55-75, trousers $35-45.

1930. 'Stetson' has become almost a generic term in men's fashion. This Homberg was made by Stetson and was known as the 'Stetsonian' model. It has a 'jaunty curve suitable for semi-formal occasions'. A dressy hat with a welt-edge brim with three rows of stitching. Hats of this type have become the rage among young men. Value with the Stetson label $45-55.

Snap brim style men's hats of 1933-34. Wool felt, usually with grosgrain band but sometimes these are found with leather bands. These hats are catching on and becoming a desirable, wearable collectible among young men. Value $25-30.

Men's Hats from the 1920's to 1950's, beaver felt. Values $35-75.

Men's shoes were less ornamented than those of younger boys. These are valued at $30-35 pair.

Square toes were what boys wore in 1933. Shoes of this type in good condition are valued at $30-35. They are not yet widely collected and are difficult to find without signs of wear.

CHAPTER IV
1940-1960

In 1939, there was no reason to suppose that fashion would go into hiding. United States involvement in the war took us all by surprise, but its reality forced much of the fashion industry to sit it out. So many people can remember the 40's, they lived through those years and many have told me that reading about fashion is not like living with fashion. The average person wore what was appropriate, what had been dictated by some designer and made available.

In general the rather static state of fashion in the early 1940's stemmed from uncertainty and a sense of the fitness of things, drastic changes would have seemed unpatriotic. "From now until the war is won, we won't have radical changes in fashion" was the fashion decree.

Waste of anything, including material, was to be avoided, and the Government asked the designers not to use unnecessary lengths of fabric, not to make extreme changes, not to use excessive trimmings, in short, let the silhouette alone. One of the results of this dictum was cuffless slacks, and patterns of that date proudly stated the limited material it would take to make such and such a garment.

The lack of new directions for clothes did not quench the everlasting feminine search for chic. Jon Whitcomb, the talented illustrator (whose work is now being collected) delineated the 40's female in the idealized way the Gibson Girl spoke for the nineties. In time this fascinating female he depicted will become the nostalgia buff's pin-up.

It was a time when evening wear was seductive, and day wear had a neat simplicity. The dirndl skirt went well with a shirtwaist top, and the jacketed suit dress could go anywhere comfortably. Necklines were varied, choices were many, but the plunging neckline was a favorite.

Joan Crawford's squared shoulders speak for the time. This padded, wide shoulder was typical, but there were dresses with soft folds which fell gracefully, the black dress might have white lace edging on the revers and short sleeves, and the 'dickey' was considered a "high spot" of many frocks. It was worn under the dress so it presented a collar on a collar usually in contrasting colors. Anybody who ever owned or wore a 'dickey' can tell you it was one of the handiest things ever designed.

"The suit dress is the civilian's uniform for summer," said a popular magazine. It could be severely tailored or made in softer materials and draped, but the shoulders were padded and square. Saddle stitching was part of many dresses and the princess line was evident in the early 40's. The shirtwaist dress was given a new twist – "something different in the 'shirtfrock' " were the suspender like tucks, with the curved pockets following the line of the saddle stitching. There were luscious colors in dresses and dress suits, and there were still some prints.

As with most coats, there seem to be few collectors. The boxy coat of the 40's was padded at the shoulders and could be had in almost any length from waist to hem. The classic town coat was sometimes called a 'reefer' and was a fitted and flattering style. The technique of using long, narrow panels to make it slenderized the figure. There are many still around, and being rapidly pulled out of closets.

It may very well be the square shoulders that attracts, but whatever the reason it is toward the 40's that today's younger collectors are aiming. From the vantage point of those who wore them some of the exaggerated styles of the 40's do not seem that long ago, to those who were born in the 1960's they have such a different look as to be almost 'camp'.

Everywhere the vintage clothing stores are catering to this younger trade, some of whom are buying to wear, some to collect. The early 40's costumes were military oriented – in feminine attire this was reflected in the wide-shouldered, nipped-in waist look.

In men's clothing gabardine and khaki were being worn and colors were rather muted in keeping with the times. The military uniforms were seen everywhere, and now they are a big segment of clothing collecting. There are military shops devoted to the sale of these as well as anything connected with any of our branches of service. A lighter touch during this period was the porkpie hat, which was well liked for its flat crown and snap brim. It proved to be an enduring fashion.

Slacks, which had become necessary in the factories, were gaining favor, but slowly. It was a time of Rosie the Riveter and as she riveted, she needed suitable clothing. Although, we in the United States, are hard put to remember the pre-jeans era, this was it. When slacks did start to become part of the wardrobe, they were utilitarian and comfortable. They were, in fact, a bit on the baggy side, but they opened the way for the jeans revolution. In 1949 there were 'dungarees' or 'western style pants.' No one could ever have foreseen the effect these pants would have on future fashion. If they had, probably every design house would have dropped everything and geared up for production. Now we have high fashion jeans and poor Levi Strauss must be twirling in his grave at the sexy image.

It was the young Christian Dior who created consternation with his New Look in 1947. It was introduced in Paris and was not an immediate sensation. It was distinctly feminine in feeling, a rounded look, and Dior dropped the hemline with a thud heard round the world. The shoulder was rounded and the small waistline emphasized. The fashion permeated every segment of society and the tiny flowered hats sporting veils, or the veils on frames, are now eagerly sought after. They are very flattering, are well made, and many have survived. Hat collectors adore them, they take less space than older hats and come in a wide variety. They can still be worn with confidence, since they coordinate well with almost any costume, and are still inexpensive.

This was the time of matching the color of the gloves with the outfit, and if ever there is an underrated collecting field it is gloves. Fortunately the gloves of the 40's seem to have spurred many young people to buy them and care for them and I know of several good collections. It's amazing how few collectors look for them. They are often in beautiful shades of colors, and may have embroidery, or have the hand-tied French knots. The soft kid gloves of the 40's are especially fine, but prices on these have made substantial gains, possibly because people are impressed with the 'Made in France' label many of them carry. The gauntlet type have a distinctive look and the wrist length, or the long evening gloves with the little pearl buttons have often sold to those interested in jewelry or buttons. I wonder how many gloves have been sacrificed this way?

The dedicated clothing collector should keep in mind that while the great designers were providing fashion to the wealthy, America's off-the-rack capability was the finest in the world. Indeed it was not until the very late 1950's that Europe tried this way of merchandising, so most of the clothing available to us was probably bought off-the-rack and does not bear the great designer labels. If one were to find dresses with a Hattie Carnagie or Adrian label it would be a tremendous acquisition, but excellent copies, or New York's 7th Avenue originals are what we are most apt to add to our collections. Haute Couture boasts intricate and clever tailoring which flatters the figure and thus can command astronomical prices, but surely part of the price is paying for the label. Still, Paris was calling the tune.

When Dior decreed skirts should rise only 12 or 15 inches off the ground, women everywhere responded and discarded whole wardrobes in order to conform. The new dress code required high heels so the shoe image changed from the clunky, somewhat awkward footwear of the earlier 40's to the slimmer heel. This is an interesting period in shoes, the toes being rounded but blunted. It is difficult to visualize a collection of shoes, but having viewed one properly set out, is to become a convert.

The really wonderful aspect of Dior and his 'New Look' is that we do not have to wade through transitional clothing, the whole world knows, almost precisely to the minute, when Dior announced his new style. This circumstance is unique to clothing collectors and we should be properly grateful. We also know exactly when the fashion ended, by 1949 the style was phasing out and hemlines rose and the silhouette became less flaring. We who collect, or deal in clothing, can thank Dior for making the 1940's so exciting for us.

Seeking the couturier clothing involves some canny planning. Often the best source is the thrift shops maintained by women's auxiliaries whose members claim some social standing. If their social life is busy and requires much formal wear, they will often donate their outdated wardrobes to the thrift shops to which they volunteer. Recently, such a shop, a tiny one, in Westchester County, New York, boasted dresses by Norell and Mary Quant, and labels such as Saks 5th Avenue, Marshall Field and Lilli Ann. These were all day dresses, all of 40's and 50's vintage, and all together would have cost less than $50. Each of them a great addition to any collection.

The truth is that superior tailoring does not easily become dated, and often you will find women wearing couturier clothing made years ago. It is largely a revolutionary style, such as the 'New Look' which demands an entirely new wardrobe to keep in fashion. Nowadays we tend to ignore such a dictum from the arbiters of fashion and independence in dress is following independence in action.

So it is wise to track down shops run by organizations such as the Junior League, famous hospital auxiliaries and annual benefit auctions and sales put on by groups of socialites to benefit some worthy cause. These annual affairs, which sometimes benefit museums and branches of the arts, are probably some of the more serious places to shop for vintage, high-fashion clothing.

To do this, the collector has to read the newspapers diligently to keep aware of the upcoming sales. Some organizations will put you on their mailing list for occasions of this kind and if it is possible, request this. Usually clothing at these sales cost very little, since they are essentially high class rummage sales, and you will no doubt find many good buys. It does take time and effort but this can be rewarding.

Resale Shops are often the source of good finds, but tend to be more expensive since they must buy and clean clothing and do any repairing, and must also maintain a good looking shop in order to attract customers.

Goodwill, Salvation Army and St. Vincent de Paul were once treasure troves of older clothing, but their donations are off and competition among collectors who frequent these places is much keener. There are many people who know the exact time of donated merchandise deliveries and manage in that way to secure the goodies. Recently, though, a local St. Vincent de Paul had a remarkable collection of vintage shoes with buckles and bows which were being sold for $5 each pair, and were intended for wear with costumes on Halloween. Goodwill saves some of its better donated vintage clothing for its annual fashion show put on by the Goodwill Bags, but take a look if you're passing, because vintage clothing, like any other antique, is where you find it. But in this field today, you certainly have to keep looking.

Shoe collectors have a more difficult task since shoes have often been discarded as wear and tear make them less acceptable to good dress. There are rising numbers of people who are looking for vintage shoes. Reduced availability and sometimes less than perfect condition makes the search for old shoes discouraging to the faint hearted. The find, though, is well worth the hunt. Shoes of the 1940's are wholly unique. They can be clumsy looking and in no way resemble the footwear of the 1920's or earlier periods. Studious collectors should note that footwear can be categorized by the way the sole is attached to the upper.

American Footwear Industry lists 'cemented' when the sole and heel are attached by adhesion; 'molded' when the sole and heel are formed and the attachment to the upper is accomplished within a mold; 'sewn' is when the sole is attached to the upper by a stitched seam. The old method of nailing sole to upper was considered obsolete, which is a good time judgment for collectors.

Shoe styles have evolved and changed, often quite drastically, and are among the very typical artifacts of a given era. The wedgies of the 40's, the fairly narrow open toes, the tie oxford, are all characteristic.

The bulky look shoe complemented the dirndl dress and the military looking suit was perfect with the oxford. The 'peep toes' were the dress shoe of the day. As a 'go with' to shoe collecting the old wooden shoe forms are ideal. In this area though you compete with the antique collector and the interior decorator, take heart, they can't be everywhere.

With the end of World War II came a lighter look, and the mink stole was worn everywhere except the supermarket. The ubiquitous mink stole of that period has not made the comeback that other vintage furs, such as the silver fox jacket and neckpiece have achieved, but considering the small prices at which these stoles are marked, they are an excellent investment.

The 40's from beginning to end were a special time in America. The red, white and blue color scheme was used in clothing, there were ration cards, nylon hose, when available, was a cause of long lines, the hats are collectible but when worn today are not tilted over the eyebrow as was de rigueur in the 40's, but at a more flattering angle further back on the head.

The 40's was turban time. A classic fashion which has appeared and reappeared in some form, the turban was in part an answer to the demands of safety, to keep hair out of machinery at which women now worked in numbers. They affected snoods and hair nets and they started the passion for pants.

As the 1940's began, fashion direction was uncertain, but people in general were becoming much more casual about dress. This decade really marked the beginning of informality and complete independence from rigid fashion demands.

As the decade ended it became memorable for synthetic fibers, the boxy, square shoulders and the return of the female figure, for boleros and the "New Look". For clothing collectors the indicators of 40's fashions are the smaller hat, the square, padded shoulders, narrow waist. The strapless evening gown, supposedly held up by a prayer, was almost standard. The military influence lent itself to the Eisenhower jacket both for men and women, and pea coats and khaki sportswear remained popular for men.

The years 1940 to 1950 are one of the strongest in the clothing collecting field. Several years ago it began to attract young people, both male and female, and the trend continues. No wonder, it seems to have everything a good collection demands, unique styling, short skirts, long skirts, strapless gowns, luxurious furs, coats of many designs, unusual shoes, and lovely handbags. There is very little the collector cannot find from the 40's, to fit his purse and preference. Close your eyes, make a clothing wish, then check out the 1940's.

As the country moved into a new decade we seemed to be searching for security. Conservatism was the new creed. This is especially reflected in the menswear of the early 1950's when the trim, quiet look was in vogue. This was a distinct change from the late 1940's brighter colors. Now dark shades of blue and brown and gray took over the scene. In 1953 the gray flannel suit began its reign.

President Eisenhower refused to bow to tradition at his inauguration in 1953 when he chose to wear a jacket with his striped trousers and a homburg instead of the usual top hat and cutaway. Looking back on his decision, it seems merely the choice of a man who wanted more informality, a less rigid way of dealing with ordinary affairs. In reality, it was a ripple on the surface of what was to become almost a full scale revolt by the young. It was a forerunner of entirely new directions both in clothing and lifestyle, and Elvis Presley was waiting in the wings with his Levis and suede shoes.

The second World War emancipated everyone, and fashion was on the way to becoming anything anyone wanted it to be. If the early 50's had any typical characteristics it was probably the normal waistline, narrow slim skirts at midcalf which were soon to shorten again. The A line which Dior ordained in 1958 had a very wide skirt draped from sloping shoulders, and the skirt just below the knee. As the 50's progressed so did the skirt, upward.

This was generally a period of transition when almost anything was acceptable. Some of the full skirts of the 40's persisted into the early fifties. The long fitted bodice of 1954 and 1955 emphasized a beautiful figure. The focus was on the neckline and hipline, and dresses were usually worn with the pointed shoe with high slender heels. Heels on the shoes became even higher before the end of the decade. They were considered a menace and were decried by promoters of good posture.

The bustline was accentuated, the waistline was high, and the strapless evening gown was still being worn by the end of 1958. Knitwear, especially the Chanel style jacketed dress and suit became classic and went easily from office to cocktails. The pillbox hat was sitting pertly on most female heads, but with the modified cloche hats, organza veilings, very tiny hats, wide brimmed hats, headbands, small feather confections, the hat collector can have a field day with the 50's.

Recently, while I was browsing in a small vintage clothing shop, an elderly lady approached me in a state of high excitement. "Look at this," she exclaimed, holding up a rather nondescript gray straw hat, "this is a Dior, look at the label." I did. It surely was a Dior, if rather faded, and since she explained she was a hat collector I could understand her exuberance. The label itself was large and striking, it was a vintange hat, and the price was not very high, and no doubt she felt she had a bargain. I would have recommended perhaps, a hat bearing no label, which sat on a nearby stand and was of the same vintage — a small, crescent shape with a mesh veil, flowers on the crown and a velvet ribbon flat bow, an enticing affair and costing just a bit less. There was that label, though, and we collectors have to make our choices. Vintage clothing bearing designer labels will usually cost more. "Snob appeal", one dealer says.

This is not true for shoe collectors, the label does not make the shoe, except for a few outstanding makers and the mark of an exclusive shoe store. Most dealers price according to condition and era. Collectors who buy also to wear are concerned with fit, and this is a frustrating situation. The 50's shoes are fairly easy to find, although here again, their appeal to younger collectors causes the fine examples to sell quickly. These very high, slender heels are more difficult to find, the styles without sides or cut deeply on the sides are very flattering to the foot, but the smallish, open toes are the big goal. The alligator and lizard skin shoes and handbags of this era are intrinsically valuable but condition should be good. Many closets still harbor shoes of this period.

Budget conscious collectors should visit their thrift shops more often. In a recent tour I found large numbers of the 50's coats. These were unusually attractive, especially in the late 50's. Dior (the man did everything) had introduced his A line with its wide hemline and narrow shoulders and these are found frequently. The tie neckline also is a very pretty style. There are also the very typical three quarter length coats and the shortie coats with the belt in the back. Another attractive coat from that period has the shawl collar and narrow hem which is often furred. People who buy and wear these coats profess to admire their 'old fashioned' look. People who buy them as a collectible have found a veritable gold mine.

The sheath was the big news in the 50's and in keeping with the times it was an easy and comfortable style. Women were seen everywhere in the narrow but unconfining dress. Capri pants and the skirts — circle skirts, were wide and often stiffened. The total ensemble was usually skirt and blouse or capri pants, or skirt with sweater or blouse. Handbags were casual and that was the attraction of the shoulder bag.

Handbags are a joy to collect. Not as pretty as the beaded bags or as intricately worked as the tapestries, not as spectacular as the best of the art deco, the 50's handbags have a special place. They often have unusual handles of metal, leather or plastic. Reptile skin was commonly used and some women were still carrying the corde.

As always with pocketbooks or purses, shapes are quite varied, and it is often the handles that lend interest. It is almost a cliche to say that fashion comes full circle every generation, but there is ample proof that this is true. Several times recently I have used a heavy leather shoulder bag from the 50's. It is finely made and has a heavy gilt closure. It is large enough to hold all the necessities and it still strikes a fashion note. There is a timelessness about some things and good leather, simply worked, is one. Except for the wide, braided shoulder strap which was used frequently on bags of this type in the 50's, only the most sophisticated fashion critic could date the bag.

Gifts for the men in the years of the early 50's included a Shaefer "snorkel fountain pen", which would be a great find; or a yellow and black striped Italian denim butler's jacket, which would be useful if you wanted to impress guests; and waterproof deerskin slippers with foam rubber lining, at $12.50 a pair.

Ski parkas were being touted in bright colors and 'warmly lined for warmth'.

Clear plastic umbrellas cheered the rainy days, and a wool jersey scarf lined in hand printed silk was the offering from 'Vera'. Today a complete and very thorough collection of scarves by 'Vera' could easily be made, they seem to turn up everywhere.

Mother and Daughter dresses were popular. A charming collection this would be — the adult's dress and the matching child's dress displayed side by side. Almost like collecting in pairs, the large and the miniature. To date,

I have found only two such pairs and they are in a private collection. Should a person happen on a set and the dealer would be foolish enough to break it up, don't hesitate, buy both. Not only were they eye-catching in their day, and interesting to us today, but think of the future and how unusual the matching pieces will be.

Hats of both mother and daughter often matched too, but it is almost too much to expect that four such articles will be found intact. Still, it's intriguing and cries out for a determined collector. Someone with an eye for the unusual. It is these fads which sustain popularity for awhile and then disappear which sometimes become the basis for the most valuable collections.

Plisse was an oft-heard name in the early 50's, but we don't hear it too much anymore. It is cotton, with a crinkle effect and usually patterned. It was 'easy iron' and was widely used in nightwear and some of the nightgowns from which it was made, are attractive enough to be worn for summer evening wear. Many plisse garments are striped or have small prints and almost all are very pretty. When some young collector decides this is the case, you may see a brightly colored plisse printed nightgown of the 1950's doing double duty.

With the variety of fabrics available in the 1950's, it is probably safe to say that lingerie could be made of almost any material. It is also safe to say that it was exceedingly lovely for the most part. The shortie nightie which ended just below the knee sometimes had tiny sleeves or cape effects and touches of lace and ribbon which made for a dainty, delightful morsel. The colors, petal pink, or heaven blue, or even buttercup are delectable. Longer gowns were also worn, many of them made of nylon tricot which boasted the same 'easy care'. Nylon is a high-strength, resilient synthetic, so many survive today. This is a great time to collect these pretty things including the full underslips and the handy half slips which have wide lace trim.

Barbizon was the big name in lingerie if you are label conscious, but there were many manufacturers producing beautiful underwear. Some of the fancy slips are made in the gored fashion which prevented bunching at the waist. They were expertly tailored and make a wonderful collection. It was one of the best of times for women's undergarments and before these get away from us we should make every effort to include them in our collections. They require little care and make a colorful display.

The undergarments fitted well under the clothing. One of the most delightful of fashions in the 50's was the two piece suit, jacket and skirt, in rayon gabardine. The jacket was short, with a flare and a Peter Pan collar with double rows of buttons, the skirt was straight and fairly narrow. It was one of those outfits which went everywhere, and I have seen several similar outfits lately, so it must have been a big seller. It was practical, maybe that's why. Women were losing their zest for using a different garment for every occasion and a dress that went through the day was a plus. With this two piece suit the whole look could be changed with a new sweater or blouse and with the jacket left open.

Dolman sleeves were still being worn in the 50's and the loose, and longish sweater often had them. The Dolman sleeve is one of the most comfortable ever devised, so it's easy to see that we have moved even deeper into our desire for ease and practicality in clothes.

The Italian fashion collections became very important and without doubt they had a flair for color and design which began to take the lead in certain directions. They introduced innovative ski wear and magnificent shoe style. It wasn't the Italians, though, who created a sensation in the tennis world. It was Ted Tinling who dressed Gussie Moran in lace trimmed panties which caused a furor. She played at Wimbledon in 1949, and those panties banished forever the image of the staid and proper tennis buff.

A small development really, that Moran outfit, completely modest by today's standards, but it led to a new fashion standard for tennis players and more enjoyment for fans. One reporter maintained that people were going to watch tennis when Gussie played only to see what she would wear.

Tennis gear is collectible on all levels, the tennis wear itself is an excellent collectible because it did not change much until 1949. Since that time it has become as varied as one could want. The dresses were usually white, one piece and belted and pleated. By the 40's the one piece dress was shorter, and soon the outfit became two pieces. Tennis dresses are distinctive and to a sportsminded person would present an exciting challenge. I do not know anyone with such a collection so it has a relatively open future. As with anything that has not yet really caught on, prices should be minimal.

Many things from the 50's are ideal collectibles. The eyeglasses are strictly for fun and profit. Rhinestones or brilliants were set into plastic frames which were called 'harlequin' and looked like a giant butterfly. Until about 1984, these could be bought for a dollar or two anywhere, now they are commanding prices of $25-65 depending on their amount of decoration and how bizarre they are. Women are wearing them and there is a trend to buy a pair and replace the lenses with your own prescription. They are certainly conversation pieces. These wild spectacles did not much influence men's eye wear, they were still sporting the horn rims.

There is much to commend the 1950's as a collecting field, but for many it is still too close.

Designers appreciate it and many adaptations of the 40's and 50's styles are evident in the new clothing.

The 1950's are a closed chapter which many of us remember vividly, and that makes it easy to dismiss the 50's as yet too recent to be considered vintage fashion. The collecting world has become so competitive and unpredictable that it is almost dangerous to discard anything made yesterday.

On that note, the 1950's seem akin to the dinosaur age. Much of the clothing has not yet come out of the closet, and thrifty women everywhere have saved a quantity of it, now hanging neatly all in a row and never worn. Yet they cannot part with it.

When more of it comes into the marketplace, potential collectors will be surprised at its beauty, its charm or its whimsy, depending on the mood.

Collecting is largely a point of view. From the vantage point of 1995, it may be difficult to keep the 1950's in perspective. Try — the fashions of those years may bring big rewards.

1960

A peek into the 1960's should send collectors scurrying about to try to amass a collection of that decade's most controversial style — the mini skirt. It looked great on young, long-stemmed American beauties, on all others it was an abomination.

Mary Quant evoked it, and has been quoted as saying that she felt at the time that the 1960's needed "a revolution" and frankly admits that it was intended as a fashion for the young. In fact, it seems to have been an acknowledgement that young people were a major market, they had plenty of money to spend and were more than willing to spend it.

There were other styles and other happenings during the following years, there are other clothes and other accessories to search for, but at this time, before they disappear, the collector should be alert to the mini.

Fifty years from now the uninitiated are going to look at all those minis and think, Gosh, people were short in the 1960's.

Everyday or house dress of 1942. Printed percale coat frock, modified torso style with white binding trim on yoke and pockets, square padded shoulders. Value $35-50.

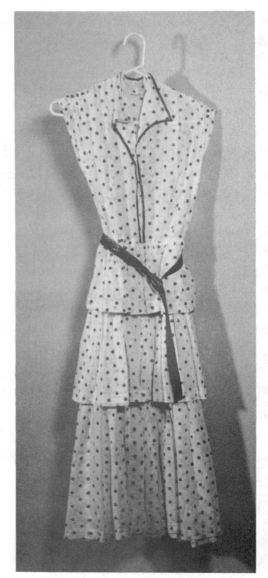

Two piece jacket dress, self cuffs, raglan sleeves, sateen. C. 1944. Value $140-165.

1940s white organdy, with red dots, three tiers, red binding trim. Red belt. Value $75-95.

Left: Tan flannel dress with asymetrical button closing on waist. Tucks, collarless, square padded shoulders, bracelet length sleeves. Shoes are the well remembered loafers. Dress 50-65.

Center: Another three piece suit. The suit is blue and white check, matching coat of solid blue. Nipped in waist and wide shoulders distinguish the suit, the coat has a boxy look. Value of 3 pieces $150-185.

Right: Purple crepe dress with square neckline, padded shoulders, elongated tucks at waistline, belted in self material. Worn with black wrist length gloves and the hat with the popular front large standing bow with veil which is so typical of the period. The pageboy hairdo was well suited to these hats. Value of dress $60-75

Another deceptively simple looking dress of the 40s. It is black crepe and black taffeta with a large bow at the neckline. Long waisted and mid calf length it molds the figure in a provocative way. 3/4 length sleeve. Although this dress bears no label it was bought in Lord & Taylor's, New York. Worn in 1942 with black suede pumps. Value of dress $225-295.

This beautifully crafted tissue-taffeta blue-green dress of the 1940s displays all the qualities which are making the clothing of this era so collectible. The zippered front closing is carefully hidden beneath the fly which lies perfectly flat, the Peter Pan collar is covered with small white beads, the waistline is long and fitted to the hips and over all while this dress would seem to have a distinctly demure look, it is in fact quite seductive on the right figure. Mid calf length. Value $250-325.

1950s dark brown faille dress with self cabbage roses on shoulders. Cap sleeves, belted. Skirt falls just below knee. The attention to detail in 'off the rack' clothing of the 40s and 50s is often meticulous and to today's new collectors rather unexpected. Value of dress $175-225. The brown lizard shoes have very high heels.

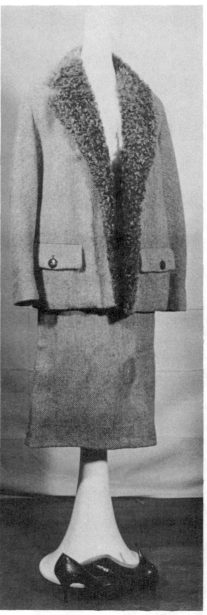

Turquoise faille, empire style, full skirted dress of the 40s. Plastic buttons, V neck. Ann Fogarty label. Value $225-300. The greenish-blue enamel necklace of the 1930s blends perfectly with the dress.

Two piece outfit from the 1940's. Quilted blue midi length skirt worn with Lilli Ann of San Francisco jacket, dark blue textured wool accented with white bead work on collar and on the wide cuffed sleeves. Skirt, value $65-95. Jacket, value $65-100. Model is wearing a snood

A classic Chanel type suit of brown tweed with brown caracul fur collar which runs down to waist. 1950s. Still wearable and in perfect taste for almost any but the most formal occasion. Value $250-325.

The silhouette of 1949. Two piece dress, double breasted with large self-covered buttons, gauntlet cuffs, wide revers and standing collar. Very wide, circular skirt. Gorgeous and eminently flattering to the wearer. Silk and worsted combination. Value $200-300.

In 1948 dresses were longer, fur pieces were still very much in evidence, veils and the same high front decorations were visible on the hats, gauntlet gloves were popular and the suit continued fashionable. Wool with gabardine, beautifully tailored, simple lines, nipped-in waist, small double collar, straight skirt. Value of this wonderful suit, $250-295.

Although we all like to think in terms of couturier fashions the fact is that most everyday wear requires sturdy, comfortable shoes and clothing. In 1944 the suits were a bit looser, this is left unbuttoned at the waist, the skirt was fuller, but the handbag and furpiece dressed up the rather mundane outfit. The shade of green is a plus, being very attractive and the matching hat lends a festive touch. The shoes are arch supported and obviously ready for this traveler who is probably off to a club meeting or luncheon in town. Value of suit $45-65; Shoes $8-12, this hat which is rather interesting should have a starting price of $12, but hats prices are more and more depending on labels.

241

A two-piece taffeta dress with short jacket and back bow interest. Full skirt, thoroughly typical of dresses of 1949. Value $195-250.

A nautical look wool flannel dress with a bow tie, dickey top and sleeve edges of linen-like rayon, fitted bodice to hipline and a box pleated skirt. The back has a row of glitter buttons. Value $45-50.

A Princess dress of wool flannel has flare-away skirt with vertical gores. High neckline, long back zipper. Value $45-50.

An orlon-wool blend jersey dress with a rolled standup collar over a front stitched yoke bodice. Accordion pleated skirt and a self belt. Emerald green. Value $45-50.

The fiftie's clothing had a somewhat romantic look as these glamorous dresses prove. An acetate flower-strewn print, the differently shaped cummerbund narrows the waist and ends in a large back bow. The billowing skirt is interlined with nylon net. Dress is lined with acetate taffeta. Value $45-65. A cotton velveteen in Princess style. Bateau neckline, gored skirt, draped back cowl falls from the neckline over a low scooped neckline. Red. Value $45-65.

This lustrous brocade of cotton and rayon has brief sleeve caps, with a smooth fitting bodice scooped high in front, then V'd in back. The big satin bow rests just below the waist, caught front and center with a rhinestone button tab. Back zipper. This one dress personifies the way we remember the glamour dresses of the 1950s. There are many still out there, waiting to be bought at giveaway prices. They can be stunning and the best of this era should be picked up now. Value $35-55.

Sapphire blue cotton velveteen has a flattering scoop neckline and a midriff circled with matching satin bands. Unpressed pleated skirt, back zipper. The model carries a muff. A muff in 1958? Indeed yes, and she looks quite elegant. This lovely dress is valued at $45-65.

242

Knits were popular in the late 1950s. They travelled well (still do) looked trim and were easy care. Left: Ban-Lon with a bulky look, center is Arnel Triacetate. (Have you asked for anything in Arnel Triacetate at Saks Fifth lately?) Upper right a tightly knit cotton 3 piece 'travel suit', lower right another travel suit of cotton knit. All of these have the slim skirts and shorter jackets. Value of any good knit suit of these years should be $30-40.

The ubiquitous cardigan was popular in the 1950s as well as every other year you can think of. This green banlon textured nylon is fully washable and non-wrinkle. It has a matching short sleeved top of the same material. This skirt is 'stem slim' wool flannel with a side cluster pleat. These sweater sets could be teamed with the tapered leg, front pleated slacks, or any of the skirts of the same period such as this box pleat wool flannel in muted plaid; a pencil slim wool flannel skirt with a back kick pleat and a self belt or the wool flannel kick pleat 'arrowhead' motif. Front pocket. Willow green. Value of skirts - $15-20, slacks $15-20, cardigan set $20-30.

A wonderful grouping of 50's fashions.

Wool tweed, cape collared with a removable dickey, Skirt is lined and has a concealed zipper, Gray.

Wool and worsted crepe dress. Soft blouse with a glitter button holding the tab. Self buttons close in back. Lined. Pine green $25-40.

Wool and rayon combination boucle weave sheath with a colorful jacket. $30-35. Sheath is gray.

Wool, nylon and rabbit hair combine to fashion this really elegant dress. The bow below the midriff, the skirt has unpressed front pleating, and lovely neckline make this very chic. Beige $40-45.

Wool and worsted crepe Princess dress. The neckline and sleeves are piped in satin. Royal blue, the pin is part of the original outfit. $40-45.

Remember the duster? A very handy garment, very comfortable and easy to care for. They were made primarily of cotton in various sparkling prints, checks and stripes either lightweight for summer or heavier material for winter. They are still available and still reasonable and still useful. Dusters were usually 45" long, some were trimmed in lace, others were tailored. All are collectible now. Value of any of these $20-40.

We tend to forget the fashion statements of the near past. So it is with the 1950s although there are certainly signs of collector stirring. The formals of 1958-1959 are really lovely. The models here show the typical formal dresses in a variety of colors and styles of the period. A very good cross section.

Top: Floor length 100% sheer nylon Jersey topped with a cotton lace jacket. Remove the jacket and the dress shows a scooped neckline back and front and rhinestone studded straps. The waist shows a shirred midriff. This has a billowing skirt with a nylon net underskirt. Shrimp pink. This dress also could be bought in a ballerina length. Value $50-125.

This sheer nylon jersey looks like chiffon. A rhinestone pin nestles at the draped bodice, Shirred midriff, V neckline, back zipper, flowing skirt over nylon net. Also came in ballerina length. $50-125.

This dress was designed for 'juniors'. Delicately patterned nylon acetate lace floats over rustling acetate taffeta. Molded bodice with tiny cap sleeves.

The neckline is scooped in front. V'd in back. Ruffled nylon underskirt and acetate satin cummerbund. The stiffened hemline emphasizes the "stand away" skirt. Value $60-145.

1946. These contrasting skirt and blouse outfits were sometimes referred to as 'plaid and plain'. Cotton and rayon-linen, they were cool and easy to keep for summer. Value $50-75.

The fleecy wool short coat was a style that went over everything and could be worn for years and years. Women who wore these in the 1940's and still own them can be seen wearing them on a given summer evening. White. Value $65-75.

Another jacket dress of 1949. Wool and worsted suit in hunting green. This is 2 piece with the jacket covering a collarless dress. Value $150-200.

One of the biggest fashion notes of the 1940's was the ladies' three piece suit, the coat matched the suit or was in a contrasting color. This navy blue 3-piecer has the 3/4 length coat which is a very flattering coat length on some figures. Wool, the suit is collarless. Value of 3 pieces $195-250.

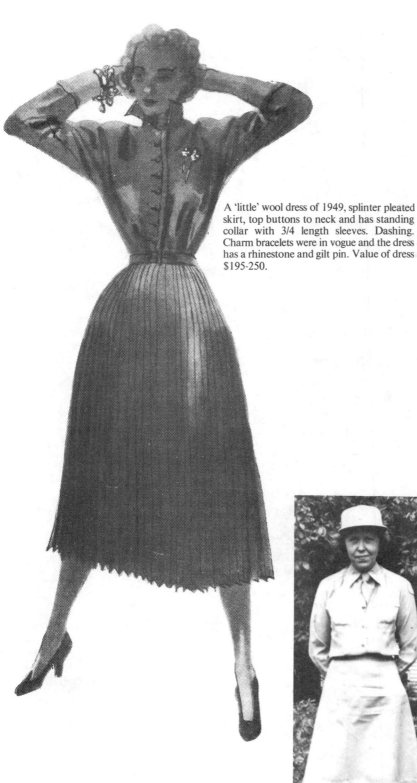

A 'little' wool dress of 1949, splinter pleated skirt, top buttons to neck and has standing collar with 3/4 length sleeves. Dashing. Charm bracelets were in vogue and the dress has a rhinestone and gilt pin. Value of dress $195-250.

1944. Blue wool coat, fitted, white fox collar, $250-325. Brown felt envelope handbag, satin lined, brass engraved triangle on flap, $100-145. Brown brimmed felt cloche hat, $50-65. (WW II) military uniform, jacket with decorations, $135-150. Complete uniform, $185-225.

WOMEN'S ARMY CORP. UNIFORM, WWII, 1945. This WAC uniform is cotton khaki, standard army issue-skirt, blouse, tie and hat. Uniform jacket not shown. The shoes are standard brown oxfords. This WAC served as a supply sergeant in the Philippines. The complete uniform has been donated to the Smithsonian Institution.

The still popular silver fox jacket, c. 1941. Value, $650-750. Black satin evening dress, c. 1935. Value $350-500. Satin shoes, worn originally with the dress shown, buckles are part of shoe itself, $150-195 (shoes).

1940's dress. Black crepe with peplum and sleeves trimmed in sequins. Accessories include black cotton cut-worked embroidered gloves, sequined hat with feather, snood and a stole of four stone martins. Values: dress, $110-120; fur piece, $200-225; gloves, $15-20; hat, $40-45.

1940's dress of brown crepe with beige flowers, low waistline drape ends on left side. Mid calf length. Value $135-195. Worn with beige and bone kid shoes which have an ankle strap. Beige straw hat with wide brim by Mr. John. Value of hat $50-85. Stone marten fur scarf $250-275.

Full length wool coat with classic white fox collar; brown with bands of contrasting darker brown. C. 1950. Value $750-850.

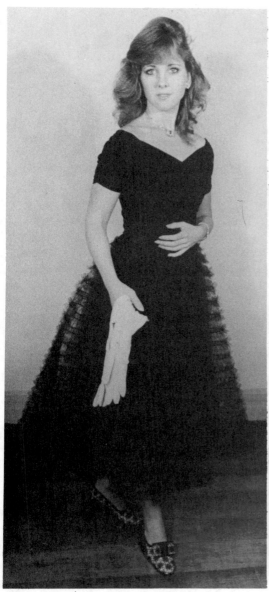

Black crepe mid-calf length dress, V-neck, belted. c. 1949, black satin shoes with self bows, original to the costume. Double strand pearl choker, pink. Values: dress, $175-225; shoes, $60-80.

Cocktail dress, 1945. Black crepe top, V-off the shoulder neck, ruffled tiers of black net over taffeta skirt. Net and embroidered see-through shoes. Value, dress, $175-225; shoes, $45-65.

1950. Light pink strapless taffeta evening gown with large bow accenting one shoulder. Full skirt lined with a stiffened attached slip. Value, $150-195.

Below: Mainbocher short evening dress, c. 1955 of black broderie anglaise over black net, with boat neckline, fitted bodice and full skirt, appliqued up the center with a black satin band curving to form a second shoulder strap on the left with black cotton and net slip. Label: Mainbocher, Inc. The value of this dress should be in the $850-1250 range but the dress brought less at the recent Ruth Gordon auction at Doyle Galleries in New York. This is what motivates collectors, the bargains which consistently occur in this still undercollected field. Pre-auction estimate of this dress was $200-300. The 1950's really fine garments are just beginning to come into their own.

Above: Blue cotton lace with attached taffeta underslip. Cocktail or 'Mother-of-the-Bride' dress. 1952. Tasteful, small rhinestone patterns on collar. Value, $175-195. Blue gray kid shoes, worn with dress originally. Value $40-50.

A spectacular formal cocktail dress from Frederick's of Hollywood, 1958-1959. Silver lame with wide black taffeta ruffle on skirt, large black taffeta rose on left side above hemline. Value $300-350.

250

Above: Mainbocher cocktail dress, 1960's of deep blue velvet-cut-to-satin, the sleeveless dress with a slightly gathered skirt, no label. Value $200-275. The future of dresses of this quality is unlimited.

Above: Chanel cocktail dress, late 1950's, early 1960s, of minutely tucked black chiffon with bootlace straps and fitted midriff of black satin, skirt stiffened with horsehair at the hem to flare out in a pleated ruffle. Label: Chanel $1,000-1,500.

Mainbocher evening dress, c. 1955. Pale mint green silk chiffon over aquamarine tulle, with halter bodice and full skirt, the bodice trimmed with ball-edged satin ribbon in pink over yellow and with an ornament pin of green and turquoise jewels. Label 'Mainbocher, Inc.' Value $600-850.

Pink gabardine two-piece suit. Jacket was high necked collar, corded bows, and rhinestone buttons, and is lined with crepe. These suits from the 1940s are so well tailored and fitted they were almost a uniform and they did almost every wearer proud. For the most part, in some mysterious way that style seemed to 'suit' everybody. Value $200-250. The hat is a soft grey felt with pink taffeta trim, and a green rhinestone buckle. Value $30-40.

Sundress with jacket of printed waffle pique in the "Nantucket Harbor" pattern. Waffle pique was an enormously popular fabric. Its texture makes it a tactile pleasure. This dress has a scoop neck and all is trimmed in brown with brown spaghetti straps under the tight, short, over the shoulder bolero jacket. This little bolero comes to a point and reaches to the midriff in back. These little dresses have to be acquired with alacrity because as with most everyday wear, they tend to be ignored, discarded and they simply disappear. Value $45-65. The model sports a ponytail, carries a brown quilted boxy purse $15-25, spike heeled sandals. Late 1950s.

When beaded dresses are mentioned, all thoughts turn to the 1920s. But other years and other styles also featured beads and beads and beads regardless of vintage and aside from the clothing itself beads and beadwork are becoming a major collecting field so any beaded dress should be bought when found and preserved. This beaded black silk velvet dress is from 1955 but it is strongly reminiscent of the 1930s, as if the designer went back to those glamorous fashion years for inspiration. The neckline and front panel of this cocktail dress in intricately beaded with black bugle and strand beads. Capped sleeves. Zipper is located on the side up under one arm. Bottom is flounced. Shades of 1816. Flouncing is a wonderful device, it attracts attention to body movement, gives a garment a flowing look without a lot of extra fabric and finishes a hemline in great style. The model wears a matching silk velvet clip hat which fits on the back of the head with side swirls of matching beading to the dress. This outfit is outstanding. Dress $300-400, 1955.

Hat $55-75. The model carries a lucite rhinestone-studded box handbag and has a pearlized compact and mother-of-pearl lipstick in her hand. These accessories are extremely collectible and expensive today. The purse is valued at $150-200 and already large collections of these have been made.

A classic tailored gray heather wool 2-piece suit. Made by Kolmer, lined with crepe. Accessories include a blue velvet clip hat, blue gloves and blue suede shoes and purse. We were much more coordinated fashion wise in those days and it worked well, when done tastefully the look was neat, elegant, fashionable and often even in daywear, glamorous. This suit was worn by the model's mother at her high school graduation. 1950s. Value $65-100.

An exciting black taffeta formal. Tight fitted bodice is low-cut to the shirred beige satin cummerbund. The sleeves are tight and darted at the elbow to allow freer movement. The full swirling skirt is graced by two large slit pockets which are sewn to the outside of the gown and lined in the beige satin. 1950s. The 1950s are a fast moving collectible period and gowns of this excellence will grace any collection. Value $250-300. She wears crystal jewelry, a draped black velvet evening turban and clear lucite evening shoes adorned with a large rhinestone ornament on the vamp. Turban $75-95.

A late 1950s heavily corded dress in black cotton. Sleeveless and belted. An unusual design, the dress is overall swirled with heavy cording. A very effective dress, shorter than fashion decrees now but the owner still wears it occasionally. Lined with silk. Good quality $50-60.

An interesting dress from the late 1950s. It is charcoal gray, sleeveless and has bands of fine white beads which at first glance look like fringe. The accompanying wide scarf or shawl is also banded with these same small white beads and has a large pocket on each side. Value $50-60.

The short fitted and contoured jacket dress of the 1942-43 period hugged the hips and nipped the waistline. The fashions of this period were ultra feminine and flattering to the figure. This is blue, with silver trim, Peter Pan collar and bracelet length sleeves. Jacket value $15-20; Dress $40-50.

Formal dress. Blue floor length sheath with a short bolero type jacket which has metallic thread embroidery and long sleeves. A simple but effective gown. Probably 1950s. Value $250-400.

Top, L to R:

An Italian tweed of rayon, wool and nylon with a straight jacket with a club collar, simulated pockets, the lining is acetate rayon taffeta. Slender skirt has a back walking pleat. Black and white.

This is a 'dream suit' of reprocessed wool and nylon with a collar of imported black Italian lamb. The jacket is boxy with a Peter Pan undercollar, sleeves which can be pushed up, and novel side tabs. Slim, back pleated skirt. Blue.

A boucle type tweed suit with a short casual jacket. Big buttons. Rust colored.

Bottom, L to R:

This suit is ribbed wool on cotton backing. Shawl collar of black Italian lamb. This fur is sewed to the undercollar. Jacket is lined with rayon pile. Slim skirt. Red.

The 'station wagon suit'. Three pieces to mix and match. Topper-like jacket of suede finish. Camel colored.

Deep shawl collar of raccoon on this 'car coat' suit. Velvety cotton wale corduroy, box jacket, 30" long. Matching skirt but jacket can be worn with almost anything. All these suits date from 1959 and each would be priced at $40-50 in today's unappreciative world.

The back interest of the 1930's (which has never entirely gone out of style) continued to some degree into the 40's. In 1945 this sophisticated lady was wearing black with halter neck and low cut back accentuated with a large satin ribbon bow at the waist. The dress is fully draped in the back, rather straight in front. A stunning garment. Value in silk chiffon $600-750. Worn with long kid gloves.

Strapless gown of 1952. These are now in the category fast approaching the beaded dresses of the 1920's. Although almost every prom saw a profusion of these in the 40's and early 50's many must still be in the closet. Much depends on the material, tailoring, trim and general effect but the more extravagant such as this commands $350-450. Every collector should be alert to the strapless evening gown that dominated evening fashions for so long.

Formal wedding gown, 1951. Candlelight satin, appliqued leaves and seed pearls at neck. Train. Saks 5th Ave. Value $1500-2000.
The lace veil is the same as that worn by the 1928 bride shown on pg. 211. This illustrates the nature of Vintage Clothing collecting as its heirloom potential.

Lingerie, 1940. Nightgown and bedjacket of rayon crepe in a floral pattern. Maize and white. Original Bennington label, a manufacturer of fine lingerie. Value of set, $150-175. These have been known to be worn as formals.

A rayon nightgown with lacey bodice, bare midriff and lace 'cocktail' bottom. Value $75-125. 1948 name of this fashion was "Diversion".

Mother and Daughter play outfits of 1946. These could be worn for sunning, or at the beach, to play in, even as pajamas. Sanforized combed cotton, small prints of kittens. Pink. Adult size $35-45. Child's size either one piece or two pieces $30-35.

Pajamas with matching scuffs of 1949. Cotton broadcloth, coat could be used as a 'brunchie', striped trim on collar and pockets. Scuffs have same trim. Set $50-75 in excellent condition.

Lingerie. Pink pleated nylon nightgown, usually referred to as "Marilyn Monroe" nightwear; turquoise short slip with attached garters, spandex, pleated; value of these is $45-55 each; ivory satin nightgown bias cut, pink embroidered rosebuds on bodice. Long length value $45-65.

Taffeta housecoat of fine houndstooth check with embroidered collar and pockets. Self belting, jet buttons, 3/4 sleeves. Late 1940s. $95-145.

Lingerie. Stretch girdle, 1940s, unworn, attached garters. In 'as new' condition these are a worthwhile addition to a collection and as yet no real surge is on to find them. Value $10-20; silk crepe teddy, 1920s, $85-120. 1920's silk bandeau $55-75, 1940s rayon crepe panties with hand crocheted ornament, value in unworn condition $20-25; gorgeous teddy of silk and lace with satin ribbons. $125-155.

Plain and striped denim mark this outfit of sturdy beach wear. Pedal pushers with wide banded-at-the-waist flared jacket. Pink and white. About 1948. Value of set $25-28.

Playclothes in 1942-43. Full flared shorts with belt, worn with striped cotton top. Set $30-40.

260

A maternity bathing suit of the 1950s, blue cotton with blue and white printed scarf belt. Expansion elastic under front panel. $25-35. Somewhat unusual.

Hemp-tan shorts banded in red. Matching halter and jacket c.1948. Value of set $20-30.

1940s skirted bathing suit. White with green print. Jersey. $25-35, old 'Kleinert' bathing cap. $10-15.

A rather modest bathing suit of the early 1960's, two-piece, polyester. Value $20-25.

The two 1950s half aprons are made of cotton. The small checks and everyday sort of trim is designed to give them a 'homey' look. One in red, one in blue, they are attractive and easy to care for. Still much underpriced at $5-10.

The 'cork clog' was distinctive and uncomfortable yet for a time in the early fifties was a big hit with faddists. These shoes can be found in all colors including yellow, fuschia, kelly green, violet and multi colors and are made of genuine kid or suede. Anyone who loves bizarre shoes (and they are legion) must have a pair of these. Value in excellent condition, $30-35.

1940. Pretty and efficient, the apron should not be underestimated as a clothing collectible. Cotton. In good condition, $10-20.

Shoes are a distinctive indication of any fashion period. These two of 1943 will jog memories because they were extremely popular at the time. The right model was considered equally well tailored for daytime or evening wear while the more mundane oxford tie was strictly a daytime shoe. The saddle stitching was a nice touch. Value in excellent condition, each pair $30-35.

A fancier apron of 1942. Woven dotted swiss in pastel blue. Smocking in deep bands at the waist and pockets. Original cost $1.50. Value $10-20.

These wedge (wedgies) heeled shoes were often very well made and extremely comfortable. This shoe was made in Italy, has a low-slung wedge and is made of hemp net and leather covered cork. Natural colored with a festive bow. Ferragamo. About 1950. Value in excellent condition $20-25.

The shoes of the 1940's are quite distinctive. Toeless and sling back vied with the rounded toe pump. All of these are suede. Value $25-35.

A high heeled, platform shoe of 1948. Black suede trimmed with black satin. Value $30-35.

In 1949 "wedges or wedgies" were the rage. They were advertised as "dramatizing your proportions with the perfect height" although many people considered them ugly. An interesting fashion note nonetheless. Value $35-40.

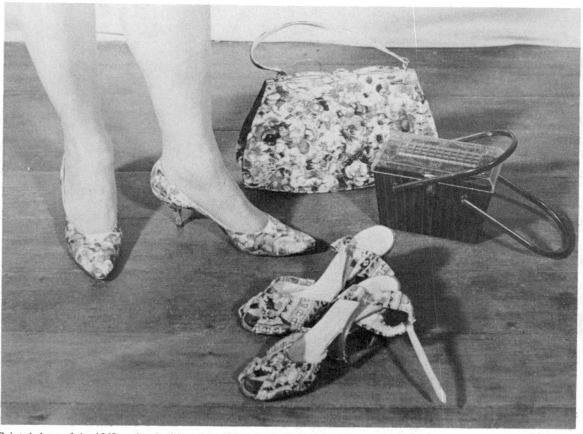

Pointed shoes of the 1960s, printed with multi-colored silk, 2½" heel, $30-35; matching handbag $25-35; Ankle strap printed sandals of the 1940s, 3" heel, $35-50.

263

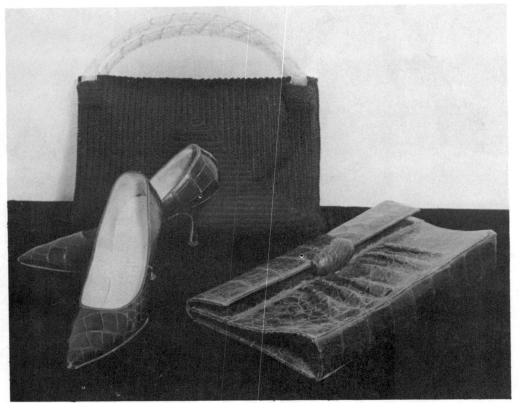

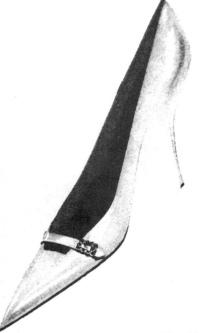

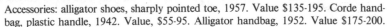

Accessories: alligator shoes, sharply pointed toe, 1957. Value $135-195. Corde handbag, plastic handle, 1942. Value, $55-95. Alligator handbag, 1952. Value $175-200.

The shoe toe in 1959 was almost a stiletto. Kid with buckle trim and spike heels. Value of these is soaring. $40-55.

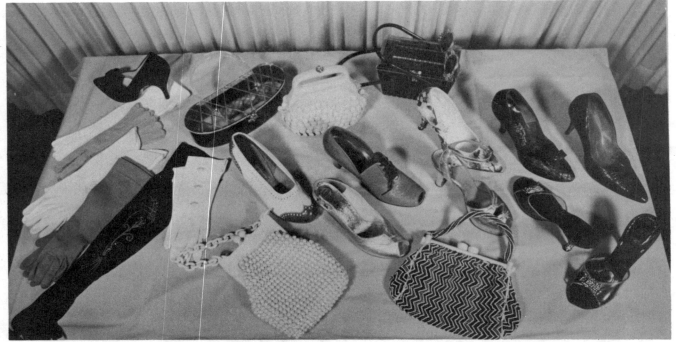

Accessories of 1940-1960. Gloves of various lengths and adornment from this period are remarkably well made and ornamented. They are still very easy to find, quite inexpensive and make a pretty, rather fascinating collectible. Values vary depending on length, material and trim but the long kid gloves with small pearl buttons, the nylon and the crochet are all moving up in price. Starting price is about $5-10 on ordinary types of cotton, $15-25 on others. Now is definitely the time to start searching for the unusually colored, decorated cotton gloves.

Shoes: Black silk with faille bow knot, 1960's, value $15-25; black and white 'spectators'; leather silver sling pumps with open toe; brown leather tie; silver leather ankle strap; 60's print pump; alligator with bow; 1950's lizard pump; lucite with rhinestones embedded into the shoe as well as the entire heel. Shoes are also variable in price, generally begin around $20 for the ordinary types; $45 for the reptile and higher for the well-made rhinestone.

Handbags: left top is purple and clear lucite of the 1940's. These bags are becoming expensive, are often bizarre and are valued at a minimum $35-40. A brown and clear lucite of the 40's; crochet handbag on a yellow plastic frame which embodies the handle. Yellow plastic discs are attached to the crochet, 1950s, $15-20; handbag of crocheted raffia, plastic beads on a crochet base, plastic chain handle $15-20. These bags are charming with a unique look, quite colorful and still available. The bag on the right is 1950's beaded red and white, blue, green on blue rayon. Plastic top and closure $20-25.

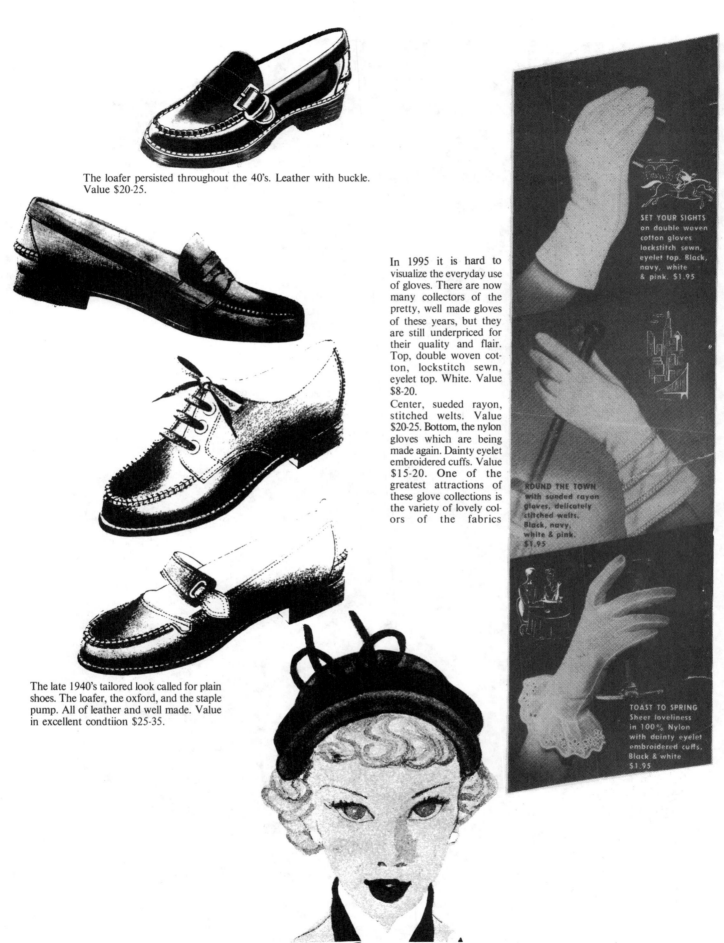

The loafer persisted throughout the 40's. Leather with buckle. Value $20-25.

In 1995 it is hard to visualize the everyday use of gloves. There are now many collectors of the pretty, well made gloves of these years, but they are still underpriced for their quality and flair. Top, double woven cotton, lockstitch sewn, eyelet top. White. Value $8-20.

Center, sueded rayon, stitched welts. Value $20-25. Bottom, the nylon gloves which are being made again. Dainty eyelet embroidered cuffs. Value $15-20. One of the greatest attractions of these glove collections is the variety of lovely colors of the fabrics

The late 1940's tailored look called for plain shoes. The loafer, the oxford, and the staple pump. All of leather and well made. Value in excellent condtiion $25-35.

SET YOUR SIGHTS on double woven cotton gloves lockstitch sewn, eyelet top. Black, navy, white & pink. $1.95

ROUND THE TOWN with sueded rayon gloves, delicately stitched welts. Black, navy, white & pink. $1.95

TOAST TO SPRING Sheer loveliness in 100% Nylon with dainty eyelet embroidered cuffs. Black & white $1.95

The little felt hat, a wardrobe staple. This is 'smooth-as-silk felt' with velvet trim and butterfly bow. 1949. Value $20-30.

The hats of the late 1950s come in a great variety but they do have a distinctive look. Top left is a creased crown cloche of wool felt with a sequin band. $20-25. A deep telescope crown cloche, wool felt brushed to a beaver like finish. Rayon grosgrain ribbon band with a bow. $20-25.

Tucked and shirred cloche. Wood felt with a shiny, mirror like finish. Rayon grosgrain band with a bow. $20-25.

Feathered toque. Feathers cascade over brim of this felt hat. $25-30.

Deep crown cloche with a softly draped crown and stitched brim. Rayon velvet bow. $25-30.

Rayon velvet scalloped shell. Trimmed with shiny nailheads and pearl like ornaments. Mesh veil. $20-25.

Pleated capulet with a rayon velvet crown encircled with pleated rayon grosgrain ribbon. Mock pearl accents. Value $20-25.

Pleated cloche of rayon velvet with double tiers of pleated rayon satin with fringed edge. Satin band, bow. Value $25-30.

Everyone is seeking the bonnets, the huge floral decorated hat, the elegant Edwardian and very few are buying and preserving the hats of the 1950s. They are a great bargain, are well made with good materials and attractive.

Many people are now collecting handkerchiefs commemorating holidays, these two Christmas examples are becoming prime collectibles. Value $18-25 each, top right is a silk English coronation commemorative, value $20-30. A beautiful lace hankie, value $20-30, one of the colorful, print handkerchiefs of the 40s. Value $8-15.

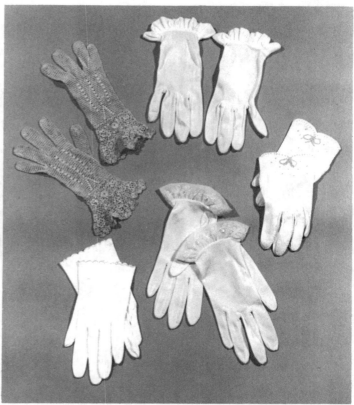

Gloves from the 1940s. While the forties does not seem that long ago to people who lived through them, the wearing of gloves for everyday certainly does seem dated to us now. Which is exactly why they are so collectible. These are all from the 1940s and very early 1950s, clockwise: wrist length cotton with hand stitched accents (value $8-15) elbow length tan cotton (value $15-25) wrist length black nylon with ruffle ($12-18).

A selection of brightly colored 1940s gloves. Clockwise: Pale blue crochet, these are most often found in white (value $15-20) pink nylon with a wrist ruffle (value $7-12) short cotton with pearl and bead trim ($7-15) lavender nylon with embroidered wrist ruffle ($12-18) short white kid with a scalloped edge. Marked MADE IN FRANCE ($20-28)

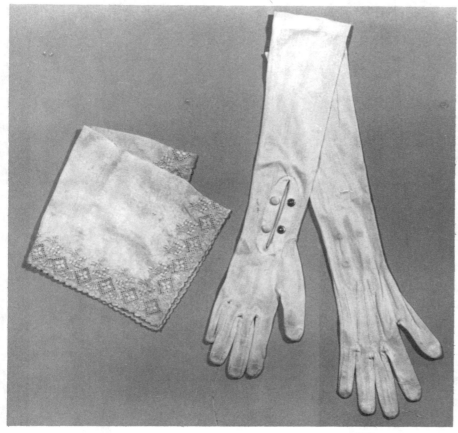

A pure silk Victorian wedding handkerchief. Value $30-40; a pair of silk wedding gloves from the 1940s, obviously worn. Value $20-30.

267

The whole trend in 50's men's clothing was toward the casual. Left, an all rayon gabardine suit worn with a coconut straw hat, suit $95-150; hat with printed band $15-20; denim shirt and slacks, set $35-45; cord sports jacket (rayon, nylon, cotton blend) $25-45; Glen plaid slacks $20-25; sports shirt in dual colors with long sleeves $20-25. Men's ties now fill a variety of functions – quilting, skirts, reconstructed as ladies' ties, belts, these older wide ties are a versatile hobby item. The silk material can be either subdued or quite wildly patterned to fit any taste. Value of each tie in silk $10-25. socks in pristine condition are almost impossible to find but if available are $5-10 especially in bold plaids.

The wide ties of the early 1950s can make a beautiful collection of fabric and pattern. They are wide enough to enable a good display and as with many ties of all recent eras, they are highly colorful. The tie on the left is a vivid blue with a well defined bird and foliage. Ties with such scenes are desirable and have a value of $15-22, the rather business-like tie on the right is of excellent pattern and the coloring indicates it was probably designed for the holidays with its reds and greens and tiny snowflakes. Good quality. $10-12. Both date from 1951.

Men's hats in 1959 were quite debonair, and were having their last hurrah. Now the rage is the baseball cap, (usually turned backwards) so remember hats when you are out shopping for vintage. The hat at top is gray with an open crown and of a fur blend.

The next two down are water repellent, deluxe beaver fur felt. Left has a center dent, right has an open crown and matching band. These good quality hats were not inexpensive when originally sold.

Pre-bent crown with a pinch front. Brown, water repellent felt fur.

Pre-creased crown, pinch front, water repellent fur felt.

Tight telescope tapered crown, narrow brim, braided band with brush feather trim. Brown.

Tapered level top, tight telescope pre-shaped crown. Medium Gray. All of these hats have satin rayon linings, genuine leather sweatbands. Value of each hat $20-40.

Men are obliged to add color to their wardrobes by various strategems since wearing a bright red and yellow suit is not considered quite the thing. Socks therefore have been a source of brightness to the gray flannels and navy blues. These jaunty stripes and plaids are from 1950, and although they have gained and lost popularity over the years, this type of sock has never entirely left the scene. Unworn, or in excellent condition $5-10 each pair.

269

This shirt of the same type and vintage but is not labeled as a vargas design. It too is of tan and brown but features an Oriental scene and is labeled AUTUMN IN KYOTO and was made by the same manufacturer as the Vargas - CHEMISE ET CIE. It is 100% nylon. Value $40-45.

Just when we think all vintage has been uncovered we find shirts such as these. Not only are these important because they deal with mens' vintage which is coming into its own, but also because they are a special type and feature a specific very collectible artist. This is a Vargas design shirt of rayon from the 1960s or very late 1950s. Although the owner remembers exactly where he bought them and why, the exact date is hazy. It is labeled VARGAS FLORAL COLLAGE, CHEMISE ET CIE and has a smaller label 'PLAYBOY'. It is not only colorful but the artist's work is clearly delineated. in fabric shades of tan and brown nylon. Imagine walking down the street with this lady on your back. Value $145-195.

The dandy of 1949. He wears a lightweight summer suit of tropical worsted with an unlined jacket. Snappy bow tie, pocket handkerchief and summer straw hat with wide brim. Wide shoulders on suit jacket. Value of suit $125-195. It is interesting that men's clothing of this period is as popular if not more so with collectors and potential wearers, than the female apparel.

Couple wearing the rather loose clothing of 1952. Men's trousers were wide and cuffed, jacket long, snap brim fedora; woman wears a full back 3/4 length coat over dark skirt, large fitted beret, stockings have defined heels and seams. Shoes have rounded toe. Clothing of this type still available and inexpensive. The open toe was prevalent in 1952 and shoes were not too much changed from previous years. Price ranges previously noted.

In the late 1940's men were fond of pin stripes. This is gray and white, has a neat, tailored look and has the usual tie and handkerchief combination. Value of this wool suit is $150-185.

Another article of men's clothing which has reached classic status is the white sports jacket processed for either rainy or sunny weather. Longer length it is of twill with zippered front closing, two large pockets, wide collar. Value $55-60.

The men's clothing in 1946 featured pullover sweaters, flannel slacks, long sleeved shirt. This was the time of the 'gray flannel slacks' worn with a tweed jacket, bright bow tie. The gabardine topcoat doubled as a raincoat, it was a standard. The sleeveless sweaters are most collectible in plaids – value $15-25; the slacks are eagerly sought after $45-65; the topcoats $40-50.

A wonderfully dashing coat of 1947. All weather; a longish but flattering length; a sleek fur collar; wide belt, camel colored leather buttons; altogether a sophisticated man-of-the-world look. These coats were popular but not too many seem to be available. Value $45-75.

The collectible 'Hawaiian shirts' of the 1950. These were inspired by the Islands but made on the mainland. Rayons and cotton, the patterns are colorful and 'easy care.' Sport shirts of this kind are $60-75. Authentic Hawaiian shirts of the 1930's are commanding very high prices, into the thousands.

Woolen robes for men which had a high attrition rate in the constant battle with moths. They are invariably comfortable and the more expensive ones are superbly tailored. In good condition, flattering and wearable. Value $50-55.

Male version of the loafer or moccasin in brown or antique red leather. Value $25-35.

The shoes show great variety considering the structured styles of men's clothing - left, perforated; wing tip; woven; crepe soled loafer. Value of this type shoe in excellent condition, $25-45.

CHAPTER FIVE

1960-1980

From the vantage point of the mid-1990s, 1960 seems a world away. If you lived through the 1960s your viewpoint is that it was only yesterday, such is the selectivity and folly of memory and the swift passage of time. If you were not yet born or very young in the 1960s it has become never never land in the history books. And fashion was as much its tool as its credo.

The clothing of the 1960s is a collection of philosophies as much as a panorama of fashion. Depending on your political stance in those days your closet may still house dresses which indeed you are still able to wear without raising eyebrows, or if you were young and active then your clothing may have long since been discarded with some of your opinions. Perhaps not, perhaps somewhere there are closets full of headbands, or bandanas, torn jeans and other symbols of unrest which shook the land and still cloud our fashion memories. It is not possible to discuss fashion of the 1960s without at least touching on the political climate because, incredible as it seems, the clothing genuinely reflected the politics of a large segment of the younger generation. And in the United States in the 1960s, the younger generation was the prevailing bellwether of fashion propelled by an over active media.

It is very difficult to define the 1960s in a fashion sense, it was like no other period in our history the atmosphere cannot accurately be transferred to paper. As 'they say' "you had to be there". In the beginning of the decade we had Jackie Kennedy, with her elegant, opulent wardrobe orchestrated by the genius of Oleg Cassini and commanding world-wide attention which one part of our psyche will never forget; and by the mid 1960s we had the scruffy, rebellious look fostered in the streets and parks and which another part of the American psyche can never erase.

All of this clothing has been well documented (after all, TV was there), the behavior much written and talked about, the chaos, the outrageous street scene, the whole is history and well recorded history. What can never be brought to mind with precision is the attitude which pervaded the times. Everyone alive seems to have been affected in some way, an emotion, a tension seemed to engulf this whole land, and nowhere were the distinctions between us all better delineated than in the clothing.

What made the best remembered history in the 1960s? Things certainly happened that were unique and their traces still remain. The hippies, the cults, the riots, the spirit of rebellion, the ascension and assassination of a young President, all of this and more affected our fashion memories and influenced us in ways too subtle for analysis even now, but without a doubt our fashions were subverted forever.

We can talk of fashion, of style, but what marked the 1960s in our memories is the absolutely unstructured look - it was costume, it was rebellion against order, it was cacophony in textile, and it was as far from Jackie Kennedy and her cool image as it was possible to get. Both were important, both help to explain the fashion of the decade in a way no treatise ever could. It is classic allegory. And over all it was a political and sociological statement that had nothing to do with fashion as we know it. Fashion was being used, fashion in its way has always been a tool, here fashion was not only a tool, it was your uniform. It was 'thrown together' and in its unformed way it was as uniform as anything every conceived.

The impact of all this, the upper echelon magnificence and the deliberately scruffiness of the young left a visual impact so enormous that today we tend to overlook the finer fashions which the 1960s and 70s gave us.

In 1960 when John Kennedy was elected president the mood of the country reflected the upbeat, dashing image he projected. Mrs. Kennedy was interested in fashion and this too brought world wide recognition to Oleg Cassini her designer and her ability to wear his wardrobe with panache. All the pretty daywear, and of course the hats, (the famous pillbox which is a Cassini concept) seemed to suit every head and went with almost any kind of costume and even today is still wearable and attractive, underpriced and neglected by collectors. The pillbox is a perfect example of a basically simple design, a classic, good design, made well and easily adaptable to any outfit. It is one of the proofs positive that good design overrides almost any factor in clothing, we may yearn for the laces and gossamers but it is the simple line and easily adapted design which endures. Dior, with his A line, was a master at this idea, A line he said is the most flattering, most easily worn of all fashion. So the A line prospered and still does even when given another designation.

The 1960s world was certainly interesting. In 1962 John Glenn was our first man in space, fashion designers are still reacting to that. The mini skirts of Mary Quandt were in vogue. This English designer was in the new wave of those who were wrestling the fashion stranglehold away from Paris, at this time too the Irish designers with their unusual fabrics were making an impact and those designs are now sought after, Milan was rearing its fashion head and altogether an international flavor was rife in the fashion world. It lent an air of piquancy to a field that had become somewhat static and restricted to the wealthy few. This fashion revolution which was a long time coming, was a genuine upheaval, even upscale clothes became much less expensive, they became much more informal and they were in truth more interesting, they also sported more unusual features than would normally be seen in any one period.

It was also the first time in history that youth dominated the fashion market to such an extent, the young had money and were literally 'spending machines'. Anyone who had seen Carnaby Street in London in the 1960s can easily recall the really bizarre outfits and their purple, orange-haired wearers, but also the way large sums of money for this clothing was changing hands in the boutiques. No longer were older women with huge spending budgets dictating what we wore, no longer were we paying much heed to what some famous designer based in some ivory tower told us what we should be wearing, it was the beginning, in earnest, of the new philosophy, "do what you want, wear what you want, when you want". That 'me' generation had arrived and had reached their fashion plateau. Fashion not only catered to their needs, but continued to create their wants.

Not all of Paris abandoned high fashion, some of the designers were astute enough to realize where the new money and power lay. so there were a few who catered to the young clientele such as Ungaro and Pierre Cardin, but it soon became apparent that Levi Strauss, unfashionable designer but merchandising genius that he was, continued to corner the market on pants. This generation, unique as it was, was still captivated by the jeans although now they had to look ragged. This 'casual' look is still around, some countries abroad spend many rubles and yen to own a piece of that particular fashion.

Flower children was such an apt name for most of the Woodstock generation. Most of them believed in 'flower power' and often carried or wore flowers, they wore long skirts or short skirts, sandals on their feet, or bare feet, which spawned the warnings seen everywhere in stores "No bare feet allowed", they danced and frolicked in the streets. This aspect of 1960s clothing personified what they thought of as "free spirit", but the garments they wore reflected nothing so much as a total rejection of all fashion as we knew it, indeed all rules of society as we used them to keep society intact. The big cities were host to most of this Peter Pan generation, but the clothes they affected trickled down to all parts of the United States and had a stupendous effect on fashion for the young.

Many of these same aging hippies are now totally mainstream, have even amassed fortunes and no doubt wear couturier clothing, most of them have fallen victim to the collar and tie and suit and suburban outfits most of us affect.

There have been periods in history when fashion mirrored society's mores, but none which dominated (at least in our mind's eye) a generation so completely. Think back, when you recall those years what comes to mind (aside from the assassination) - no doubt TV coverage, showing a person with long hair, the headband, the requisite sloppy clothes. It is an image etched forever in the American psyche, reinforced by heavy media coverage. No designer fashion show, no matter how opulent, could buy that kind of publicity. The era was unique and nothing stamped it so indelibly as the clothing the young rebels wore.

Fashion has never quite recovered from the 1960s and in a way that is a plus. We have become completely independent as to what we wear. We are no longer bound by rules of fashion conduct except those dictated by common sense. We no longer worry about things like a hemline - is it a bit too long, a bit too short? We no longer worry about which color is 'in' we no longer consider the social consequences if heaven forbid, our outfits should not be properly coordinated. We, most of us, care about how we look, but we do not spend too much time worrying about it.

Although all this fashion independence has its roots in the 1950s, the 1960s was its time of refinement. Every aspect of life was in a state of flux. High fashion designers are still the wellspring from which most of our available costumes originate (in more expensive versions), it still has its wealthy coterie of clients, it still impresses us with the famous names of people such as St. Laurent and Calvin Klein but it can never influence most of us in any significant way again.

This is a marvelous opportunity for collectors, some of the dresses, suits and hats of the 1960s are wonders, and well worth buying and preserving. Don't be sidetracked by the emphasis on the unkempt, all the good clothing of that time is still way underpriced and has not yet begun to be collected in any serious way. Now is the time to begin acquiring it. But not only the clothing itself, begin right now to assemble a collection of the accessories, for in truth you might categorize the whole period as THE ACCESSORY DECADE. Possibly the most fun you will ever have as a vintage clothing collector will be dashing around trying to find the low-slung, big buckled, hip belts; the headbands (in good condition) many still adorned with feathers, or beads, or rhinestone pins; the totally bizarre shoes, the big, bold jewelry; the chatelaines of brass or silver plate; some of the ethnic accessories are marvelous. Do try for the accessories if you need to start on a small scale, to list them makes them seem more unreal than many of them really are, but you will have a great time seeking them, many of them still lodging undisturbed in thrift shops. Try, keep trying but don't neglect the dresses, especially the dainty formals, you will be surprised at the quality and elegance.

The 1960s fashion look was quite characteristic, you will very soon become an expert. It is an unusual period in textile history, so many new fabrics made their appearances, many have since disappeared or are now used minimally. This can be a mini education, for example, whatever happened to polyester?

The designers of the 1960s were names we recognize. Marc Bohan assumed control of The House of Dior late in that decade, Balenciaga who closed his business in 1968, St. Laurent a highly imaginative designer who was a very young man himself when he took over at Dior (who had died in 1957) and who anticipated Twiggy and her short skirts way back in 1959. Chanel was still around in 1960s having reactivated her business in the 1950s, Jacques Fath was a factor. So many truly great designers whose clothing will surely grace museum collections (although a friend recently found a Jacques Fath in a small shop) that only an encyclopedic fashion history can testify to their legacies. What the serious vintage clothing collector should hasten to do is preview every clothing auction of which you are aware, even there prices are rising very rapidly but the consigned clothing often allows an opportunity to acquire a treasure.

These designers created clothes aimed at their own market niche which they understood and appreciated, but it was the young people who took fashion out of that narrow groove and moved it forever into a place where we are all comfortable, where most of those fabled designers could never go. Be forever grateful to the collectors who rush here and there trying to find their fabulous clothing.

Black cotton eyelet 1960s dress, lowered waist defined by a wide satin ribbon tied in a bow. Sleeveless, higher in front than back. Shows wear, but basically good condition. A very attractive 'little' dress. $45-55.

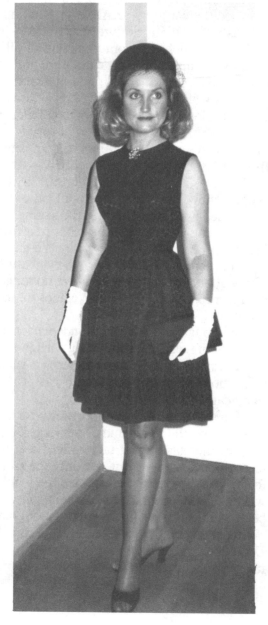

Black embossed satin cocktail dress. Satin piping trim around the neck, waist and down the front middle. $40-50. Worn with a black velvet pillbox with short net veiling $25-35. Black satin clutch handbag, 1960s. $15-20.

1960s red draped chiffon cocktail dress. Fully lined, this dress features a v-neck and low v-back with a loose flowing chiffon scarf over one shoulder $65-100. Enhanced by rhinestone jewelry and a slinky feather boa, this outfit is completed with red satin Saks Fifth Avenue shoes with rhinestone buckles valued at $30-45. Although the great rhinestone jewelry period had passed by the 1960s, much good jewelry was being made and vintage clothing collectors need to be aware of this, so the 1960s costumes can be coordinated with the period jewelry.

The utterly classic 'formal'. Timeless and simple. This could have been anytime within the memory of most collectors. The blue color is striking, the taffeta has the requisite rustle which is supposed to stir mens senses, the fit is tight without being vulgar, the bateau neckline accommodates well to almost any kind of jewelry - what more could any deb ask? This dress with its capped sleeves, fitted midriff and full skirt is a delight. Value $175-250.

A stunning dress by the standards of any era. It is almost timeless but it did indeed come out of the surprising 1960s, 1969 to be precise. A red silk shag long evening gown with pink satin square collar trim, and six satin buttons on the midriff. It has a low cut back neckline. The hemline commands interest. This was originally worn during a stage performance by a singer in concert. The pink satin pointed spike heel pumps and pearl accessories give the dress an added dimension. Dress $200-250; Shoes $20-30.

If you study the photograph and subtract the lovely accessories you will realize that while the gown itself is quite beautiful the accessories help frame it, not only in context, but in interest to the beholder. A good example of how to collect in context. This becomes increasingly important in museum display.

A fairly typical 1960s cocktail dress, but the bright red color and good tailoring make it quite effective. These are still available and make for a delightful collection, especially with proper accessories. This dress has a tie belt in front while the midriff is shirred with red rhinestone bands. This dress is very well made and the skirt gives a feeling of fullness without adding inches to the figure. Dress $45-65. The model carries a rhinestone studded tapestry clutch purse and her shoes have clear plastic heels with a large rhinestone jewel on the vamp. Purse $15-25; shoes $50-65.

The inevitable 1970s pants suit, this one with a different focus. Black polyester suit worn with a striped polyester knit coat casually draped over one shoulder. One great advantage of this clothing, aside from comfort, was the non-wrinkle, do-anything-with-it aspect. The black pants are matched with a long black tunic with long sleeves. The shoes are platform sandals with high heels. The jewelry is shell. Shell jewelry of this period is easily picked up now, but who knows for how long. The suit is valued at $35-50, the coat $25-35, the shoes, $20-25.

Party dress of 1960's. Dotted organdy embroidered with satin ribbon inserts. Short gloves. Value of dress is $55-95. This is the time to be seeking the clothing of the early 1960's.

A stunning gray velvet cocktail length dress with finger tip length jacket. The jacket is trimmed with a wide band of rhinestones of excellent quality and is worn over an ivory satin top which in turn is worn over a gray velvet skirt attached to a slip top. The whole is fully lined. IRENE SARGENT LABEL.
Sargent is a well known name in the California Bay Area fashion world. A lovely garment of high quality. 1960s. Value $195-250.

1965. Dress of houndstooth check with white pique flat collar and cuffs on long, rather loose sleeves. Knee length. Very high band of contrasting color maintains the straight line of the garment since it takes the eye away from the waistline. Value $45-55. Courtesy of Butterick Archives.

Late 1960's one piece dress which resembles a two piece outfit. Polyester and cotton. Value $40-50. Clothing of the 60's is not yet a genuine collector's item. Courtesy Butterick Archives.

1964 Mini skirt dress is cotton. Value $50-65.
Photo courtesy of Butterick Archives

1968 - Knitwear full length coat. $100-125.
Courtesy Butterick Archives.

The collarless rather elegant coat of the early
1960's in polyester and cotton. Short; large
pockets. Value $55-95.

281

The early 1970s was really a time of adaptation, it was also a full flowering of separates; pants, jackets, tops, skirts, blouses, all could be mixed or matched. It is fairly difficult to build a definitive collection of 1970's clothing because of this wardrobe of many pieces. The best starting point is color, this is a lovely blue three-piece cardigan suit that has a gently flared skirt. A coordinated pair of pants, either in blue or a complementary shade, a patterned top of blending colors and you've got two separate outfits. These two models show the perfect way a good wardrobe could have been built in the 1970s. These two outfits are washable, packable, all season, all occasion knit coordinates. Clothes of the 1970s are still a great bargain and not yet widely collected, values on almost all of them are low.

Suits, of course, have never lost favor no matter what the era, but they have certainly been adapted to the needs of the times. This could be called a 'non suit' since it does not have the classic approach. It is a soft suit, with a relaxed look. It is a white washable unlined double knit. The flaring skirt gives it an unstructured look. The scarf over the collarless top adds to the casual effect. Large brown and beige buttons to match the beige suit. Value of suit $25-35.

This is a classic blue blazer, 1970's style. It can be worn over nearly anything, and has quite distinctive wide, low lapels and pockets with flaps. Navy blue worn with a red and white print blouse, the jacket has two button closing. The blue and white buttons coordinate with the bracelets the model wears. Value of jacket $20-25.

Rayon and nylon lace and rayon chiffon makes this a rather bewitching garment. The bodice flows into the hip-slimming pleated skirt. Not enough emphasis has been accorded the flattering tailoring which marked these early sixties dresses. This is rayon taffeta lined and should be dry cleaned. The length of the garments in those years was quite kind to most women and the black lace gives this dress a festive, elegant air. Dress $50-85.

A flattering long vest (which is what the various jackets were often called in those long ago 1970s). Interesting that in the mid 1990s vests, the men's traditional vests, are a big fashion item, and are being adapted and marketed heavily toward women, but they are not nearly so flattering as the Jacket vests of the 1970s. This long vest has curved seaming and patched pockets. Went very well with straight pants. Dark blue with a plaid shirt and a red and white small bandanna. White belt on the pants and red and white bottoms. Long vest $20-25.

Right, one of the many types of jackets worn in the 70's. The shoulder line is extended, and the bodice is full so it can be belted or left to hang loose. Red, worn with matching pants, a blue belt and a scarf of red, white and blue. Value of suit $15-20.

283

The silhouette of the sixties sometimes resembles a modified version of the silhouette of the 1940s. Natural nipped in waistline and a shorter, swinging skirt.

The model on the left wears a 'gala bouffant' in sheer, combed cotton lawn. Embroidery wreaths the bodice and the sweeping skirt. It is wash and wear which seems unbelievable in such a stunning dress and it is 'wrinkle shy' according to the Spiegel company. Shown in dazzling yellow, the shoes are also in the same color. Notice the typical jewelry of the 1960s which the models wear.

Right: This dress is a brilliant draping of sheer silk organza in an eletrifying emerald green. A crushed pleat cummerbund and a dramatic envelope collar make this a figure flattering garment. Note the gloves, sling back matching colored pumps and the jewelry the models wear. Some of the events of the 1960s have erased recollections of the very lovely fashions which were being worn in those years.

Dresses of this type in excellent condition are valued at $55-95.

This striking dress is all one piece, completely lined, flared skirt, the bib front is stitched to the basic fabric and it has a jumper look. Dress $20-25. Navy blue and white, with navy and white shoes, white hat and jewelry.

284

Red, white and blue has always been a classic combination in fashion, although not always a style leader. Spring always seems to inspire sales in this color combination and here we have not only the classic colors but the entirely classic shapes of fashion in the Spring of 1961.

A very elegant outfit in wrinkle resistant rayon, acetate shantung flashed with a detachable dickey. And was there ever a more useful fashion accessory than the dickey? Navy blue with red accessories and button trim. The obligatory short white gloves and the very flattering hat. Dress $30-40; Hat (straw cloche with red grosgrain trim) $15-25.

A 'date sheath' in the classic mode of Coco Chanel. Of 'lineny' wrinkle resistant rayon, hand washable in navy blue and red with the accessories required in the not so distant past. This model wears a red straw cloche with a red grosgrain trim. These are altogether surprising costumes viewed from our vantage point, we tend to forget some of the elegance of that time. 2 piece dress $40-45; Hat $15-25.

A wonderfully definitive pair of outfits which typify the 1960-62 period. On the left the model wears a walking suit of worsted looking rayon acetate in navy blue with white detachable collar. The coat is taffeta lined and has large mother-of-pearl buttons. The straw hat and gloves are white. Walking suit Valued at $50-95.

The gray coat and slim skirt on the right is Italian flannel with a 32" long coat which is taffeta lined. An excellent choice for the taller woman. The fancy buttons are eye catching. Both models wear the wonderful hats of the period. Value of flannel suit $75-100.

A machine made lace pants suit of flesh colored cotton. Wide flaring pants with a scalloped edge, in a large size. 1960s. $25-30. This is a vintage gem.

Early 1960s chic. Bright and beautiful. This is an any hour costume in a rich textured rayon and silk blend, bound in braid, the coat is taffeta lined and is worn over a classically simple sheath. The coat is sunflower yellow, the sheath and accessories are navy blue. A gorgeous outfit. Coat $35-55.

This sultry pose emphasizes the allure of the mandarin collar and stunning hat. This 'couturier-inspired' all wool coat has the mandarin collar and funnel shaped sleeves giving this coat a high fashion look. It has an ornamental button and a wrap front. Rayon crepe lining. The lilac color completes the sophisticated look.

Pleats were also popular in the early 1960s period as this really beautifully designed and crafted dress shows. The color is outstanding - a lively violet with a skirt of 'stay-in pleats' topped by a bodice which cries out for accessorizing, the passion of every jewelry loving woman who breathes. This is wrinkle resistant arnel triacetate jersey and miraculously is hand washable. The same shoes and handbag fit this very different costume nicely. Dress $40-50.

It is incredible how so many really older garments have surfaced which could be worn today without too many people looking askance at the oddness of the attire, while the 1960s spawned so many different looks many of which seem dated and even bizarre. This couple are typical of the fashions of 1968 and while they look fairly high fashion, the clothing is certainly out of place in the 1990s even though it is very well tailored. The many pocketed jacket of the rose colored suit has a safari look, belted and with a short skirt, beige square toed low heeled shoes, handled leather handbag this model is wearing a huge blue silk scarf which fills in her neckline and ties in a big bow at the back. Suit $55-75.

The male model wears the narrow shouldered jacket with narrow lapels, striped tie and matching handkerchiefs and narrow trousers without cuffs. He also wears tan square toed loafers a shade lighter than the trousers which in turn are much lighter than his brown herringbone tweed jacket. Jacket $30-35. Trousers $15-20.

Right:
A man's white Palm Beach dinner jacket and black tuxedo trousers. As a complete suit, value $145-225.

Left in photo: A black satin bias cut evening gown with a black velvet jacket. Termed 'cafe society' clothing. The coat is lavishly furred. Dress $700-950, coat $400-500.

Lady wears a jumpsuit of c.1965. What dates this photo more than the clothing is the man's hairdo and his tie. This photograph proves though that almost any type clothing could be worn today without comment. Value of jumpsuit $40-60.

The casual clothing of this period is difficult to collect since its very offhand approach resembles much that has gone before and come after. And indeed much of it is still being worn. This is a white ruled lilac cotton pullover with a fringe hem. It is a washable material. The wash and wear deep iris capris are cotton chino. Lilac top value $5-15; Capris $10-20.

This is debteen clothing with a western motif. A villager shirt of combed cotton gingham with rolled sleeves, multi plaid pattern. Shirt $4-8.
She wears tapered beige slacks in fine washable cotton cord, smooth front line, western tabs and square pockets. Wide cowhide belt. Slacks $15-20.

Center model wears a combed smooth cotton blouse with multi colored striped Jamaica shorts of lustrous sport cotton. Multi colored stripes. Value $5-10.

Model on right wears a tunic blouse and capri pants in smooth cotton in a gold color, worn with a belt. Value with belt $10-15.

BOTTOM LEFT:

A two piece 'sarong' suit in a batik print cotton sateen. Boned bra is built into the halter top. Blue, early 1960s. Value $7-15.

CENTER:
Top left: Sun and swim set in lustrous combed cotton sateen has a tie front jacket and a pleated middy skirt suit. The bra top is boned and has an elasticized back Peek-a-boo panties. Beige multi stripe. Complete set $30-35.

RIGHT:
This acetate faille latex suit has a matching cotton jacket with two pockets. The multi pleated suit front does wonders for the figure. Built-in bra. Value of complete set $30-35.

The beach scene is always interesting to the fashion conscious and is a tremendously barometer of society's mores. This early 1960s family group is modestly attired in matching swimwear. These were called 'cabana sets' and not many seem to have survived. The males wear cotton terry lined jackets over trunks which have elastic back waists and extension tab front. Mother and daughter wear form fitting bathing suits with shirred elastic backs and detachable straps. All are done in a deep sea motif in a blue cotton percale. To assemble a complete family ensemble such as this would be a marvelous coup. Ladies' bathing suits $15-25; Man's outfit $20-30; Boy's outfit $20-30.

1968 was a torturous shoe period for women. The stiletto heel was 'in' and the sharply pointed toe was also the vogue. Together they represented back trouble if worn too often as well as pinched toes but everyone admits they did have a sexy look. Patent leather with a saucy bow. Value in excellent condition $18-28.

TOP LEFT:
This shoe is multi toned silk, slim pointed toe, 1½" heel, the shoe does remind one of Mardi Gras, its official name. Value $25-30.

TOP RIGHT:
A favorite, utilitarian but pretty shoe, the plain pump. Soft leather on a 1½" heel. Black patent. Value $12-18.

BOTTOM RIGHT:
A necessary adjunct to any shoe wardrobe, the walking shoe. In the 1960s this good looking model was popular. Beneath the big, bold button is elastic which flexes with each step. 1" 'stacked' heel. Soft leather in beige. Value $15-20.

Top left: scalloped filigree pump, supple leather, fully leather lined. This is a sharply pointed fashion shoe designed for frothy fashions. Black patent leather. Value $10-20.

Finest calf. Italian. Pleated accents, leather-lined. Sharply pointed toe, 2⅞" heel. Value $15-25.

How soon we forget. Many people have deliberately put these 1970s wedge shoes out of their mind and seem surprised to learn they are collectible. The high braided heel and sole surround the canvas and give it some distinction but these were not considered a 'comfort' shoe although some were advertised that way. This is in black, and in summer they did coordinate well with some of the costumes. Value $12-18.

In each era and each area of interest there is one defining object. In the early 1960s in the important but neglected field of footwear it was the silk covered, multi-patterned, sharp pointed, high heeled shoe. Here is a good example of what you should be buying while the prices are negligible. Calf leather with a 2⅛" heel this pure silk covering is in a bouquet pattern. Fairly large collections of these shoes, properly displayed are breathtaking. Surprisingly, shoes of this type can often be found in unworn or almost new condition. Value in excellent condition $30-40.

Jeweled bedecked 'softie' - rhinestones and faux pearls on supple blue leather, tapered toe, this is turquoise but it is a common type of the early 1960s, many are still around in good condition and they are pretty and colorful. Value $10-12. A shoe collector recently bought a pair in mint condition for $6.

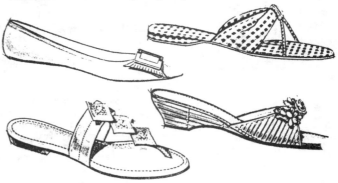

Casual shoes are most apt to be discarded and in the 60s these were bright and pretty. This is orange canvas with tropical trim, rope covered crepe sole with wedge heel. Very well made with cushion insoles. From Italy. In good condition. Value $12-18.

These sandals and 'loungers' were the ultimate in comfort and in the 1960s were a very big part of the fashion picture.

Top to Bottom:

Blue checked cotton gingham. Wedge heel, cushion insole, great for the beach. Value $5-10.

This capeskin leather is soft and flexible wonderful for travel. It tucks into its own plastic case and is elastic bound for fit. Value with case $4.

Supple textured vinyl with a 1 1/2" chamise style heel. This 'bamboo' mule cost around $4 new in the early 60s. Value now $4-8.

The ever popular thong. This sports an array of multi colored vinyl patches which give it a bright look. This has a standard low heel. Value $5-10.

Imported Italian raffia straw scuff. 2" cork covered wedge shaped heel, floral ornament, foam cushioned insole. Natural. Value $15-20 in perfect condition.

Imported raffia straw and leather look vinyl in a double cross design. 1½" cork covered wedge heel, pillow cushion insole. Contemporary foot wear is often made in this same pattern, so learn to recognize the 60s materials. Value $5-12 in perfect condition.

This scuff was labeled 'Siesta Sling' and it does have a lighthearted and comfortable look. Italian raffia straw on a carved wooden heel. Cushioned insole and multi-colored pom pom. In excellent condition $12-18.

In 1960 this smocked coral linen sports bag was a very fashionable item. It has a mock tortoise chain handle and a mock tortoise frame but these could be had with a metal frame. It is smocked on the wrong side of the fabric with a lattice stitch. It is lined and interlined. This type of handbag came in a variety of styles, some of the evening styles embellished with stones and pearls are attractive. They all have the same overall look however. Value $15-20.

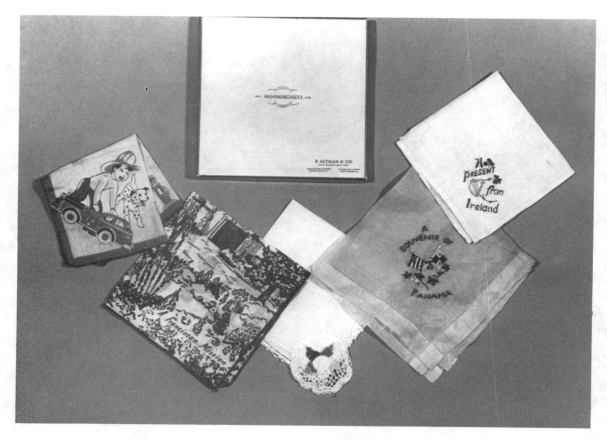

One of the really great new collectibles. Handkerchiefs are fun and still inexpensive but prices are beginning to rise fairly rapidly. These are easy to care for, easy to display and can tell myriad stories - where you've been, what you've done, it's endlessly fascinating. From top - a handkerchief box from B. Altman, NY, one of the world's most beautiful store which itself is now a thing of the past; An older hankie, linen, marked A PRESENT FROM IRELAND, which was bought in a small shop on the Dublin road in 1975 (value $10-15). A souvenir of Panama, with two flags, pure silk (value $20-28). This handkerchief was a labor of love, plain cotton with hand edging and an applied hand-made Women's organization logo. Value $20-25, a very colorful hankie with garden, buildings and labeled FRANCISCAN MISSION. Bought in California. Value $8-12, a child's hankie of the late 1940s, small size, it was a gift to a young boy and depicts quite vividly the dream of every boy under 6, to be a fireman. Even to the requisite Dalmation. Value $7-12.

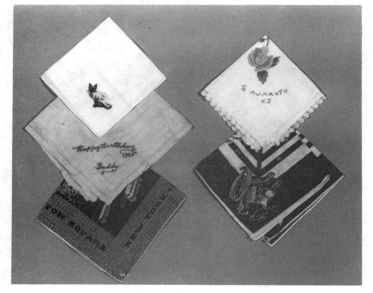

You can take your pick of specific kinds of handkerchiefs which interest you. This group features a collectible cat $12-17; a Happy Birthday Daddy $10-18; a large geographic type, New York with buses, trains, buildings, all in black and white, value $15-22; a pretty hankie bought in New Zealand and proof that these make great momentos of any trip, easy to pack and certainly cheaper than airport dolls or key chains. Hand edged. Value $12-18, western motif hankie with all the cowboy accoutrements in red and white, value $15-20.

1963 headgear is forever imprinted in our mind, primarily because of Jackie Kennedy and her trademark pillbox. The two shown here are typically shaped. Both are blue and in a smocked design. In good condition, each $20-25.

Designer scarves are another item which is fast achieving high collectible status. Prices have already risen, and even thrift shops which used to be a wonderful source have now raised prices. The basic material of the scarf has some bearing on price of course, but primarily the designer name is all important. Patterns do not matter as much as the name recognition. Silk scarves with designer names should have a starting value of about $20, scarves of other materials with good names should begin around $25. Prices upward then depend on other factors mentioned, material, pattern, size and name recognition of the designer. Prices can easily reach $125 on some of these.

No one needs to ask what STETSON is. A hat of course, although now it often denotes the cowboy variety. Stetson is one of the great names in the industry. These 1968 versions of the famous Stetson man's fedora are one of the most sought after gentlemen's clothing artifacts. Hats in good condition and of this quality should have a starting price of $25.

This gentleman of the early 1960s wears a wash and wear shadow weave easy care tropical weight suit. It is of dacron polyester and rayon. Single breasted with a vented back, cuffed trousers. Polyester became despised and hence immediately collectible when the cotton and wool rage took over men's wear. Value $25-35.

This multi-colored, very busy men's shirt of the 1960s is by Lily Dache. The label reads LILY DACHE, PARIS, NEW YORK, CALIFORNIA. Value $40-50.

Ties, while not precisely a brand new collectible, are just now achieving wide collecting appeal. For some time now crafts people have been buying older ties, particularly the wide ones, not for their labels or materials but for their patterns for use in quilts, jackets and as one friend of mine says, "for wall hangings which really catch the eye". The wild patterns of some older ties will certainly do that. Coupled with the designer names, often the pure silk of the material and you have a real reason to seek out these vintage offerings. Until recently any self respecting flea market was a treasure trove for old ties, now even their prices have risen. The plain Lily Dache tie is most notable for its label, the center mono-patterned blue tie is pure silk, marked 'Paris' the uninhibited FOREMAN AND CLARK tie is a collectible not only for its pattern and age but for the label, a foremost American maker. Designer ties are valued at $20-30, unlabeled ties of good quality and bizarre (the most bizarre the pattern the better) can start at about $5. It is important to catch this brass ring while others are still unaware.

An early advertisement for Levi Strauss and Co.'s copper riveted 'overalls'. Recently I watched a sale of early 501 jeans, the price paid was $850 and the buyer is ecstatic, he feels he got a rare bargain.

This advertisement by Levi Strauss Co. shows the cut of the early clothing. It seems unlikely this could ever be found in good condition since this sort of thing was made for hard wear and was certainly worn hard. Levi Strauss Co. has a museum at its headquarters in San Francisco which features some of the earliest 'overalls'.

These miners photographed in 1882 in California wear the original Levi's 501 jeans. These were first made by Levi Strauss in 1853 and the company says 'they have changed little over the past century and a half'. Each still carries the button fly and is made of rugged "01" denim that shrinks to the wearer. These hard working-hard living miners didn't know they were 'fashion pioneers', nor that they were trend setters. Now in 1995 their counterparts can be seen on any big city street. This styling is beyond timelessness, it suits every man and woman. And as usual Shakespeare had is right: "Fashion wears out more apparel than the man", jeans were never fashion, jeans were and are a rugged, wearable American symbol.

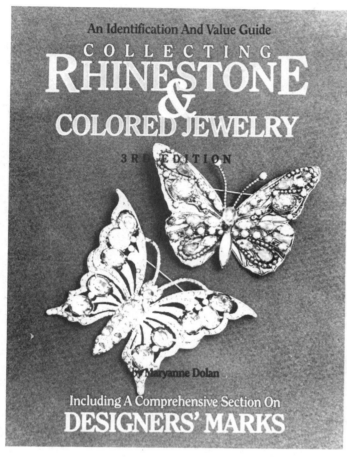